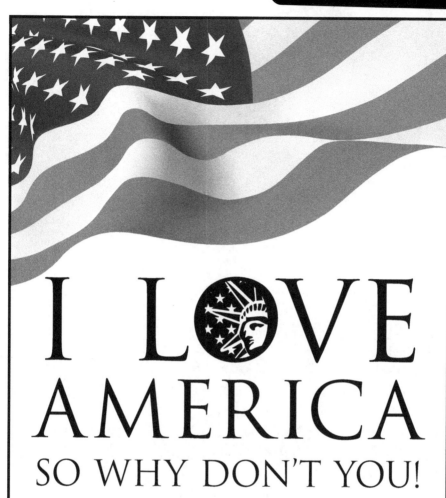

I LOVE AMERICA

SO WHY DON'T YOU!

A Young Immigrant Transformed by
Living the American Experience.
His Views on Why America is Great,
and His Assessment of the
Rise of Muslim Terrorism.

MUBARAK CHOUHDRY

Published by
GlobalWeb, Inc.
Roswell, GA

Library of Congress Control Number: 2013937635

ISBN: 978-0-9891320-0-8

Interior and cover design by Jera Publishing

Printed in the United States of America

DEDICATION

*To my, father Mohammad Akram Kahlon, my adopted American father
Bob Johnson and my father-in-law Joseph "Joe" Sterneman.*

And

*To the brave men and women in uniform
who volunteer to defend our freedom and liberty.*

And

*To this great country whose citizens enjoy,
"life, liberty, and the pursuit of happiness."*

And

To the youth of America on whom our future rests.

Visit my website at

www.iloveamericasowhydontyou.com

Follow me on Facebook

www.facebook.com/iloveamericasowhydontyou

CONTENTS

COMMENTS FROM
GREAT AMERICANS

"You don't have to be in Mubarak's presence very long to be impressed with his deep love of America and unbounded faith in America's future. Were America populated with more Mubaraks, his vision of our future would be a certainty. His confidence and love of country are inspiring and more often seen in people who have deliberately chosen America as their mother country as opposed to many who are native born and have little appreciation of the price that has been paid in blood and treasure to build this one and only America."

—LTC DANIEL ROSSMAN, USAF, RET., ROSWELL, GEORGIA

Mubarak is a great human being and global American. If you would like honest answers to worldly questions, you have come to the right man. Mubarak not only understands the history of the world and Middle East but is very knowledgeable about the USA and he loves this country. This is a courageously written history of his early beginnings and love for family with respect for all, and his quest for knowledge and to be significant. I think, "I Love This Country So Why Don't You! Is one of many books he will be asked to write because he is a Thought Leader with sound answers for our future.

—PAT HALY, PRESIDENT NATIONAL PERSONNEL, DUNWOODY, GEORGIA

"Not only was Mubarak a fine employee, a splendid citizen, and a good friend, but he certainly qualifies to me as an American patriot. You cannot be around him long before you discover that as an American and former Pakistani he is very concerned about the situations in the Near East and areas where he is particular familiar. His approach is, in my opinion, one which we need to examine, it is noteworthy."

—WESTON BERGMAN, JR., RETIRED HOSPITAL ADMINISTRATOR, VIDALIA, GEORGIA

"I met Mubarak in 1991 and was quickly impressed with his desire to be involved in our Vidalia Community. He joined our local Kiwanis Club and wasn't merely a participant but a very busy Kiwanian that participated in many projects to make our community better. He was a valued citizen of our city for seven years. He continues to serve this country through his community involvement and asserting his love and pride for America by writing this book. I have found him deeply devoted in discussing the dangers of and solutions for Muslim terrorists, especially since September 11, 2011. He is a genuine American through and through!"

—STEVE BROWN, OWNER, BROWN INSURANCE GROUP, VIDALIA, GEORGIA

"When I met Mubarak, I was very reserved as he came from a different country, grew up with a different religious background and had spent most of his time in America north of the Mason Dixon line. However, it didn't take long to see that he had a very big heart and cared for other people. He was a person you wanted to spend time with because he made you feel better about yourself and about what you did. God used Mubarak in my life to teach me many things about myself and how to deal with others. Many of these lessons learned brought about changes in my life, changes that made me be a better person and helped me grow in my desire to be more like Christ. I am blessed to call Mubarak both a friend and family."

—BOB DIXON, VIDALIA, GEORGIA

"During the summer of 1974 Mubarak was chosen to reside at and manage the International Student Center house at Vincennes University, Vincennes, Indiana. From this position of responsibility he extended a welcoming and helping hand to new and current international students. Mubarak made an excellent peer student advisor and leader. No one was a stranger to him and he made himself available to all students."

—PAT MINDERMAN, MEMPHIS, TENNESSEE

"As I didn't mean to meet Mubarak on purpose, I can't remember exactly how it happened. However, I am sure he spoke to me first because that is the kind of person he is. He certainly became immersed in small town America and the notion that with hard work and education anything is possible. I on the other hand became open to many new and global ideas and the fact that although cultures are different there is a common thread that runs through us as human beings."

—CAROL KEUSCH, VINCENNES, INDIANA

THE MYSTIC

"As the lightning was snaking through the sky and the thunder was rumbling in my ears, I remembered the days when I was an old man and almost ready to depart from this world. Then something strange happened as my eyes were shutting down and the angel of death was ready to take me to the unknown kingdom. There was this burst of energy which flashed through my eyes and what happened next, I can not to this day fully recall."

—MUBARAK CHOUHDRY

Acknowledgments

In the process of writing this book many friends and supporters have counseled, questioned, prodded and cheered me along the way to its completion. No matter what mere words I could put together it would not be sufficient enough to describe my deep gratitude and appreciation. I am indebted to you all.

My heartfelt thanks to Danny Rossman, Bob Hilton, Wes Bergman, Patrick Minderman, Carol Keusch, Steve Brown, Bob Dixon, Earl Norton, Howard Holman, Ronnie Smith M.D., Syed Sajjad Haider, Syed Abrar Ali M.D., Pat Haly and Jody White.

To my mother and father for being the best parents and providing me a wonderful childhood, to my brothers and sisters for helping me along as the youngest of the siblings, to all the Midwest Angles that guided and nurtured me along during my formative years and to my teachers for encouraging me to ask questions in advancing my knowledge.

To Jera Publishing; Kimberly, Jason, Stephanie and Ryan for their laser like focus in getting things on track and done.

To all of you who have contributed so much in my life, I am ever so thankful for your love, kindness and generosity. You know who you are.

To my loving wife, Jenny, and my son Ali for their assistance and contribution to this book.

I ask for forgiveness of all those I may have offended over the years knowing full well that as a part of human race, at times I must have been weak, sinful and arrogant.

THE THOUGHT

This is my story; a story of the dreams of a young boy who wanted to make something of his life. It is a story of the boundless, unconditional love given to me from the great people of an even greater nation. But most importantly, it is the story of humanity and perpetual optimism in the face of uncertain challenges that we all face today. I wish that everyone in the world could have felt the warmth and hospitality I did when I came to America, the greatest country that God has ever created.

It transformed me into the mature person that I am now by shaping my world, revamping my thinking and making me a true believer in the American dream.

I love this country and am in awe of its achievements since its independence a little over 200 years ago. I have written this book to give inspiration to both Americans and non-Americans alike. No nation is perfect but there is no doubt that America is a beacon of hope for many, and I pray for it to stay that way for centuries to come.

"Feelings of worth can flourish only in an atmosphere where individual differences are appreciated, mistakes are tolerated, communication is open, and rules are flexible — the kind of atmosphere that is found in a nurturing family."

—Virginia Satir

My Inspiration,
How It All Began

The seeds of this book were planted within me in 1993, when I was invited to give a presentation to the Kiwanis Club of Vidalia, Georgia about "Coming to America." My feelings were further reinforced after my presentation won both the quarterly and yearly program awards. Several times since, I can recall waking in the middle of night, trying to figure out how best to put my thoughts to paper. However, what propelled me to fruition is my profound love and deep gratitude, and this is a way that I can somehow give back a little to this remarkable country.

The diversity, opportunities, freedoms and acceptance that this country offers is a direct result of the genius minds that met in the halls of Philadelphia, and these characteristics are now enjoyed by most of its citizens today. There is no other example of such extraordinary experimentation in the history of mankind. The spirit of early settlers and the pioneers of the west still live on and thrust us forward to overcome obstacles and make this a better world.

The events of September 11 brought us face-to-face with terrorist activities, a terror not known in the annals of history books. Having migrated from the peaceful Muslim Pakistan in which I grew up, just like my fellow American citizens I was equally repulsed by the sheer cruelty against the innocent people that fateful morning. This also put in motion my thoughts and theories that I have put into this book.

Now that this book is complete, my hope is that you too can share my proud immigrant's journey, ponder my views and see why you should love America too.

I left Pakistan in the summer of 1973 and arrived at Vincennes University in the terrific small town of Vincennes, Indiana. My two years in Vincennes were filled with adventure, exhilaration, learning and meeting all the angels that God had sent to guide and protect me through my immature years. The love and kindness that I experienced was so amazingly genuine that to this day, at times, I wonder: why me?

Once I completed my freshman and sophomore years at the Vincennes University, I transferred to the University of Evansville, located 50 miles south of Vincennes, upon receiving an academic scholarship for my junior and senior years. Evansville, Indiana was much larger than Vincennes, but again, I found it be full of the same affection given to all strangers. After receiving my B.S. in Business, I continued on with the MBA program and was awarded a Graduate Assistantship by the University of Evansville in my pursuit of higher education.

In 1979, I married Jenny, who also graduated from the University of Evansville. In 1982, our first son, Aki, was born; he brought so much joy to our lives. In 1989, I was fully immersed in my American Dream while living in the Deep South in Vidalia, Georgia. In 1990, my second son, Ali, was born. In spite of my foreign background, I was well liked and respected in Vidalia and was dedicated to serving the community through my involvement in several community programs, including Kiwanis, United Way, Toombs County Against Child Abuse and few others. I had it all: a good job at the local hospital, a terrific wife, and two handsome sons who were blessings. I was also celebrating the 10th year of my American citizenship and the 20th anniversary of my landing at John F. Kennedy International Airport in New York City as a green and apprehensive teenager.

I had not come to stay in this country. My plan was to complete my education and go back to be with my loving family and, most importantly, my mother and father. However, once I decided to stay, I carefully studied the American citizenship process along with my obligations for being a good citizen. On October 6, 1983, I proudly took my oath alongside other aspiring immigrants in Evansville, Indiana. And as my young son, Aki, waved his little American flag from his stroller, I finally became an American citizen.

NATURALIZATION OATH OF ALLEGIANCE TO THE UNITED STATES OF AMERICA

"I hereby declare, on oath, that I absolutely and entirely renounce and abjure all allegiance and fidelity to any foreign prince, potentate, state or sovereignty, of whom or which I have heretofore been a subject or citizen; that I will support and defend the Constitution and laws of the United States of America against all enemies, foreign and domestic; that I will bear true faith and allegiance to the same; that I will bear arms on behalf of the United States when required by the law; that I will perform noncombatant service in the armed forces of the United States when required by the law; that I will perform work of national importance under civilian direction when required by the law; and that I take this obligation freely without any mental reservation or purpose of evasion; so help me God."

(FROM U.S. CITIZENSHIP AND IMMIGRATION SERVICES)

THERE ARE FIVE PRINCIPLES MANDATED BY THE IMMIGRATION AND NATIONALITY ACT OF 1953.

1. Allegiance to the United States Constitution

2. Renunciation of allegiance to any foreign country to which the immigrant has had previous allegiances

3. Defense of the Constitution against enemies "foreign and domestic"

4. Promise to serve in the United States Armed Forces when required by law (either combat or non-combat)

5. Promise to perform civilian duties of "national importance" when required by law

As a first generation immigrant, I took the above oath freely and I am continually humbled to live in this magnificent country.

I hope that my writing is an inspiration for all American born citizens and immigrants, as well as those who have yet to set foot on American soil, so that together we can continue to serve and keep this country strong until the end of time.

PART I

CHAPTER 1

MY BEGINNINGS

"Some men see things as they are and say why. I dream things that never were and say why not."

—ROBERT KENNEDY

MY INDO-ARYAN PUNJABI HERITAGE

MY HERITAGE IS PUNJABI. THE Punjabis are defined as the people who come from the Punjab region of the sub-continent of India. The Persian word Punjab literally means land of five rivers. The Punjabi identity is primarily linguistic, not a religious affiliation. There are about 120 million Punjabis worldwide (Muslim, Sikh and Hindu), about 650,000 in the United States.

The Punjabi people belong to the Indo-Aryan group of the Caucasian race. It is believed Indo-Aryans from Eurasia reached Assyria in the west and the Punjab in the east before 1500 B.C. The ancient Indus Valley Civilization of Harappa in Punjab became a center of early civilization. King Porus, the earliest known notable Punjabi king, fought the famous Battle of the Hydaspes against Alexander the Great.

Punjabi is spoken as a minority language in several countries where Punjabis have emigrated in large numbers, such as in the United Kingdom where Punjabi is the second most commonly used language. In Canada, Punjabi is the fourth most spoken language after English, French and Chinese.

SOME FAMOUS PUNJABIS

1. Bobby Jindal– Governor of Louisiana

2. Nikki Haley– Governor of South Carolina

3. Kalpana Chawla– a mission specialist and was one of seven crew-members killed in the Space Shuttle Columbia disaster

4. Deepak Chopra– physician, a holistic health and new age guru

5. Manmohan Singh– current Prime Minister of India

6. Har Gobind Khorana– won the Nobel Prize in Physiology or Medicine

7. Dr. Abdus Salam– won the Nobel Prize in Physics

8. Sir Muhammad Zafarullah Khan Chaudhry– served as a judge at the International Court of Justice in The Hague

9. Nusrat Fateh Ali Khan– a famous singer

10. Shahid Khan– American billionaire businessman, the owner of the NFL's Jacksonville Jaguars and owner of automobile parts manufacturer Flex-N-Gate Corporation

MY FAMILY BACKGROUND

I was born the youngest of eight siblings in an affluent and prominent Punjabi family in Lyallpur (now called Faisalabad), Punjab in Pakistan. My Rajput ancestors were Rajah, or Raja, and were followers of Hinduism and later Sikhism in the Sialkot/Kashmir area. The title "Rajah" is from Sanskrit and is a term for a monarch, or princely ruler.

By the early 15th century, my forefathers had converted to Islam and taken the title of Nawab (Lord). The exact reason for the conversion can't be said for sure, but I am speculating that it was the Muslim encroachment from the Northwest that may have led them to join the new powers of Delhi. This was most likely politically motivated with the purpose of keeping order to protect their lands and to continue to rule their Princedom.

As the wealth and land continued to get smaller after being passed on through generations, it was sub-divided among various members of the family. My great grandfather assumed the title of Chouhdry (also Chaudhry, Choudri, etc.) or, as the British called them, Landlord. Instead of a small kingdom or state, they now ruled a village comprising 500–1000 inhabitants.

The title of Landlord, which was created by the British, was largely for the psychological compensation of various established families who were once the power brokers before imperialism but still had enough power to help the British govern the vast Indian Sub-Continent. A Landlord (also Lambardar, Numberdar) in his village was responsible for the day-to-day administration, resolving both social and legal issues, collecting taxes, and keeping peace among the populace. They generally owned most of the land in the village, which was used to grow crops and generate wealth. Having a culturally rich ancestral background along with the ability to manage a small or larger population was considered a virtue in the days of the past.

My grandfather moved from our ancestral village in Sialkot (Chahoor) and established a new village named Chahoor near the city of Sangla Hill. The city of Sangla Hill is near a peak that is visible for miles around the countryside. I can recall hearing stories about Alexander the Great visiting the prominent hill and spending some time around the peak.

Upon the unexpected passing of my grandfather, my father, the eldest son, became a landlord with the title of Chouhdry at the young age of 17. As the head of the clan, he was not only responsible for all the subjects of his village but also took care of his widowed mother, three brothers, four sisters, and two orphaned cousins. My father handled these responsibilities adroitly and was considered wise and just by everyone he met.

GROWING UP

We moved to Latifabad, Hyderabad in the southern province of Sind in 1958 after my father had bought farmland in the South of Pakistan. The city of Latifabad, located near the famed Indus River, was newly built, sparsely populated and mostly inhabited by the Muslim immigrants from India after the 1947 partition of the Indian sub-continent. The roads were fresh but there were very few automobiles to enjoy the bump free ride. The most common modes of transportation were bus, horse buggy and bicycle. As a new city, the water and electric departments were running behind, and our house had no running water or electricity. The stream behind the house provided the water, and numerous kerosene oil lamps would light up the house in the evening.

I was the youngest of eight siblings, five brothers and three sisters. We lived in a large house with a big courtyard where we always played. Our home employed several servants that included a cook, errand person, cleaning person and a driver. As a five-year-old, I was neither fascinated by the house nor by the servants but totally mesmerized by the brand new green "Willys Jeep" that father had bought soon after we had moved into the house. My world was small and carefree. I was living in heaven with so much love and attention from my family. I lived an ideal life in a Utopia that gave me everything I needed or wanted provided by my dear, dear parents.

My mother was a kind-hearted woman who was always happy and had many friends and visitors. She had a soft voice and infectious giggle that would melt anyone's heart. She was always full of energy and laughter and was a compassionate person. She was the perfect wife for my father, and their love for each could be clearly seen. She was also a tremendous storyteller and was especially gifted in describing the climatic parts of any story. I was always spell bound with the stories she would tell my sister and I before we fell asleep. I never saw her get mad or yell. I did see her cry at times and that would always break my heart. Before I left for America, my mother was worried that I might get married there and not come back. Of course I originally had no plans for this, and I never worried about it; however, once I did get married, I realized how prophetic her worries had been. I have always felt bad that I did not go back and take care of her. Thinking about it now, I still get a lump in my throat even though she was at peace with my decision to stay in the United States and raise my two sons with my loving wife.

My father was a stern but pious man. He was a kind-hearted and a unique, forward-thinking mind. He believed in always increasing ones' knowledge through education, science, and modern medicine. He taught us to respect everyone no matter what his or her color, religion or language was. He also prayed regularly and believed in a loving and compassionate God. On many occasions in my youth, I saw him gather people from our village to pray for rain when there was a drought, and when he visited the sick, he was always the leader of group prayers. He went to bed early and would wake up between 3 and 4 in the morning and pray for his siblings, children, family, friends, and humanity. There would be times in the night when I would wake up and hear him crying while praying to God. I would ask my mother why father was crying and she would always calmly say, *"Your father wants all the suffering and problems of the world to go away, and this is his way of asking God."* It took me a while to realize the reasons behind my fathers' prayers and the answer my mother gave me. When I was older and would hear my fathers' prayers and the soft weeping coming from his room, I noticed that he always prayed for everyone but himself. I still think in amazement at how unselfish, benevolent, and charitable he was.

Both my parents were extensively involved in helping others. They would always send money to needy relatives and friends, visit the sick in various hospitals, and would never hesitate to feed complete strangers. Our house was always full of people who would stay for months, including relatives and my father's prayer buddies. Sometimes, my father would ask my sister and me to ride along with him in the Jeep. At the first intersection we would come to, father would notice people standing and waiting for any means of transportation like a bus or horse buggy. Father would immediately ask the driver to stop and pick up as many strangers as our Jeep could hold and give them a ride to wherever they needed to go.

Oftentimes, relatives would camp at our house and my mother would welcome them with open arms, make their sleeping arrangements, prepare the necessary meals, and tend to their basic needs. Luckily, having servants helping with the daily chores made it easy for my mother to manage our busy household.

I was introduced to many languages at an early age. I spoke Punjabi at home and learned English and Urdu (now the national language of Pakistan) at school. English was the official language of Pakistan until 1972. As a Muslim, I learned to pray in Arabic. Since we moved to Sind, a southern province of Pakistan, I learned to communicate in Sindhi on the streets. Persian was the official language until British took over in 1857, so I took a year of Persian in the high school. I can also speak Hindi.

Punjabi, Sindhi, Urdu and Persian all belong to the Indo-European language tree. *"Indo-European languages are spoken by almost three billion native speakers,"* [1] which represents the largest language group.

"Of the twenty languages with the largest numbers of native speakers according to SIL Ethnologue, twelve are Indo-European: Spanish, English, Hindi, Portuguese, Bengali, Russian, German, Marathi, French, Italian, Punjabi, and Urdu, accounting for over 1.7 billion native speakers."[2] Arabic does not belong to the Indo-European language tree.

My Early School Years

My father was well versed in both Arabic and Persian languages, along with Punjabi, Sindhi, Hindi, Urdu and English. I clearly remember one Arabic prayer that my father would repeat to me over and over each week. *"Rab-e Zidni Ilema"* in Arabic or *"O, God help me to increase my knowledge."* With this said, he never hesitated to add that this requires hard work along with following a well thought-out plan.

I started my education in a co-ed school until the 5th grade, where boys and girls were allowed in the same classroom. We wore uniforms and attended a morning general assembly that involved prayer and a speech by the principal prior to starting our classes. I quickly developed a profound fascination with math and history. Having good discipline both at home and in school made me realize the value of my life and of planning for the future. Excelling in the classroom and being placed at the top of my classes also taught me that quality effort and hard work will yield positive results. Top grades made me the darling of most of my teachers, and I avoided the punishment with a cane that was pretty common for other classmates.

By the 8th grade, I was enrolled in an English school established by the Pakistan Government and the British School System. It was a boarding school, but I did not stay on campus, as my home was close enough that I could walk to and from school; therefore, I was considered a "Day Scholar" instead of a "Boarder." My first six months were rather difficult as all of the subjects that I was studying were in English instead of Urdu, the language in which I had been schooled. For several months, I found myself at the bottom of my class with no scores higher than 20 out of 100. It was very embarrassing, and I knew I had to put more effort into my studies in order to get ahead. For six months, I stayed up many nights studying everything I could cram into my mind. The hard work paid off, and after a few months, I was number one academically in my class.

The students that did live on campus had to wake up early each morning for physical exercises run by two retired army sergeants. Participation in a sport after school was also required. The "Day Scholars" were required to participate in a military style parade on a weekly basis. Each Monday, the entire school from 6th to 12th grade held a parade with either the principal or some other dignitary inspecting the entire student body. This process would take 2–3 hours, and then we would be dismissed to head to our classes. The school consisted of four dormitories, several grassy fields, common areas, housing for teachers on campus, a tall clock tower, antiquated buildings, manicured lawns and various other amenities not found in other schools in the area. The school owned over 100 acres of land. It was a pretty school, and I liked it very much.

I played cricket regularly and participated in the school theater production, playing the role of Sir Francis Chesney in the famous British comedic stage production based on Charley's Aunt.

DREAMING OF THE USA

I was in love with history throughout my schooling. At age 10, I became a fan of President Abraham Lincoln after reading his autobiography. My young mind was totally enamored with his persona and the challenges he faced in keeping this country together. At the time, I did not comprehend the details of the American Civil War, but I knew that he provided the necessary leadership during a tumultuous time in American history. With this in mind, my very first childhood dream was to go to the Cadet College in Petaro to finish high school, join the Pakistani Army, and one day become a democratic leader of Pakistan. I would daydream of working hard to create a kingdom where all the citizens were happy and everyone was treated both justly and fairly.

This dream came to an unfortunate end when, at the age 11, I was struck with Typhoid fever. The experience deeply impacted my vision and ultimately left me needing to wear glasses. Despite this, I still applied to the Cadet College in Petaro. I passed all the educational requirements and physical tests but ultimately failed the eye exam. I was devastated and did not know which direction to take my life. The answer to this would come once I entered the 9th grade. Upon taking my first physics courses, I fell in love with Newton and Einstein and decided to pursue a degree in engineering. Significant credit is due to my excellent physics teacher, Mr. Anjum, who convinced me that pursuing a higher education in the United States would be a better alternative to staying in Pakistan or going to the UK. He was well versed in world affairs and admired the USA. When Robert F. Kennedy was shot on June 5, 1968 in Los Angeles, California, Mr. Anjum spent the whole class period describing the whole incident in detail while all of us were spellbound.

Anyway, I appreciated the logic and reasoning of Mr. Anjum and made it my new goal to get a degree in Engineering from an American university with the ultimate goal of returning to Pakistan and taking care of my parents. I could have lived away from them but, being the youngest of eight, I felt it was my duty.

By the time I was 17, I had completed high school and began searching for routes to accomplish my new dream. Unfortunately, my father still thought I was too young to be going so far away right after high school. With the USA option being put on hold, I enrolled at the University of Engineering and Technology (UET) in Lahore, which was considered one of the top universities in South-Central Asia at that time. Thanks to my good grades in high school, I was awarded a scholarship. At the urging of my brother, I had not revealed this to my father, so I found myself double dipping monetarily and having a terrific time in Lahore. I lived on campus in a dormitory and had a servant who fixed my food and took care of my domestic needs.

As an 18-year-old experiencing total freedom for the first time, I was enjoying myself immensely. I would take my friends to Mall Road in Lahore pretty much every day. It was the place to see and be seen, to shop, and to eat. We would dine at various restaurants or watch English movies at the local cinemas. Other times, I would take the train to visit my sister Qudsia who lived about fifty miles away in Sangla Hill, where my uncle was building a sugar mill and my brother-in-law worked. I had grown my hair long, wore tailor-made bell-bottom pants and had my own transistor radio to listen to music while traveling.

Once, as I was traveling from Lahore to Sangla Hill, the train broke down and had to make a stop at a station where it normally did not stop. All of us came out on the platform to eat snacks or drink hot tea while they fixed the unknown mechanical problem. I was wearing dark sunglasses, bell-bottom trousers, and a t-shirt. Standing by the snack stand with my long, flowing hair and radio on my shoulder, I became aware that I was slowly being surrounded by many young children. They were all talking in Punjabi and commenting on my looks, clothes and overall persona. At first, I did not realize why I was being encircled and deserving of their commentary. Then, a couple of kids started betting about the country of my origin. It suddenly dawned on me that in this rural town where few trains stopped, I was standing out like a sore thumb— an oddity— and therefore, I was being declared as a person of a foreign land while at a train station that was not far from my ancestral village. I decided to play along for a few more minutes and asked them in Punjabi, *"How are you all doing, what are your names?"* I vividly remember the utter shock and surprise on their young faces. They ran like fawn from a cheetah, and I had a good laugh. Soon after, the conductor announced that the train was ready to depart, and I slowly climbed aboard with a sheepish grin, trying to figure what had transpired.

Within a few months of easy living, the charm of this lifestyle had worn off. I was quickly becoming a restless soul with no sense of accomplishments. From my early days in school, I had learned the spirit of competition and associated rewards with achieving success. Seeing my father as a respectable leader of our clan and village, I wanted to grow up to be a leader who did something good for my fellow citizens. Luckily, the higher powers that be were at work and would force me back into the running for completing my dream of coming to America.

After a few months of classes, there was political strife from the recent loss of Bangladesh (formerly East Pakistan) with political parties blaming each other to gain the upper hand (more on the history of Pakistan later in the book). These parties had infiltrated colleges and universities and had set up student unions by providing monetary support to bring the young men, and sometimes women, on the street to agitate the government while destroying property. This was an unfortunate partnership that exists to this day: the older generation exploits the young minds for their selfish causes. As a result, the universities and colleges were closed for the next nine months including my school, The University of Engineering and Technology, and all students were sent home until further notice. There was nothing the students who wanted to study could do but bow to the whims of the few bent on violence and destroying not only their future but also the future of others.

On the positive side, this irrational and destructive behavior provided me with a better argument when I was trying to convince my dad that I needed to go to America. My dad strongly believed in higher education but was somewhat hesitant for me to leave because of my young age. Despite this, I was sticking to my dream of going to America and concocted an elaborate marketing plan to convince him to give me his approval. I met with all of my seven older brothers and sisters and asked them to write a letter to our father pleading on my behalf for his permission for me to study abroad. Fortunately, all of my siblings obliged. I was losing precious time, and no one knew when the educational institutions in Pakistan would re-open. In the meantime, my father upped the ante by offering to buy me a brand new car if I would only stay at home and drop my plans to go abroad to study.

After reading letters from my siblings and seeing the overwhelming support from the rest of the family, my compassionate father agreed with my request and even offered to provide the necessary financing and prayers that would be required. He had only one condition: I would have to make all the travel arrangements. This was his way of teaching me to stand on my own two feet. I was overly excited with the thought of my dream coming true and agreed whole-heartedly with his requirement.

When I mention that I had to make all the necessary travel arrangements, it is important to note that it wasn't as simple as buying a plane ticket. There was a lot of work one had to do in order to even become "qualified" for traveling to the United States. These included:

1. Taking the required TOEFL (Test of English as Foreign Language) through the Educational Testing Service (ETS). ETS, based in Princeton, New Jersey that also administers various other tests including SAT, AP, GRE, etc.

2. Applying to various American Universities, mailing high school transcripts and waiting months for letters of admission.

3. Taking an EPT (English Proficiency Test) administered by the American Embassy or the Consulate in Pakistan and scoring at least an 80%.

4. Applying for a visa from the American Embassy by providing an official letter of admission from a university, EPT passing score and financial statements proving that my father could support me for four years while getting my degree.

5. Completing a face-to-face interview with a Visa Officer.

6. Filing with the State Bank of Pakistan for the tuition and living funds approval once the visa was issued. In those days, the dollars were available through two means: legally, through the State Bank of Pakistan, and illegally, where they were available through the black market at a much higher price. I never used the black market route even though it was illegal but openly acceptable.

In the six months that it took me to get these steps completed, I never felt frustrated or hopeless because I firmly believed that I would eventually make it to America.

I finally received acceptance letters from Marquette University in Wisconsin and Vincennes University in Vincennes, Indiana. After talking with my family, we determined that the weather in Wisconsin was much colder than Vincennes. With that simple logic, I made final preparations to leave the land of my birth and the arms of my loving family behind to wade into an unknown world to pursue my dreams in the great state of Indiana and, best of all, the United States of America.

Over the years, many have asked me why I chose Vincennes. I really never had a good answer until I started writing this book. As I look back now, I believe that Vincennes chose me because it had many angels in place, ready to help and guide me in learning the American values that laid the groundwork and ultimately led me down the path to becoming a citizen.

The Power Of Prayer

By 1972, I had accepted my admission to Vincennes University and was now was ready for the final step: getting my passport. I believed in praying but had not yet realized the exact power of prayer.

I wanted to leave for America as soon as possible, so I talked with my father and asked him to call some of his influential friends to help me attain my passport on time. His simple reply was that instead of calling his influential friends, he would call upon the most influential power he knew of in the universe. This answer was not what I wanted to hear, so I went to my mother and asked her if she could talk with my father. Seeing my disappointment, she agreed to intervene on my behalf, but she got the same response. Obviously, having been with my father for a long time, she had seen the miracle of prayer and urged me to trust in his efforts and be patient.

In that part of the world, getting a passport isn't as simple as walking into the passport office, filling out the necessary forms, attaching your picture and waiting a couple of weeks for them to mail you the finished product. It is a corrupt society where you either pay the bribe upfront to initiate the process or get some influential person to call the head of the passport office to get things done ahead of everyone else. With this thought in my mind, I was feeling dejected and decided that I was going to give it a shot by myself.

I completed all the necessary forms and got an appointment with the passport officer after several calls. When I met with the passport officer, I explained to him that I had already received admission to a university and that in less than six weeks I needed to be there. He listened to all of this, but after I was done, he replied, *"Young man, this will not be possible as there are hundreds of applicants ahead of you, and your passport should be ready in six months."* I tried to reason with him, but he wouldn't budge and said that there was nothing he could do. I came home fuming and furious at both the system and my father and decided that all I could do was wait.

The passport office was only few blocks from my house. It was an easy walk, so, having no other option and nothing to do while I waited, I would walk there every day to see if my luck would come through for me. There was always a circus-like atmosphere in the evenings when they would announce the names of the lucky people who would finally get their passports. Since I was now a part of this shared ordeal, I would often walk there in the evening to watch all of the festivities. It now made more sense to me how big of a deal it was to get a passport. There were a few young men like me there who were hopeful that they too would soon be headed for schools in America or Europe; however, the overwhelming majority of people in the passport office were in their thirties or older with their own personal hopes of heading to various Middle-Eastern countries as laborers. They were responsible for supporting their families and had a big burden placed on their shoulders. Some of these men had several family members with them and, upon hearing the announcement that their passport was ready, shouts of joy and exhilaration would erupt from their groups. Despite all the excitement, jealous eyes would watch them with apprehension. But now, these groups of jealous and apprehensive travelers included me.

One evening as I finished my dinner, my father informed me that he and his prayer buddy would be using my room for a few hours to pray. Then he smiled and said, *"We are especially going to pray for your passport."* I respectfully listened to this and tried to hide my dismay as best I could. As they went to my room to pray, I left my house and began my daily journey of walking to the passport office so that I could keep myself busy for the evening.

The atmosphere was festive as usual, and another evening was bound to end with joy for some and despair for others. The sea of people included men, women and children occupying every inch of available space. Kebobs were being hawked by street vendors, and hot tea was sipped by many to stay warm after a cold front had moved in from the Northwest. Impromptu fireplaces were built by a few to stay warm. As the night progressed, there were many celebrations, and the crowd started to get smaller and smaller.

Finally around nine that evening, as I was lost in my own thoughts, I heard the window clerk announce from a distance, *"Mubarak!"* I was looking around to see who this lucky guy was that had the same name as mine, but no one moved forward. After calling a few other names, he called again for *"Mubarak"* and added that this was the final call. Suddenly, it hit me that it could be me. I ran to the window, and the clerk seemed somewhat grumpy. He asked me why I did not move faster as he slowly opened the picture page of the passport. The clerk asked me to step closer. He looked at the picture and then at me. The entire time my heart was beating so hard it felt like it was ready to jump out of my chest. After what seemed like forever, he pushed the register forward and asked me to sign. I signed with trembling hands, and then he placed the passport in my hands. I quickly backed away from the window and stood in disbelief for several minutes trying to focus and understand the enormity of what had just occurred. I opened the passport and checked the picture, name and address. Everything was mine! At that instant, I jumped in the air with a shout of joy and ran back home. I had obtained my passport in less than two weeks instead of six months.

As I approached the house, I remembered my father's earlier conversation during dinner. I remembered that my father had talked about praying with his friend and, among all the places he could have chosen, he chose my room for prayer. Against all the odds of getting my passport in time to start my schooling, it was this one evening that he prayed for it, which made my dream come true. I wanted nothing more than to tell him that his prayers were heard and answered. The first person I saw as I came home was my mother. I ran and hugged her and waved the passport in the air. She just smiled and said that she was so happy for me. Then I ran to my father's room and exclaimed, *"Father I got my passport!"* He gave me a big smile, congratulated me, and while he hugged me, he said softly, *"Son, always trust in God."* That was and still is the best lesson that I have ever learned.

Over the years and in my darkest hours, I have reached out to God, always remembering His special blessing on that wonderful day in November 1972.

Coming To America And Vincennes, Indiana

My journey began on August 21, 1973. It was a very hot day as I began my trip to Karachi International Airport. As the heat encircled me, my eyes welled up with tears at the thought of leaving my family behind. However, that thought did not stay in my mind for long as I also felt a rush of adrenaline at the idea of the adventure that awaited me. The time had finally come. After five years of planning, getting my dad's approval, completing all the paperwork and navigating the bureaucratic system of visas and passports, I was finally getting on the plane that would take me to America.

While saying my goodbyes, I could see the tears in my mother's loving eyes and the pride on my father's princely face. I also said farewell to my sisters who had been my guardian angels from the day I was born, my brothers and their wives who had been instrumental in persuading my father for his approval for my journey, my cousins with their moral support, and my many nephews and nieces with the thought of missing the uncle who would always play silly games with them.

My flight wasn't a direct flight and included stops at Dhahran, Saudi Arabia; Athens, Greece; Frankfurt, West Germany; and London, England. When I landed in London, I changed planes for my final flight to John F. Kennedy International Airport in New York City. The plane landed at JFK around 11:00 PM. I took a taxi to a hotel, checked-in, and found that I couldn't turn on the lights in the table lamps next to the bed. For the next 15 minutes, I checked everywhere with my fingers but had no luck. I was embarrassed to call the front desk for help on my first day in this country. Finally, I gave up, dialed zero for the operator and told her my plight, acting as innocent as I could. After about 10 minutes, a maintenance person came to the room. He went to the lamp, and the light came on like magic. He left the room mumbling, and the few words reached my ears quickly. I was mortified. He spoke about *"foreigners not knowing much."* This really got me roiled up, and with the lamp lit, I clearly saw the reason for my inability to turn it on. I grew up with off–on switch on the base of the lamp whereas this switch was located near the bulb. Somehow in the dark and traveling for the last 30 hours, my neurons were not communicating with the brain in order to look outside of the box.

I locked the door and the dead bolt with the anticipation that I would not be able to open the door from inside. However, as I turned the handle, the door opened without any hesitation. It was yet another quirk to which I had to adapt that night after growing up in another land. The long hours of travel had not afforded me enough sleep, but with the lamp and lock challenges and my high anxiety level, it was impossible for me to sleep due to my apprehension. Throughout the night, I took a total of five showers to stay awake, all the while becoming consumed with the fear that someone might rob me of the $2,000 in cash that I had with me for my travels.

The next day, I took the hotel van to LaGuardia International Airport, where I got on another plane to Indianapolis, Indiana, where I then took a Greyhound bus to my final destination, Vincennes. The bus driver, a kind man, dropped me at 6th Street and pointed me in the direction of the University three blocks away. I did not know what a block was, but it didn't bother me as I began the walk towards the direction in which he pointed. By now, I had been traveling for over 60 straight hours with very little sleep, but I was neither tired nor felt any exhaustion. I had only gone a short distance when a gentleman in a pick-up truck stopped and offered me a ride to the University's Auditorium, which was set up for student registration. I see now that this was to be the first angel of many that I would meet along my journey to find my place in America.

As I entered the auditorium to register myself, I met my first angel, Pat Mindermann, who greeted me with a big warm smile. Pat immediately made me very comfortable and assured me that the registration process was painless and very smooth. After registration, Pat, ignoring my protest, picked up my suitcase and walked me to my room. He helped me settle in and assured me that if I needed anything he would be available to help. Despite the fact that he had over 100 students to manage, he graciously gave me his time, and for that, I will always be grateful.

Meeting Angels Of The Mid-West

It took a few days to get settled into my room at 54 Harrison Hall. It was a nice corner room on the first floor with two beds and a desk for each roommate. I was under the mistaken impression that the University would provide bed sheets and pillows and went my first month without linens. I was fine with this as I still felt the rush of adventure with each experience. A kind woman known to all as Mom Hart worked at the front desk of the building. One of her responsibilities was to put incoming mail in each student's mailbox. Since my mail from home always came late, she would assure me that I would be getting many letters soon, explaining that overseas mail takes longer to process and deliver than domestic mail.

I registered for my classes, got my cafeteria card and tried to immerse myself in the daily routine of American university life. The food in cafeteria looked exciting for the first few days, and I was really enamored with the desert offerings, which included various cakes and colorful Jell-O. Chicken and Hamburgers were familiar, but I had to learn about turkey, macaroni and cheese, and all the other comfort foods common on all college campuses. After the first week, I began to feel the pains of homesickness. Calls home were very expensive (around $3 per minute), and letters took a few weeks to get to Pakistan and a few weeks more to get back to me. The cafeteria food started to taste bland, and I had difficulties keeping up my adventurist spirit.

My roommate was nice and accommodating but not yet a close friend, so I had to keep much of my frustration and anxiety to myself. When I went to the library, I would always frantically search for any news from back home but none was available. Finally, one day I came across a Christian Science Monitor newspaper with international news and was pleased to at least find something that brought me closer to home. That is, until I read about floods that came close to my home. It didn't help my already desperate state of homesickness, and I was overcome with worries about the safety of my family. The more I let these thoughts consume me, the more depressed I became.

After these feelings became stronger and I seriously contemplated going back to Pakistan, Pat Minderman took it upon himself to help me. He would spend about an hour each evening listening to my rationale for leaving while providing gentle and well thought out rebuttals. He challenged me to think through my feelings and objectively evaluate if my decision to leave was beneficial or harmful for my future. It wasn't long before I realized that Pat was right in his counseling and I should honor both my family and my dreams and complete my education. However, I still hadn't heard anything from home. After three weeks of no mail, I opened my mailbox and found a letter. In my excitement, I opened it without even looking to see whom it was from. To my utter surprise, it was a letter of encouragement signed by Mom Hart. It was such an inspirational letter that I quit worrying about getting mail any longer. A few days later, as if Mom's letter had magically made it happen, I started getting mail regularly from my family and friends.

Finally, my homesickness was slowly giving way to new excitement and curiosity. I had finally overcome my emotions and reached deep inside to commit to finish my studies. Adopting this attitude was one of the best decisions that I have ever made.

One day, while I was walking in the Administration Building looking for the room of one of my classes, I met Carol Keusch. She was responsible for managing the phone switchboard in the evening. After a quick assessment, she guessed that I was not familiar with the building. She proceeded to describe everything in such detail and made sure that I had all the necessary information that I needed. I was really impressed with her desire to help me.

We talked for few minutes, and she asked me how I liked the University and the town so far. I responded that I would be back after my class to discuss my experiences and thoughts. This started our friendship and over the next several months, I would stop by to see Carol and talk about my family, growing up, my classes and Vincennes. She became a sister to me and was an excellent listener. She was genuinely inquisitive about my learning and would help me understand the subtleties of American culture and life style. She also helped me tremendously with my conversational English, and I owe both her and her husband my deepest gratitude for their friendship as I grew to understand the American way of life.

Anticipation was building as the newly arrived international students learned that we would soon all be matched with a host family. These marvelous and compassionate families of Vincennes had volunteered to open their homes to one or two students at a time. They sought to help lessen our homesickness and emotional stress by acclimating us to American culture.

Naturally, I was very anxious with the thought of meeting my host family. Would they like me? Would they understand my accent? Would they be able to pronounce my name? There were a hundred questions rolling through my head even though there was no doubt in my mind that I would love whoever my host family was. I needed them more than they needed me, and being the youngest of eight, I was yearning to be part of a family.

On the day we were to be introduced to our families, I got a haircut, pressed my shirt and suit, chose a matching tie and polished my shoes so many times that they could not absorb any more polish. I shaved and splashed on enough English Leather aftershave to make a dramatic impact.

Around forty of us were taken to Gregg Park on a Saturday evening. Right away, I was mesmerized at seeing so many cheerful families, their genuine manners, their pretty dress and clothing, and all the tables piled up with food. I had not eaten well for the past few days, and I was ready for the feast and good company. The organizers started to match each student with their assigned family. Introductions were made, hands were shook, hugs were shared and smatterings of laughs were heard. I could feel the happiness and joy in the air and eagerly stood by watching while waiting for my turn to be introduced.

After about twenty minutes or so of not hearing my name being called, I started getting panicky as I saw one of the organizers who had just arrived go over to the table and look over the list. Then someone pointed her towards me. The look in her eyes made my heart sink. She slowly walked towards me and said very tenderly, "Sorry, your assigned family is not coming today. They will get back with you later." After seeing the shock and despair on my face, she quickly added, "Don't worry, my husband I would like for you to join us for dinner this evening." I accepted and sat down to think about what had just happened.

After a short while, a distinguished and elegantly dressed gentleman walked over to me and said, "Hi! My name is Bob, what's yours?" I extended my hand and replied, "Mubarak." Although he had no problem getting my first name right, my last name was another story, and we gave up after few tries. After some conversation, he took me over and introduced me to Alice, his wife. A month after meeting Bob and Alice, I got a call one evening from him inviting me to dinner at his house for "shish kebobs." Always being thirsty for knowledge, I knew right away that this would be a special evening. Bob always relished in showing people around and making them comfortable. He showed me how to fix shish kebobs on the grill, how to heat up water in the microwave, how to get ice and fill a glass directly from the refrigerator door, and other basic skills that I never had to learn while growing up with servants and my doting sisters. This was also the first American home I had been inside, and I was totally fascinated by everything that Bob and Alice showed me.

Once the dinner was over, both Bob and Alice asked me if I would be interested in coming back and cooking a native Pakistani dish. I did not tell them that I had never cooked before, but I was so humbled by them and their house that I readily agreed. It would be the first time I had cooked anything on my own, but at this point in my adventure, I had already overcome so much that I assumed it would be an easy challenge.

When I came back to their house to cook for them, I did everything on the fly and off of memory from what I saw the cooks do in my own house growing up. The result of my labor was a chicken dish the likes of which I had never eaten before. I knew that Alice had recognized my naïveté, but I did not expect the reaction that she and the rest of the family gave me. When the food was served, Bob, Alice and their children all kept telling me what a great job I had done and how delicious everything tasted. This was true hospitality, and from their actions, both Bob and Alice instantly became saints in my eyes. Years after this incident, I would joke with them about my first ever cooking experience at their home. Their response was always the same; they loved the food, and it was delicious. I knew that they had made up their minds and that they never wanted me to feel embarrassed.

Bob and Alice eventually became my unofficial adopted parents, and in the spring of 1976, I lived with them for few months. It was my best learning experience since coming to America. We would talk about religion, philosophy, psychology and the human experience for hours every night. I would also go to church with them and pray. I learned a lot about American life from them, including how to eat raw oysters (Bob's favorite), how to appreciate and eat a good medium-rare steak with only your fork and, most of all, how most American families work hard to provide for each other.

In the spring of 1975, I was invited to give a speech about Pakistan and its culture to a ladies group attended by another dear friend I had come to know, Peggy Scott. I traveled to Sullivan, Indiana to talk to the group of about 30 ladies and followed it with a lively Q&A. Afterwards, I ate lunch with the group and Peggy handed me an envelope with $40 as a thank you gesture. I did not intend to make money off of the speech but, understanding the importance of the gesture, graciously accepted it.

A month after my speaking engagement, I got a call from Peggy. She said that after talking with Alan, her husband, they wanted to offer me a chance to stay with them for the summer to facilitate a job they had gotten for me at a nearby farm. I kindly thanked Peggy for this generous offer but, since I had already planned to go to Nashville, Tennessee for a job selling Bibles door-to-door, I graciously declined.

After two days of attending sales classes, I realized that the Bible salesman job was not what I had been led to expect. The tactics that were taught bothered me the most; I was told that as soon as the lady of the house opened the door we had to put our foot in the door so that it couldn't be closed and that we had to be let into the house. Once inside, the next tactic was to pressure her to buy the Bible if she was a good Christian. I felt that this was a con job and I needed to get out of it immediately. I called Peggy, and without any hesitation, she told me to come home right away.

Peggy and Alan treated me just like one of their sons. My picture was put on the desk in the foyer alongside photos of their two sons. I slept on the family room couch, which was a pull-out bed. The next two-and-a-half months were fabulous. I worked at a local orchard pruning apple trees. Peggy would fix my lunch each day, and at break time, I would eat my sandwich with the other help. Even though I came from a farming family, I had never worked on the farm. Sometimes while I was on the ladder, I would marvel at the opportunity to work as it was teaching me the value of earning money and being a responsible person. It didn't matter what the job was. Amazingly, for a kid who had really never worked a day in his life, I was enjoying the whole process of getting up early, heading to the orchard and earning money.

As mentioned earlier, after completing two years at Vincennes University (a two-year college), I transferred to the University of Evansville in Evansville, Indiana. On the day of registration and after completing the process in less than 10 minutes, I learned who the International Students Advisor was and walked up to him to introduce myself. He welcomed me, told me his name was Dr. Marvin Hartig and asked if I needed anything. I replied that I didn't but asked if he needed my help with the new students who were arriving to this country for the first time. I explained that I could pick them up at the airport, take them to a store to buy things they needed or just be on-call for any help in general. After seeing my enthusiasm, he gratefully accepted my offer, and this began one of my greatest friendships.

Dr. Hartig had contracted polio in his teen years, leaving his left arm and leg disabled. His full-time job was "Dean of Academics" for the University, and he had cordially volunteered to serve as the International Students Advisor without an increase in pay. Of course, I did not know all of this when I met him during registration; nonetheless, I immediately got a vibe that this person was an angel doing God's work. Dr. Hartig had a very calm demeanor. I never saw him get upset or angry. He had an open door policy for all students. He would always listen intently prior to doling out advice or a solution. He helped many Iranian students during and after the 1979 revolution. The flow of funds was disrupted for many, impacting their ability to pay either tuition or living expenses. Dr. Hartig worked diligently with the University administration to provide some relief to the needy students. At times, he would hand out cash from his own pocket. I knew he could not afford to do so, but it was not in his nature to say no. He was always willing to sacrifice in order to help out the needy. Over the next few years, Dr. Hartig and I became close. We both shared the common goal of wanting to help the new students in getting settled to their new environment. I had not forgotten how difficult my first month in this country was, and I was going to assist in whatever capacity I could.

In the spring of 1977, Dr. Hartig asked what my plans were after graduation. I replied that I would like to either enroll for an MBA (Master of Business Administration) or get an 18-month work permit (allowed by the Immigration and Naturalization Service to students on F-1 visa at the time) in order to gain experience prior to going back to Pakistan.

Dr. Hartig recommended that I get my MBA, adding that due to my helpful nature, he had a proposition for me. He explained that because of his increased workload in a dual role, the University had approved a position of "Graduate Assistant." He said that he wanted me as his "Graduate Assistant" and asked me to consider the offer.

After a few days of deliberation, I told Dr. Hartig that I would do it. I was awarded the "Graduate Assistantship," which covered full tuition in return for assisting Dr. Hartig. Even though the Graduate Assistantship required only 15 hours of work per week, I found that I was working 25–30 hours per week. I was a full-time student and had full-time responsibilities in this newly appointed role. I was also the Student Manager in the University Dining Center and put in 30–35 hours per week managing around 156 students who worked part-time along with regular civilian employees.

Dr. Hartig and I became even closer after I left the University and got married. I would call him at least once a month and was never surprised to find him always optimistic and full of life. From this man, I learned the necessary qualities of helping others and staying positive and optimistic. After Dr. Hartig passed away in 2007, Mahmood, a good friend of mine who was from Iran and had benefited from Dr. Hartig's generosity while a student at the University, called to see if we could work together to start a Memorial Scholarship Fund at the University honoring this terrific man whom we all knew and greatly respected. This project was a success, and I am happy to say that each year the Dr. Marvin E. Hartig Scholarship, inspired by a man who did so much to the students he worked for, is awarded to a student in need.

In the summer of 1978, I met Russell and Charlene Vickers through one my roommates who was from Hong Kong. They invited me for a dinner at their house, after which Mrs. Vickers asked if I would be interested in staying with them as a paying guest. After giving it some thought, I called and told them that I would graciously accept their kind offer. They lived in the historic part of Evansville on Riverside Drive near the Ohio River in a big Victorian house.

Mrs. Vickers was a motherly woman and treated me like a son during my stay. She would fix my breakfast, do my laundry, and iron my clothes. Mr. Vickers was a quiet, kind and gentle man who never complained about anything.

As a Muslim, I did not eat pork, and I had communicated this to Mrs. Vickers when she inquired about any dietary restrictions that I may have had. She was very accommodating, and I never thought anything else about it. One morning a few weeks later, I was finishing my breakfast and we were having a morning chat. I asked, *"Don't you eat bacon or sausage for breakfast?"* What she said next made my jaw drop. Mrs. Vickers said that they did not want to offend me by eating pork in front of me. Just imagine: I am the one staying at their house and eating their food, and they were doing 100 times more for me than I was giving in return. They did not fail in giving me the utmost respect. After hearing this, I clarified that I did not eat pork personally but I had absolutely no issue with anyone eating it around me. She felt better after my explanation, and I felt totally humbled by their kindness and respect.

Looking back, I believe that coming to the American Mid-West was the greatest decision that I made. I found the folks of Indiana similar to my own family back home. They were unconditionally generous, kind, and loving to everyone they met, and they never hesitated to make any stranger feel welcome in their home. This was especially true for the young international students like me. They were always genuinely interested in learning about the culture of the respective student and willing to help them learn about American culture. The great "American melting pot" was alive and well in Vincennes and Evansville.

I had no difficulty assimilating to the culture and to this day truly appreciate all those who gave their precious time for this worthy cause. The interaction was extremely beneficial for my English as well. The more I talked, the more I started to pick up on common English words and American slang. Within just a few months, I could even think completely in English.

Through all my experiences with these outstanding human beings I learned the necessary requirements of becoming a contributing, productive citizen instead of becoming a burden on society. Over the years, I have thought on numerous occasions why these folks were so kind to me. None of them asked anything of me, never demanded anything from me and never implied that they were doing me any favor. The only answer that comes to my mind is that they were following the teachings of Christ and believed in helping humanity. Simply put, they were Angels sent to help me. It was because of them that I became a responsible adult. Now some of them have passed away, and the remaining few still make me feel honored and humbled whenever I talk with them on the phone or visit them in person.

1974 – First Job And Getting Robbed

My nephew Farooq had joined Vincennes University (VU) in January 1974, after I had completed my first semester. Another dear chap, Shahrukh, who hailed from Shiraz, Iran and belonged to the Bahi faith, also joined VU in January 1974 and became a good friend. They both appreciated my help in getting them settled into campus life. We were like three musketeers enjoying our newfound student life.

As the summer of 1974 approached, I wanted to work and make some extra cash. In those days, Immigration and Naturalization Service allowed foreign students to work off-campus during summer upon receiving a written request duly signed by university officials. All three of us had received our work permits in April of 1974. My good American friend William Gates (no relation to Bill Gates) had offered to help me get a job in Indianapolis. Since I was the de-facto leader of the three musketeers, both Farooq and Shahrukh had decided to follow me to Indianapolis.

In early May of 1974, William explained the job deal in Indianapolis. He was going to work during the summer at the school for special children owned by a psychiatrist. The school owned three big Victorian homes near 38th street. The school was located in one of the houses and the other two houses were empty. The owner would provide us room and board in exchange for painting both empty houses inside and out. We were free to get a regular job in addition to earn wages. This sounded like a heck of deal, and after discussing it with Farooq and Shahrukh, I communicated to William of our acceptance.

None of us had done any work or labor in the countries of our birth, but we were totally excited and committed to learning all that came our way. Farooq and I arrived in Indianapolis in mid-May 1974, while Shahrukh went to Bloomington, Indiana to spend some time with his physician uncle prior to joining us. William welcomed us and showed us the nearby grocery store. We had not done any grocery shopping or cooked anything until now, so we went from aisle to aisle looking for things that we felt looked familiar and would create the taste we wanted. I was picked as the chef, and the other two wanted to act as a sous chef or cleanup person. We liked chicken, so selecting meat was easy. The challenge was how to pick spices. That ordeal took us a couple of hours. After opening and smelling many containers, we settled on a few. I prepared the chicken dish after spending several hours in the kitchen, and the experience at Bob and Alice Johnson's house definitely helped.

The next two days, we familiarized ourselves with the paint, paint cans, brushes, long ladders and the fine art of balancing the tools and ourselves. In the absence of a car, we walked many miles to fill out employment applications for a regular job. Finally, on the third day we landed a job in the kitchen at the Stouffer's Hotel (2820 N. Meridian St. Indianapolis, now closed). Our shift started at 6:00 AM and ended between 2–3 PM, depending on the lunch crowd. The restaurant was located on the 13th floor, but the elevator did not identify it as such. That is when I learned that "13" is considered an unlucky number and many times is not labeled on the elevator floor panel. The Stouffer's Hotel was an upscale restaurant with a nice ambiance. The pay was $1.65 per hour plus breakfast and lunch. It was a wonderful day indeed, and I felt like I was on cloud nine. This was the first regular job of my life.

We didn't have a car and were still learning about the bus system, so we walked the first week, which took us an hour in the morning and little longer in the afternoon, as we were tired. Our routine was to relax for half an hour, then climb up the high ladders and paint until dark. After eating, we would be in bed by 9 PM to start around 4:20 AM.

As soon as I saved around $700, I bought a 1966 VW bug. It was a nice car with a few holes in the floor and the heater worked all year along, but those were the least of my worries. I did not have a license, and no one had told me about car insurance. I had been driving since I was 14 years old but had not driven in the USA. I would wake up at 3:30 in morning to get on the road to practice when there was little traffic and drive for about an hour prior to getting ready to go to work at Stouffer's. Within a week, I had learned my way around and felt like a pro on the road. Now every day had become an adventure, and nothing bothered us.

Shahrukh joined us in June, and I got him job at Stouffer's. Our painting productivity rose with the passing of each day, and the owner of the house was pleased with our work. The cooking had also improved greatly. Shahrukh would fix a delicious Persian rice dish that when combined with my chicken masala became our favorite. I don't know why, but we ate chicken pretty much every day and only ate beef once in a while. Our favorite entertainment was going to the malls and drive-in movie theaters.

One day, the owner of the house we lived in asked me if one of us could start sleeping in the other empty house next to the house that we were already living in. I readily agreed; however, both Farooq and Shahrukh did not want to sleep alone. This was not an issue with me, so I told them that they both should sleep in the house next door. Furthermore, as a de-facto leader, I had to keep the troops happy.

After few days, the new sleeping arrangements had become a normal routine. One night after dinner, we all went to our stations, and I was in a deep sleep by 9 PM. Sometime around midnight, I heard noises in my bedroom room and heard steps on the creaky old wooden floor. I was groggy and thinking it was either Farooq or Shahrukh. I softly asked what was going on. I heard some muffled voices, cursing and in the flash of a second, felt an awful pain all over my body prior to passing out. When I gained consciousness, there was total silence. My head was aching terribly, and upon touching it with my fingers, I could feel blood.

Somehow, I managed to turn on the side table light, reach for phone and dialed ZERO for the operator (911 did not exist then). The operator was very nice and asked me to hold while she called the police. I could not find my Seiko watch, a gift from my father, and I asked her for the time, and my recollection is that she replied 1:30 AM I called Farooq and Shahrukh in the house next door, and they called the landlord. The police and an ambulance showed up in less than five minutes, and I was whisked away to the emergency room. After receiving 16 stiches in my head and talking with the police detective, I was released in the wee hours of early morning. The owner's sister took us to stay at her very nice apartment on the top floor of some elegant building. She was amazingly kind and did everything to make us all comfortable.

Sometime that afternoon, she brought us back. I learned that the owner had to replace the box spring and mattress due to my excessive bleeding. The owner also left his German Shepard with us, so we felt secured. The next three days, Farooq and Shahrukh were very frightened and worried about me. One of them always stayed with me, and we all slept on the same bed for the next few nights.

The detective came to see me a few days later. According to him, there were probably three to four robbers who climbed one of the ladders that we used for painting in order to get to the top of the garage. They gained access through the open window of the bedroom. Since there was no air-conditioning, I kept the upstairs windows open at night to stay cool. The robbers had taken my prized, blue Seiko watch, thirty dollars from my wallet and a stereo that belonged to the house. The robbers were never caught.

After a week, I returned to the hospital, and my stitches were removed. I had lost 10 pounds in weight, but I was regaining my strength quickly. That evening, we all decided to quit our jobs and leave. I called my Godmother, Mrs. Iva Novak, who was the dormitory director at Vincennes University but was visiting her home in Fort Wayne, Indiana for the summer. Upon learning what had transpired, she told me (or ordered me, rather) to pack up and get to her lake house near Fort Wayne. With that, we said our good-byes to William, owner of the house, and to our friends at Stouffer's with a real sadness in our hearts. The next day, we put all of our belongings in my VW bug, and with my newly acquired driver's license, we legally hit the road. As soon as we left Indianapolis behind us, we all started feeling better and were looking forward to spending time at the lake house, yet another new adventure for us. I remember that day vividly because as we cruised along we listened to President Nixon's resignation speech on the car radio. The date was August 8, 1974.

We stayed with Mrs. Novak at the lake house for a full week. She took care of us like a true mother; we relished each moment. She fed us, played cards with us and took us around Fort Wayne. We swam in the lake and had the time of our lives. She was another angel that came into my life and helped me along the way. The last time I talked with her was in the late 80's or early 90's, and then we lost touch.

Now looking back, I realized how close I came to dying that fateful day in the summer of 1974. The good Lord had other plans, and I am thankful for all His blessings.

OVERCOMING PREDUDICE AGAINST PEOPLE FROM INDIA

During my second year at Vincennes University, I was helping out as many international students that I could. Pat Minderman, International Students Advisor, would send whoever needed help my way, and I also sought out the needy on my own.

One evening, Pat called to ask if I could help a new student who was having considerable difficulties adjusting to life on campus. The student's name was Madhukar Bhatt. He was in his late 30's and had won a Gold Medal for his art in India. I told Pat that I would contact him to see what I could do. The things that I could not tell Pat was that I had never met a person from India and that I had some reservations about meeting a fellow from India.

Pakistan had two wars against India while I was growing up. I was both an idealist and nationalist at that time. I had grown up with the idea that anyone from India was an "enemy." Obviously, it was "brain washing," but I did not know any better back in August of 1974. Even though I had responded to Pat in the affirmative, I did not know if I could overcome my own biases. I went to bed struggling with how I could bow out of this ordeal gracefully. When I woke up in the morning, I picked up the phone and called Madhukar Bahtt's room number. I hoped that he would not answer and that I could call Pat to tell him that I could not get hold of him. I still had not figured out how to handle this but definitely hoped that this would buy me more time until I could find a better way.

On the second ring, I heard a soft and anxious voice on the other side. I introduced myself, and he said that he was expecting my call since Pat had called him the day before. Pat had talked highly of me, and he was looking forward to meeting me. Suddenly, all of the apprehension that I had felt for the last 12 hours was gone. I inquired when a good time would be to meet, and he asked if we could do it right away. Knowing that his room was only about 30 feet away, I told him that I would be there in couple of minutes.

I took a deep breath and started walking towards his room. I knocked at the door, and what I saw next was totally unexpected. I did not see a monster standing in front of me but a short-statured, nice looking man. His face was full of fear and excitement as he softly said, *"Namaste."* Namaste is a non-contact form of Indian greeting, commonly accompanied by a slight bow made with hands pressed together, palms touching and fingers pointed upwards and in front of the chest.

All my fears, biases and prejudices evaporated. So, we sat down to discuss his difficulties and needs. Number one was the bland food in the cafeteria. He loved spices and peppery, hot food. We also talked about going to a retail store, bank, etc. and agreed to meet at 2 PM after our classes.

I discussed this meeting with Farooq and Shahrukh and enlisted their help in finding a place that served spicy and hot food. Vincennes is a small town of approximately 20,000. In 1974, there were no Mexican or Chinese restaurants, let alone Indian. After struggling for about an hour and checking with all of our American and international friends, we could not solve this riddle.

Then suddenly, it occurred to me that we should take him to eat pizza. That evening, Madhukar Bhatt (henceforth known as Mr. Bhatt or Bhatt

Sahab out of respect, as he was 18 years older than us and our elder), Farooq, Shahrukh and I piled into my car and went to the Pizza Restaurant. Mr. Bhatt, being Hindu, was vegetarian. We ordered a non-meat pizza for him and beef pizza for us. Once the pizza came, I handed Mr. Bhatt a jar of hot crushed peppers, normally available in all pizza joints. His eyes lit up with joy. I was amazed to see that he finished the large pizza with the entire jar of hot peppers all by himself.

I purchased a couple jars of hot peppers from the pizza restaurant for Mr. Bhatt to use in the university cafeteria. He was delighted and kept telling me that this was the best meal he had had in the past seven days. After a couple of months, the university administration moved Mr. Bhatt to a house where he could cook or eat according to his tastes and desires.

We became fast friends. That day, I realized that most of our biases and prejudices are not only ridiculous but also cause undue hatred and do no one any good. If I had stayed in the box of prejudice, I would have never known such a fine person as Mr. Bhatt.

In 1976, I drove Mr. Bhatt to the Amtrak train station in Terra Haute, Indiana. He was headed to India and was not sure when he would be coming back. We hugged, and tears were shed as we said our good-byes.

Over the years, we stayed in touch through letters. Then one day in 1992, I learned that Mr. Bhatt was back in Vincennes for a visit. He came to visit me in Vidalia, Georgia and stayed with us for a week. After a few months, he left, and again, after few letters, we lost touch. I have no idea what has happened to him or even if he is still living. However, I am always grateful for meeting my first Indian friend and overcoming the hate and brainwashing that is a part of life.

Marriage And Family

I met Jenny in the spring of 1979, and we were married in the fall of the same year. While we dated, Jenny knew that my ultimate plan was to go back to live in Pakistan, and much to my pleasure, she was happy to go back with me! After our first week of marriage, the reality of my new life sank in, and I realized that during this entire time I had not informed the two most loving and caring people in the world, my parents, about the most fantastic event in my life. When I told Jenny about this, she reminded me that I had told her that I was going to call my parents before the wedding. Understanding the situation in which I had put myself, she encouraged me to call them as soon as possible.

I can't remember why I had procrastinated and did not inform my parents that I was getting married. A couple of years earlier, I had even asked and received permission from my father to marry someone of my choosing rather than having an arranged marriage. Regardless of whatever reason I had for not calling them, I am not proud of it. Without my parents, I could have not have come to the USA, and this was a lousy way to pay them back.

I vexed for a few more days and repeatedly rehearsed the imaginary conversation that I would have with my father. Then, I gathered my courage, picked up the phone and made the call. After the first two rings, I thought about hanging up and calling back the next day. However, there was an absolute lack of coordination between my brain, arm, hand and fingers to act quickly enough, and before I could do anything, I heard the voice of my father on the other end of the line. I quickly tried to make small talk, but after a few minutes, I couldn't hold it back any longer. I blurted out, "Father, I have gotten married!" I stopped and was holding my breath, bracing for the scolding of my life or worse; but what I heard next was a total surprise to me: *"Congratulations, Son! I am so happy for you!"* He said it almost immediately. I then heard him yelling loudly and joyously to my mom and anyone else who was in the room, *"Mubarak has gotten married, and it is a wonderful day!"* As I held on to the phone and listened to all of this, I knew, again, that I was truly blessed with a great father and a wonderful mother.

In subsequent conversations with my father, he surprised me by declaring that he would visit me in 1980. Naturally, I was completely delighted to hear this plan and began to make arrangements for his stay. Sadly, he passed away in February of 1980, never getting a chance to see the life I had made out of the enormous opportunity he had given me. It still bothers me when I think that I could have done more to share my successes here in America with him, but I trust in God's plan and continue to honor his life. After the initial mourning period, I had several discussions with Jenny and my family in Pakistan about the direction of my future. It was then that I decided to stay in this country and apply for citizenship. Looking back, it was the best decision I have ever made.

Aki, my oldest son, is kind-hearted and has worked to help the homeless and the needy. He graduated from Georgia State University and is currently working as a Project Manager for a cutting-edge 3-D Technology Company in Atlanta, Georgia. Ali, my younger son, has achieved the dream that he had since 6th grade, graduating from the United States Military Academy at West Point. He is currently a 2nd Lieutenant in the United States Army.

EXPERIENCING LOVE, KINDNESS AND SOUTHERN HOSPITALITY IN VIDALIA, GEORGIA

In August 1989, I moved to Vidalia, Georgia upon receiving a job offer from Meadows Regional Medical Center. This was my first time in the Deep South, but to me, it was all a part of the same great country. Jenny and I had one son already, Aki, and our youngest son, Ali, would be born the following year in the hospital at which I worked.

The job interview process involved a meeting with two psychoanalysts to evaluate my personality traits, intelligence, analytical and management abilities. The management felt good about my candidacy but wanted to confirm through this process that I would fit in culturally within the local community. This was the first personality test that I had taken in my life, so I was interested in all the information I could learn about myself. The test involved a two-hour interview and three hours of various tests. Both psychoanalysts concluded that I was flexible, highly adaptive and had the ability to fit in pretty much anywhere, and that was good news!

The seven years that I lived in Vidalia were amazingly rewarding. I was provided with another opportunity to learn about the United States while increasing my knowledge of the American South. My role as a part of the management team expanded, and I was rewarded for my hard work. My boss and CEO, Wes Bergman, was not only a terrific boss but also a great teacher, mentor and leader who helped me become a better leader myself.

I was fortunate enough to get involved in the community and serve on various boards, including Kiwanis Club, United Way and Toombs County Against Child Abuse. One day during a management team meeting, my boss informed me that he had nominated me for the upcoming United Way fund raising event. Naturally, I agreed without any further questions. Much to my surprise, however, I later learned that the event was called "Beauty of the Beast" and that each participant would dress up as a woman to perform a comedic act of singing or dancing. Given my upbringing, my initial reaction was that I needed to back out; however, I did not know how to tell my boss of my unfounded reluctance. After all, it was for charity! How could I say no? I told Jenny about my feelings of the situation, and she continuously encouraged me to do it and overcome my apprehensions. I would also like to clarify that I admire women deeply. My reluctance had nothing to do with the gender but with the mental hang-up of me acting as a woman. The thought of displeasing my boss, bowing out of a chance to raise money for a good cause and not heeding to Jenny's good advice finally gave me enough strength to overcome my fears and mentally commit to this event.

The character that I decided to act as was appropriately named "Laila Jasmine." I also decided to dance to the tune of a Lebanese song with Jenny helping me with the choreography, of course. I am not a natural dancer by any means, not even with all my practice during the days of disco fever. After many hours of hard work with the disco queen Jenny, however, I finally felt confident and comfortable.

There were over 10 acts in the event, and the who's who of Vidalia were attending and donating their time and efforts to this cause. The whole ordeal was top notch, including professional make-up artists and hair stylists. Vidalia's top male citizens never looked so pretty.

While we were back stage during the Master of Ceremonies' introductions and the speech one of the participants motioned for us to follow him out to his car. He opened the back of his pickup truck, and inside there was a plethora of bottles of whiskey, wine and beer. I couldn't have been happier to get some liquid courage running through me and was pleased to see that everyone else was almost as anxious as I was. It was an interesting bonding experience as this group of men contemplated what they were about to do in just a few short minutes in front of almost 500 people.

By the time the event started and my name was called, I was ready to get on the stage and show off Laila Jasmine's talent. It was only a two and a half-minute routine, but it felt like an eternity. I heard the laughs, enthusiastic clapping and then the tiny voice that rose above all the others, yelling loud and proud, *"That's my Dad!"* Jenny, Aki and Ali were sitting in the second or third row from the stage. At the tender age of two, Ali could not contain his excitement and wanted to assure me that I had his support. On the other hand Aki, who was nine years old at this time, was mortified, as I learned from Jenny later on.

That night we raised over $10,000 dollars for the United Way. I feel lucky to have been a part of that wonderful event. I made new friends, overcame my own personal fears and, most importantly of all, was able to contribute in a small way to help out my community. As awards were being given out after the festivities, I was delighted to hear my name called as a runner up by the audience's vote. Imagine a kid from Pakistan being declared runner up for a "Beauty of the Beast" pageant in Vidalia, Georgia. It's hard not to believe that this is the greatest country in the world!

PART II

CHAPTER 2

THE EXCEPTIONAL
MINDSET

"A little knowledge that acts is worth infinitely more than much knowledge that is idle."

—KHALIL GIBRAN, 18ᵀᴴ CENTURY POET

WHY NATIONS DOMINATE

FOR SOME TIME NOW, I have been struggling to understand why Muslims have lagged behind in economics, sciences, manufacturing and innovations despite their large population and significant past accomplishments. Perhaps there is an even more important question to answer: what made the Europeans and the Americans so great in achieving illustrious advancements since the 1500s?

The Chinese Shang Dynasty prospered from 1700 B.C.E. to 1046 B.C.E. From 618 to 907, over a thousand years later, the Tang Dynasty created a golden era with significant advancements in art, literature, poetry and technology. This dynasty was succeeded by the Qing Dynasty from 1644 to 1911. However, the period leading up to and the decades leading out of the era of communist revolution saw a stark decline in China's power. This trend continued until the slow de-thawing of its economic system after President Nixon's visit in 1972, which led to the mending of adversarial relations thus opening the path for China to become an industrial giant.

In contrast, the Muslim world reached its zenith in the 1800s and then started a slow decline. The Muslim world's emphasis on conquering lands did not match well with the industrial revolution of the West, and they refuse to understand the reasons behind Western ascendency. The Muslim leaders and their historical accounts lay all blame on the colonization by the West without blaming their own past leaders and poor governance.

How is it possible that in 1857 Great Britain, an island nation of less than 30 million people, overtook the richest nation of the time, India, which had a population of 175 million (six times that of Great Britain) and was over 5,000 miles away by sea? Just like the Greeks, Romans, Persians, Arabs and Mongols in the past, it was time for the rise of Europeans. However, Europeans did not simply rise on passion and manpower alone. They used technology and critical thinking to embark upon the dominance that still stands after its rise in the early 1500s.

The Muslim world, with its reliance on flawed leaders who have used religion and culture to establish a division from which they have not still fully recovered, now appears to the world as rigid, violent and backward. Except for the oil wealth that was discovered with the help of the Americans and the British, the Muslim world has contributed very little to the greater scheme of humanity. The Normal and Violent Mindset has become prevalent in the Muslim world.

This is the theory that I have developed to analyze why the Americans became so great; Japan and Germany rose from the ashes of World War II; and China, India, Brazil and South Korea are well on their way to becoming economic powerhouses.

Muslim countries show little interest in manufacturing and industrial production. They do not participate in the mass production of automobiles, televisions, refrigerators, computers, tractors, light or heavy machinery or any of the consumer goods that the world population demands. They have only one goal: to become a military might without first becoming an economic might. This is a direct result of a lacking of a critical mass of the Exceptional Mindset as well as an oversupply of critical mass that both falls within the Normal Mindset and Violent Mindset category.

THE MINDSET THEORY

As a student of history, I am an avid fan of any theory that is put forward on the rise and fall of nations. Niall Ferguson, historian and Professor at Harvard, uses a brilliant theory of "Six Killer Apps" [1] that helped the West dominate rest of the world. According to Mr. Ferguson the Killer Apps that helped the West to surpass the rest are:

1. *Competition*

2. *Scientific Revolution*

3. *The Rule of Law*

4. *Modern Medicine that doubled life expectancy*

5. *Consumer Society*

6. *The Work Ethics*

Since reading this theory, I have been exploring ways not only to explain the rise of the West but also to find answers that led to the decline of the Muslim nations and their subsequent rise in violence. With that objective in mind, I will use the various states of mindsets that may shed further light in better understanding this phenomenon. I propose that the mindsets of the general population of any country can be divided into three categories:

1. **The Exceptional Mindset** (EM). The adjective "Exceptional" means "Brilliant" and "Outstanding."

2. **The Normal Mindset** (NM). The adjective "Normal" means "Average" or "Ordinary."

3. **The Violent Mindset** (VM). The adjective "Violent" means "Cruel" or "Brutal" The noun "Mindset" means "Approach" or "Outlook."

I have intentionally avoided using the word "Superior" in place of "Exceptional" as it could insinuate a dominance of or inferiority in a race or ethnicity and may confuse the message that I want to communicate. Therefore, the mindset categories are race, nationality, ethnicity and gender neutral. The total population of each country generally falls into one of these categories. It is crucial to point out that these Mindsets are not equally distributed and the dominant Mindset with a total critical mass that is on the rise will either positively or negatively impact the social, political, and economic behavior of that specific country. The examples below will further clarify the later chapters dealing with the dominance of America and the rise of violence in the Muslim nations.

1. The majority of Americans, British, Germans, French, Brazilians, Japanese, Indians, Chinese and Koreans enjoy law and order, strong economies, good educational systems with emphasis on science, technology and art. There is a higher critical mass of "Exceptional Mindset."

2. The majority of Pakistanis, Mexicans, Nigerians, Jordanians, Egyptians, Ecuadorians, and Mongolians fall in a "Normal Mindset" category. The citizens produce few goods, have fewer economic opportunities, law and order is questionable, outdated doctrines are practiced and educational systems are biased.

3. The Violent Mindset destroys life and property, creates chaos, kills in the name of irrational agenda or even God and may be interested in the life hereafter rather than the present. The Taliban, al-Qaeda, Mafia, Gangsters, Murderers and terror groups fall in this category.

Dr. Carol Dweck, Ph.D., Professor of Psychology at Stanford states "*that our mindset is not a minor personality quirk: it creates our whole mental world. It explains how we become optimistic or pessimistic. It shapes our goals, our attitude toward work and relationships, and how we raise our kids, ultimately predicting whether or not we will fulfill our potential.*"[2] According to Dr. Dweck, the mindset starts to blossom in childhood and continues on through adulthood. She argues that we can change our mindset at any stage during the course of our lives to achieve success and fulfill our dreams.

I have varied my approach from Dr. Dweck as she is dealing only with the psychological behavior. It is my intent to explore the reasons why:

1. West Europe and America have become dominant.

2. There is a rise in violence and stagnation in the Muslim world.

I believe that fundamentally we all come into the world with the Exceptional Mindset; however, most of us will not retain this level unless we are born within the right infrastructure or migrate to it. The infrastructure that can produce an Exceptional Mindset must include individual rights, freedom of speech, an advanced educational system, forward thinking leaders, entrepreneurial spirit, law and order, facilities for experimentation and constitutional separation of state and religion. The nations that have worked diligently towards building the infrastructure that allow the citizenry to achieve an Exceptional Mindset have taken a lead in science, technology, economics, military, industry, etc.

The West started to rise from the dark ages around the 1500s. The Magna Carta, Reformation, discovery of the new world, Scientific Revolution, Industrial Revolution, democracy, capitalism and educational advancements were just a few of the essential ingredients necessary to build the infrastructure that augmented the dominance of the West and brought about profound changes in the lives of its citizens. There was an accelerating rise in the Exceptional Mindset in the West leading to economic prosperity for millions of people, and incredible innovations were being introduced at rapid rates to improve every facet of human life. Today, one cannot begin to imagine life without electricity, cars, Internet or computers.

On the other hand, the Muslims achieved their highest critical mass of an Exceptional Mindset during the Abbasid dynasty from 800–1250 while Europe was languishing in the dark ages. The thirst for knowledge led to the translation of knowledge from Greece, Rome, India, ancient Egypt and China. The educational infrastructure and libraries led to the spread of knowledge among the masses. This allowed for critical thinking and debates among the scholars resulting in innovations in math, science and astronomy. Then the hunger for knowledge and innovations slowly disappeared from the Muslim world around the 14th century. This was a direct result of the suffocation of individual ideas (starting with Imam Ghazali, discussed later), the slow rise of fundamentalism and the struggle between forward thinkers and backward thinkers. It is no surprise that by the 1920's, the Muslim world was totally dominated by the Western powers.

My argument is that the rise in Exceptional Mindset leads to the discovery of new frontiers, enlightenment, economic growth, respect for others and high moral character. Normal Mindset leads to stagnation, and Violent Mindset leads to a rise in hatred, destruction, unproductivity, corruption and paralysis.

Today, the debate in Islam regarding innovations is being controlled through Hadith (sayings of Prophet Mohammad, discussed later) and Sharia (Islamic laws, also discussed later) under the Arabic word "Bidah," meaning it is "permissible" or "not permissible," "allowed" or "not allowed." Sharia law further restricts innovations, as it could be interpreted as heresy and punishable by death. *"So whoever innovates in it an heresy (something new in religion) or commits a crime in it or gives shelter to such an innovator, will incur the curse of Allah, the angels and all the people..."* (3)

For example, the birth of Prophet Mohammad, called "Mawlid" in Arabic, is celebrated by some Muslims and rejected by others as a heresy or not permissible. The reason for the rejection by the fundamentalist is justified by proclaiming that this practice did not exist in the early Islamic history, making it sacrilegious, while moderates argue that it is permissible since it is not changing the religious doctrines. The emphasis on such insignificant issues has given rise to division and dissention, while taking eyes off the real purpose of life: to be good and do good. Innovations require complete freedom, and the constant harking by Mullahs that the Quran and Sharia provide the answer to everything has resulted in stifling the mindset.

A few Muslim scholars have attempted to compromise by dividing innovations into two categories: "Good" and "Bad." The Mullah community must then study each innovation to determine its compliance with or deviance from the Sharia law. This oppressive process can never produce enough critical mass of the Exceptional Mindset to overcome the Violent Mindset, thus changing the sordid stage of the Muslim nations. Surprisingly, Judaism and Christianity were not immune to similar illogical arguments during their histories, but eventually they were able to burst through these walls.

In the 1992 election of President Clinton, an advisor used a famous phrase to keep Clinton focused: *"It is about the economy stupid."* The Muslim world needs to immerse itself in the sciences, technology, commerce and economics to start innovating, and thus give rise to an affluent and tolerant society with all citizens of the land producing something of value that other citizens of the world would be willing to buy. It is unfortunate that in Iraq, under Saddam Hussein; in Iran, under the present regime; and in Saudi Arabia and the UAE, with all their oil wealth, nothing is produced for the consumer market. They have wasted and continue to waste billions of dollars on military related items.

The missing ingredients in the Muslim world are basic goodness when dealing with individual respect, tolerance and allowing people to fulfill their daily routines at the very maximum level that a human being is capable of achieving.

In the Muslim countries, this asphyxiation of the Exceptional Mindset coupled with religious arguments invented by the Mullahs will keep the Muslims languishing at the bottom of the pile unless they figure out how to increase the Exceptional Mindset while reducing the Normal and Violent Mindsets.

CHAPTER 3

AMERICANS AND EUROPEANS AT THE TOP

"Four score and seven years ago, our fathers brought forth on this continent a new nation..."

—PRESIDENT ABRAHAM LINCOLN,
THE GETTYSBURG ADDRESS, NOVEMBER 19, 1863

WHY IS AMERICA AND EUROPE AT THE TOP AND MUSLIMS ARE AT THE BOTTOM?

HISTORY TEACHES US MANY LESSONS and clarifies the causes that have been instrumental in the development of humanity and our own heritage. However, there is a lack of desire among the masses and the intellectuals to familiarize themselves with historical events in order to develop a better understanding of current events. For example, if our leaders in Washington D.C. had read their history and fully understood the causes for the demise of the Greek, Roman and British Empires, there would be less bickering and more coming together to resolve our national problems. With a renewed spirit of give, take and compromise, we would avoid the same fate.

This same criticism holds true for the Muslim world. They should also be enlightening themselves by reading history not only to understand why they are stuck in the dark ages but also why and how Western Europeans became so dominant from the early 1500s and how they have stayed at the top for over 500 years. Going one step further, they could dig deeper to learn the cause of American dominance after World War I.

In the early 1500s, the Ottoman Empire was well established in Asia, North Africa and South Eastern Europe, and the Mughal Empire had just begun in the Indian sub-continent. The Ming Dynasty was powerful and thriving in China. Europe was mired in wars, the revolt against Catholicism, rampant ignorance, poverty among masses, tyrant Kings, religious persecution and witch hunting. These were indeed the "Dark Ages." No one in Europe could have imagined that the events that would soon quickly unfold would be totally astonishing.

Muslims, starting with and after the Abbasid dynasty, had become masters of large masses of land and were dominant in trade. They created cities where art and education flourished, ideas were shared openly and other religions were tolerated. Delhi, Agra, Baghdad, Granada, Cairo, Damascus, Constantinople, Tashkent and Bukhara all had bazars full of goods, opulent buildings and palaces. They discovered, translated and added on to the Greek knowledge that was lost. The rapid advance that Muslims had in science, math and astronomy led historian David Landes to write, *"and Islam was Europe's teacher."* [1]

The Chinese were using the compass, printing press, gunpowder, porcelain and silk. Chinese Emperors who considered themselves "Sons of Heaven" had created an advanced civilized society for their subjects. Today, China has once again started to rise, whereas the Muslim world has fallen many steps behind with no clear hope in the near future. China is now producing 18% of the world goods verses Muslim world production, which is minimal. Living standards in China have risen considerably, the literacy rate is almost 100%, and advancements in education, science, technology and commerce have positioned China on the fast track to become a superpower. Muslim nations are lost, confused and unable to rise up in science, technology, human rights, tolerance and freedom for their own people.

Since the time of early human civilization, the main occupation of nations has been war and violence, albeit there were short periods of peace that resulted in the corresponding enlightenment among few nations. During this time in history, when one nation became stronger both militarily and economically, it gave rise to a class of intellectuals who then embarked upon creating innovations which helped in the progression of mankind during these much needed brief periods of peacetime. The wheel, fire, hammer, nail, chariots, gun power and aqueducts are few examples of the great innovations from this era.

Many years ago, it dawned on me that Americans and Europeans have contributed significantly more in improving humanity in the last 500 years than all other nations from the beginning of times combined. These improvements include human rights, free speech, tolerance, science, food, technology, education, discoveries in medicine and health, democracy, capitalism, commerce and much more. It is easy to look around and quickly observe that we are surrounded by objects and processes that we so heavily depend upon to run our daily lives. The computer, software, TV, Internet, electricity, printer, heating and air-conditioning, Google, Wikipedia, YouTube and the IPhone used for writing this book were all invented by Americans and Europeans. You can look in your house (stove, refrigerator, bulbs, toilet, etc.), place of work (phone, copier, video teleconference, etc.), your business (bank, loan, machinery, etc.), your travel (cars, planes, trains, buses, hotels, etc.), and you begin to realize the Exceptional Mindset behind these inventions. Leaving politics and wars aside, even most antagonists cannot deny the improvements and benefits that each of us enjoy due to these inventions. Without them, our lives would be lackluster and unproductive.

So, what were the causes behind this genius that took hold in America and Europe and pushed the envelope to new heights? Historians point to many reasons, including individuals rights from the Magna Carta, property rights, reformation, renaissance, industrial revolution, scientific revolution, separation of Church and State, rise of democracy, growth of capitalism, emphasis on higher education, development of the middle-class, freedom of speech and law and order; these were the intricate cogs. They were so masterly deployed originally by the enlightened few but later enjoyed by the many in the pursuit of happiness.

THE EARLIER CIVILIZATIONS

The Mesopotamian civilization, around 4000 B.C., is credited with creating organized communities and irrigation systems around the Tigris and

Euphrates rivers. The Sumerian, the Semitic and the Amorites were the people from this era. The greatest ruler of the Amorites was Hammurabi, ruler of Babylon. He developed a central democracy rule in his Empire and a law code with a common set of rules that governed property, marriage, wages and family affairs. The emphasis was on peace and justice with the destruction of the wicked. There was protection for women, children and slaves. The spade, wooden plow, sickle and flail were the tools, and labor was provided by both the free and slaves.

The Egyptian civilization also started around 4000 B.C. Much still remains for us to appreciate the glorious past of the people who lived by Nile. The Pharaohs created a strong central government. The rich Egyptian culture developed hieroglyphics with a complete alphabet, flowering delicate stonework and amazing pyramids that reached upwards of 480 feet high using over two million stones, some weighing more than two tons. Body mummification enhanced their knowledge of the human anatomy. However, like the Mesopotamians, they were not interested in the pursuit of natural sciences nor did they feel the need to search for explanations of the natural processes of the universe.

The Persian civilization started when Indo-Europeans moved from north of the Black Sea to Central Asia, Iran, Afghanistan and the Northern Indian sub-continent. The famous kings Cyrus and Darius extended the boundaries from the Aegean Sea to Western India. They created a new religion, Zoroastrianism, based originally on monotheism with Ahura as the only God. Many historians suggest that the doctrines of Judaism, Christianity and Islam were affected and influenced by Zoroastrianism. The defeat of the Persian Achaemenid dynasty by Alexander the Great was a setback, but it was successful in creating a viable civilization.

All of the civilizations discussed above were successful in the exploitation of the rivers, agriculture, city-states, strong armies and the creation of miraculous pyramids. However, with all their achievements, the one concept they had not developed and grasped yet was the great power of the human mind, i.e. "reason to think," which flourished both in Greek and Roman civilizations and set up the base for the renaissance later in Europe.

The Greek civilization began around 1200 B.C. from its location on the Aegean Sea, and under Alexander the Great's rule, they extended their boundaries from Egypt to India. Even though the Romans conquered them later, the Romans were spellbound by their high civilization. The Romans were so enthralled that they not only adopted it completely but also spread the intellectual thinking of Plato, Socrates, Aristotle, Hippocrates and Homer, which had just entered in the realm of humanity.

The Greeks promoted the role of "reason" and "inquiry" thus influencing modern philosophy and modern science. The emergence of city-states, or "Polis," brought about new thinking in Greek politics, society, economy and culture. There were hundreds of city-states in Greece ruled by locals with no central power control. Athens and Sparta were the most powerful militarily and economically.

Three institutions formed the government: the Assembly of Demos, the Council of 500 and the People's court. The Assembly allowed citizens to express their opinion and to vote on matters at hand. The Council of 500 represented ten tribes with 50 members from each tribe to govern Athens, issuing decrees as necessary and preparing the agenda for meetings. The People's court listened to cases, voted on guilt or innocence and rendered punishments to those found guilty. Women and slaves did not have a vote.

The world's greatest philosophers, Plato, Socrates and Aristotle, founded the roots of modern philosophy. The intellectual, artistic and cultural abilities were advocated in Athens, while Sparta pursued a build-up of a strong and disciplined army. Plato founded Academia to foster education in leadership and citizenship thus producing well-rounded individuals who would be future leaders.

Greek intellectuals advanced mathematics by adding to the rules of geometry. They applied formal proofs to mathematical analysis. They discovered applied mathematics and worked on forming the basics of calculus. Discoveries by Archimedes, Pythagoras and Euclid are still taught in modern educational systems.

Furthermore, the development of astronomy led to the creation of the first known geometrical 3-D models explaining the movements of our planets. Other discoveries were that the Earth rotates around its axis, estimation of the circumference of the Earth, and the cataloging of stars. The first astronomical computer "Antikythera mechanism" was developed for calculating the movements of planets and is considered a predecessor of astronomical computing. Professor Michael Edmunds of Cardiff University stated, "*This device is extraordinary, the only thing of its kind. The design is beautiful, the astronomy is exactly right. The way the mechanics are designed just makes your jaw drop. Whoever has done this has done it extremely carefully ... in terms of historic and scarcity value, I have to regard this mechanism as being more valuable than the Mona Lisa.*" [2]

Hippocrates is considered one of the most exceptional people in the history of medicine. He is known as the "father of modern medicine" and has contributed immensely to the medical arena. Physicians today upon entering their practices recite the Hippocratic Oath, swearing to practice medicine ethically and honestly.

Greek culture slowly expanded through wars and Alexander the Great's conquests, finally migrating to Rome and the European continent. Today, "Democracy" has become the system of choice for the majority of the countries of the world. Socrates, Plato and Aristotle, through their Exceptional Mindset, produced philosophies and theories that later gave rise to the "Muslim Golden Age" and, most importantly, the eventual rise of the Europe.

The Roman Empire with its splendid capital city of Rome and covering the important coasts of the Mediterranean Sea became one of the greatest empires in the world. Through conquest and assimilation, it came to dominate Southern Europe, Western Europe, Asia Minor, North Africa and parts of Eastern Europe. It gave rise to the Greco-Roman concept that was forged by the combining of religion, government, language and culture in tandem with their love for Greek knowledge and their somewhat similar cultures and societies.

Romans invented the Republic, from Latin "res publica" or "public business." Candidates for public positions had to run for election by the people, whereas the Roman Senate represented an oligarchic institution acting as an advisory body with no legislative powers. New senators were chosen but could be removed for being "morally corrupt," for bribery or embracing one's wife in public. The Roman Republic was similar to the democracy of Greece but with the ability to govern a large population thus allowing people to express their ideas and concerns. Latin was the main language, but Greek was respected as a language of culture.

Life in Rome was care free, involving the daily hustle and bustle of a thriving and vibrant great city. Roman houses were built with indoor plumbing and flush toilets, sanitation was improved and a complex sewer system carrying waste into the Tiber River was constructed. Glassblowing and Mosaics became popular after samples were discovered in Greece. The Coliseum, the Forum and the Pantheon were the main gathering points for the public. There were theatres, gymnasiums, marketplaces, working sewers, marble bath complexes, libraries, shops, and fountains with fresh drinking water supplied by hundreds of miles of aqueducts.

In addition, the Technological superiority of Roman civil engineering contributed to the construction of hundreds of roads and bridges. Romans did borrow heavily from the Greeks for their renowned architecture. They started using concrete and marble for the buildings and miles of paved roads. Roman roads used three levels of substructure beneath the paving stones and a prescribed angle for the uplift of the center of the road, allowing rainwater to drain off. Bridges and way stations on the roads were created. This allowed for horse relays with couriers to travel up to 500 miles in 24 hours. The construction of roads and travel infrastructure allowed Rome to manage their empire efficiently, deploy Roman legions rapidly in time of need and opened up the trade routes for economic influence, giving birth to the saying, *"All roads lead to Rome."*

The Romans were obsessed with written documents and public inscriptions. They were dependent upon written material that Clifford Ando, Roman law and religion classicist writes, *"If all seas were ink, all reeds were pen, all skies parchment, and all men scribes; they would be unable to set down the full scope of the Roman government's concerns."* [3] It was very common for the laws and edicts to be read then posted on a wall.

The Romans contributed to the advancement of humanity by inventing many essential items. Some that are still pertinent to our lives today are:

- The Roman legal system
- The Republic and Senate model for modern democracies
- Architecture with arches, columns, domes, sculptures, frescoes and mosaics
- Concrete and cement
- Highway system with relay station

- Entertainment venues including stadiums and amphitheaters
- Aqueducts and bridges
- Thermal baths with central heating
- Wine-making on a mass scale
- Roman alphabets
- The Julian calendar with the current names of the months
- Modern city planning

Roman law, which has left its mark on Western civilization, started with the Law of the Twelve Tables. Roman law, as preserved in Justinian's codes, formed the basis of codifications in Western Europe. Roman law continued to be applied throughout most of Europe until the late 17th century. It was divided between "Public Law," which dealt with state issues of taxation and treason, and "Private Law," which dealt with disputes among citizens. Roman law is the basis for what is now known in the West as Civil law. Many legal terms used today in our court systems are based on Latin. The concept of "innocent until proven guilty," which is fundamental in the U.S. criminal justice system, is attributed to the Romans.

One can differentiate between Greek and Roman influences on our modern times. Whereas the Greeks gave rise to the "ideas" with their emphasis on intellectual minds, the Romans used the ideas in a "practical" fashion to manage their empire.

It can be easily concluded without any historical argument that we owe much to the Greeks and the Romans for setting the magnificent foundation that is the cornerstone for the advancement of our civilized world. They were the first of the European nations to use reasoning and pursue higher intellect and knowledge, which put us on the path to harness the full power of human brain.

THE RENAISSANCE

"Renaissance," or "Rebirth," originated in 14th century Italy and extended northward to west Europe. This promoted the discoveries of the enlighten mind and the exploration of the New World. The Greek emphasis on "reason" and "inquiry" along with the Roman push to turn ideas into "practical" conventions brought forth changes in Western civilization not experienced prior. *"Some have seen this as a scientific revolution, heralding the beginning of the modern age."* [4] *"Others as an acceleration of a continuous process stretching from the ancient world to the present day."* [5]

Renaissance is synonymous with humanism and a focus on the interest of man rather than God. The church had promoted humans as frail and unworthy of understanding the divine message through rationale and logic alone. Humanism promoted individualism by elevating the dignity of the free spirit capable of versatility, materialism and ego. Renaissance gave rise to secular interests with appreciation of art, literature, dancing, poetry and the evaluation of different thoughts that impacted human life. The study of Christianity was augmented with pagan literature and liberal arts subjects.

In summing up, the Renaissance could be looked upon as an endeavor by intellectuals to observe and advance both the worldly and secular with progressive approaches to new thinking. The most important aspect of "Humanism" provided for the purpose of life in this world instead of next world. Human beings were declared social creatures that could create a meaningful life only by associating with other beings. Instead of leading a "contemplative life," the argument was presented to lead an "active life." The public life, with the focus on serving the country with high morals, was recommended. The Renaissance brought about significant changes in the way that the universe was perceived and the modes of explaining natural phenomena. The book *De humani corporis fabrica* (*On the Workings of the Human Body*) by Andreas Vesalius *"gave a new confidence to the role of dissection, observation, and mechanistic view of anatomy."* [6]

While the Chinese and Muslim worlds did not fully embrace the printing press in fear of losing control of the masses through the spread of knowledge, the Europeans used the printing press to their advantage by spreading new ideas to the masses. Ideas and knowledge were no longer controlled by a few and spread like wildfire so the majority could participate.

The polymaths Leonardo da Vinci and Michelangelo both became known as "Renaissance men." Nicolas Copernicus became the founder of modern astronomy, discovering that the sun was at the center of our planetary system rather than earth. Leonardo da Vinci conducted experiments in medical dissection, water flow and the systematic study of movement and aerodynamics. With his new research methods and other numerous contributions it garnered him the title of "father of modern science".

THE REFORMATION

Surprisingly, not many Christians today know the history of Reformation. As a matter of fact, when you ask most Americans who Martin Luther was, they will be quick to blurt out Martin Luther King; indeed they are two great but different individuals.

The Protestant Reformation movement was the 16th-century schism within Christianity that was initiated by German monk, priest, and professor of theology, Martin Luther, who was later joined by John Calvin and other early Protestants. The Reformation led to the elimination of the strangulation by the Popes of Rome and corruption that had become rampant in Catholicism.

The rediscovery of the Greek world and 15th century invention of the printing press helped in spreading the message to the masses on a grand scale never seen before. The "Humanists" applied this new scholarship to study the Bible and doctrines in their mother-tongues. Instead of Latin only, now the Bible was printed in German and later in English, and the followers were not dependent on the priest or the bishop to interpret the message. The possibility to connect with God without the Church was a totally new concept. Martin Luther declared the Pope "antichrist," and the Church pronounced Martin Luther a heretic.

Do the Muslims have the Exceptional Mindset to learn from the internal feuds within Christianity over 500 years ago? Can they not see that the strife only created mayhem, inquisitions and destruction that impacted the lives of many innocent people? Long ago, both Catholics and Protestants walked away from the Violent Mindset and replaced it with the Exceptional Mindset. Today, the differences in doctrine remain, but the hatred and destruction is gone.

The Great Schism (1378–1415) saw three Popes at one time: Pope Benedict XIII based in Avignon; Pope Gregory XII, based in Rome; and Pope John XXIII, based in Pisa. This was the result of the struggle between Bishops, French, Germans and English. The Catholic Church was more interested in continuing to add to its vast wealth then in promoting the welfare of their flock. The Church sold "Indulgences" to allow the nobility to buy a stairway to heaven and therefore generate more income for the Church. There was no salvation without the Church, but Martin Luther argued that salvation was a personal matter between God and man. To him, the Church was irrelevant, and the sale of indulgences (forgiveness) was fraudulent. He followed this debate by nailing his 95 Theses to the door of a church in Wittenberg, Germany. Rome quickly condemned this act and declared him an outlaw.

While Luther's ideas were spreading fast, King Henry VIII, in pursuit of a son heir to the throne, broke away from Rome and asked Pope Clement VII to sanctify his divorce from Catherine of Aragon so that he could marry Anne Boleyn. The Pope, who had earlier awarded Henry the title of "Defender of Faith," refused, and the King retaliated by creating the Church of England and establishing himself as its head, giving rise to the second break in the Church separate from Martin Luther. The rich properties of the Church were seized in the name of the King and Church of England. Ironically, Anne never produced a son and was later beheaded.

The Reformation started with the idea to reform the Roman Catholic Church from within, doing so with the elimination of perceived corruption and doctrines by priests who opposed what they viewed as false doctrines and Church sanctioned malpractices.

In hindsight, it freed the masses from the monopoly of God by the close-minded few. The Exceptional Mindsets of Martin, Calvin and others gave us the gift of the "ability to think freely," declaring that God belongs to all of us and we do not require the approval from a Pope, Priest, Pastor, Minister, Khalifa, Mullah or Ayatollah.

THE SCIENTIFIC REVOLUTION

The explosion of new ideas starting in the Reformation and Renaissance periods in the 1500s created the new free human spirit. This led to the Scientific Revolution and set the stage for the human spirit to continue to expand and progress forward. Logic and reason either augmented religion or replaced it with the ability to question all that was sacred before. It was a time of observation, experimentation and investigation, instead of just revelation alone.

Copernicus rejected the age-old Aristotelian idea that all planets revolved around Earth and put forth the totally new idea that all planets revolved around the Sun in our planetary system. It was a novel but rebellious idea against the Roman Catholicism teachings. Galileo seconded the Copernicus theory through experimentation but was tried and put under house arrest for his discoveries. The scientific revolution pushed forward the learning of mathematics, physics, astronomy, biology, medicine and chemistry that transformed the views of society and nature.

The dark ages were no more, and the dawn of the scientific revolution began as soon as the sun was setting on the era of Renaissance. Experimentation led to proving various ideas and their practical applicability to human life. Some of the numerous discoveries included blood circulation, Newton's laws of motions, the microscope to view bacteria, the mechanical calculator, and the binary number system that is the foundation of virtually all modern computer architectures, the steam engine, the discovery of Hydrogen and Oxygen, and Botany.

What caused these discoveries? Why did they not happen in Asia, Africa or the newly discovered Americas? What caused Europe to wake up? Was it the "Black Death" plague of 1348 that killed millions of Europeans? *"The Black Death is estimated to have killed 30–60 percent of Europe's population."* [7]

Whatever the reason, there is no denial that something had stirred in the Western lands, leading the Europeans to make life better for all of us. By the end of 16th century, Protestantism had spread to Germany, Scandinavia, Switzerland, Netherland, England and the Baltics. The 17th century was a period of reason and experimentation. We can surmise that the new freedom of Europeans due to the Renaissance and Reformation gave rise to reason and investigation. It was indeed the Exceptional Mindset that brought about these changes.

In religion, it has always been a struggle between the dictators and the progressives. Dictators cannot comprehend reason, inquiry, logic and rationale. The Dictators have no shame in corrupting the simple message of God, as they are power grabbers with only one goal: to satisfy their own neurotic wishes rather than to do what is good for humanity.

THE FIRST INDUSTRIAL REVOLUTION

The Industrial Revolution began in the small island nation of Great Britain around the middle 1700s. This was a monumental turning point in our history that eventually impacted all aspects of our daily lives. The profound changes in agriculture, manufacturing, mining, transportation and technology improved economics and brought forth changes in cultural and social values.

The population and average income began to rise. *"In the two centuries following 1800, the world's average per capita income increased over ten-fold, while the world's population increased over six-fold."* [8] In the words of Nobel Prize winner Robert E. Lucas, Jr., *"For the first time in history, the living standards of the masses of ordinary people have begun to undergo sustained growth ... Nothing remotely like this economic behavior has happened before".* [9]

Great Britain provided the legal and cultural foundations that enabled entrepreneurs to pioneer the Industrial Revolution. There were many important factors, including a period of peace and stability, strengthening of the rule of law, the advent of stock companies in the form of corporations, the birth of a free market or capitalism, the abundance of coal and iron ore deposits and the availability of raw material from some colonies while other colonies provided a market for the finished goods.

Prior to the Industrial Revolution, most people resided in small, rural communities where their daily existences revolved around farming. Life for the average person was extremely difficult, as incomes were meager and malnourishment and diseases were common. People produced the bulk of their own food, clothing, furniture and tools. Most manufacturing was done using hand tools or simple machines in homes or small, rural shops.

Spreading from the United Kingdom through Western Europe, USA and Japan, the Industrial revolution then spanned the globe. Transition-based manufacturing started with the mechanization of the textile industries. With the increased demand for British goods, manufacturers had to reduce the cost of production, leading to the increased use of mechanization in factories. The use of rivers, canals, roads and railways improved the distribution of goods. Manufacturing had started to eclipse an agricultural based economy. The great migration of people started from rural areas to urban centers. The villages became towns and towns became cities with the great influx of people to share in the bounties.

The manufacturing moved from homes to factories. The critical manufacturing change was the production of interchangeable parts, resulting in a mass production of the same parts that, in turn, dramatically reduced the price of the product. Steam power, fuelled by mined coal, broader deployment of water wheels and powered machinery bolstered the spectacular growth in production capacity. All metal machine tools accelerated the production of parts for other industries, leading to more production.

The cottage textile industry had moved from people's homes to factories as a result of a series of innovations that led to ever-increasing productivity. Mr. James Hargreaves of England invented the "spinning jenny." This allowed individuals to produce multiple spools of thread simultaneously, and pretty soon, there were over 20,000 spinning jennys in use across Great Britain.

There were other Exceptional Mindsets at work in England. Mr. Abraham Darby figured out a cheaper and easier method to produce cast iron. Mr. Henry Bessemer discovered an inexpensive process for mass-producing steel. Thus, cheap and mass-produced iron and steel were the essential materials that gave rise to the production of tools, machines, appliances, railways, cars, ships, buildings and infrastructure.

The improved transportation led to the hauling and distribution of raw and finished goods to the factories and market place respectively. The first successful commercial steamboat built by American Robert Fulton in the early 1800s led to steamships carrying goods and merchandise to and fro on the Atlantic Ocean. Both the Liverpool and Manchester Railways became the first to offer regularly scheduled train service in 1830, and by 1850, Great Britain had more than 6,000 miles of railroad track.

There was no let up, and the Exceptional Mindsets embarked upon the discovery of better communication systems. Mr. William Cooke and Mr. Charles Wheatstone of Great Britain developed the telegraph system in 1837, and by 1866, a telegraph cable was successfully laid across the floor of the Atlantic Ocean, making it possible for the USA to communicate instantly with Western Europe.

In 1776, Adam Smith, a Scottish genius, published the book *The Wealth of Nations*, outlining the *"economic system based on free enterprise, the private ownership of means of production and lack of governmental interference."* Now was the time to develop a financial mechanism to augment the Industrial Revolution. Banks were established, and the financiers were born to fuel the engine of capitalism, giving rise to the creation of the London stock exchange established in the 1770s and the New York Stock Exchange in the early 1790s.

All of these innovations, combined with increases in production and a mass migration to the urban centers, raised the standard of living for a good many folks. There is, however, no doubt that the Industrial Revolution did not produce equal results for all. Wages in factories were low, and laborers did not reap all of the benefits. Child labor was common, working conditions were poor at times, housing in cities was inadequate and pollution was spreading. But slowly, the conditions of the working class started to improve as labor reforms were enacted and workers gained bargaining weight with the owners after winning the right to form trade unions.

By the mid-19th century, the Industrial Revolution had engulfed Western Europe and Northeast America. By the early 20th century, the foundation had been laid for the USA to become the world's leading industrial nation. A few of the pioneers of the Industrial Revolution are:

1. James Watt, first reliable Steam Engine 1775

2. Eli Whitney, Cotton Gin, Interchangeable parts for muskets 1793, 1798

3. Robert Fulton, Regular Steamboat service on the Hudson River 1807

4. Samuel F. B. Morse, Telegraph 1836

5. Elias Howe, Sewing Machine 1844

The Industrial revolution was successful in replacing human and animal power with machine power. The agricultural economies became manufacturing economies. These changes led to the start of the second industrial revolution in communication and information technologies, resulting in the computer age, Internet, space exploration, unprecedented rise in food production and abundance in consumer goods of varieties never seen before.

The Second Industrial Revolution

Around the 1850s, technological and economic progress had started to gain momentum with the growth of steam-powered ships, railways and better communication and distribution channels. This era ushered in the mass production of steel, which enabled expansive growth in various industries, including electrical, chemical, automobile, heavy equipment, large ship, airplanes, and petroleum refining coupled with mass distribution. Specifically:

Henry Ford built his first car in 1896. He is considered a pioneer of the Assembly Line production concept, in which the placement of all work tools was within easy reach of each worker, therefore removing unnecessary human motions. This resulted in the phenomenon of mass production. Each worker performed only one operation. *"This was the first time in history when a large, complex product consisting of 5000 parts had been produced on a scale of hundreds of thousands per year. The savings from mass production methods allowed the price of the Model T to decline from $780 in 1910 to $360 in 1916. In 1924, two million T-Fords were produced and retailed $290 each."* [10]

"By 1890 there was an international telegraph network allowing orders to be placed by merchants in England or the U.S. to suppliers in India and China for goods to be transported in efficient new steamships. This, plus the opening of the Suez Canal, led to the decline of the great warehousing districts in London and elsewhere, and the elimination of many middlemen." [11]

"The mass production lowered the prices for almost all good making it easier for majority to use these goods to improve their daily lives. By 1900, the leaders in industrial production were the U.S. with 24% of the world total, followed by Britain (19%), Germany (13%), Russia (9%) and France (7%). Europe alone accounted for 62%." [12]

Imagine: Americans and Europeans combined were solely responsible for 86% of the total world production, a feat never achieved in history. That was huge and will probably never be achieved again.

This mastery of the Industrial Revolution clearly shows the rise of the Exceptional Mindset to the highest level. The inventions shown on the next page and in Appendix 1 produced unparalleled improvements in the quality of human life, including health, work, home and travel.

FAMOUS MEDICAL INVENTIONS

In 1798, the discovery of the **Smallpox Vaccination**; in 1818, the first successful **Blood Transfusion**; in 1846, the first **Painless Surgery** with the use of general anesthesia; in 1847, the discovery that washing hands stops the **Spread of Disease**; in 1853, the **Hypodermic Syringe**; in 1854, the causes and prevention of **Cholera**; in 1865, the **Antiseptic System**; in 1866, **Genes** were discovered; in 1868, the first diagnosis of **Multiple Sclerosis**; in 1889, **Rubber Gloves** for surgery; in 1892, **White Blood Cells** identified; in 1895, **Psychoanalysis Techniques**; in 1895, **X-Ray** was used; in 1897, the causes and prevention of **Malaria Fever**; in 1898, **Typhoid Vaccination** was developed; in 1899, **Aspirin** was introduced; and in 1899, the causes and prevention of **Yellow Fever** were discovered.

In 1901, **Four Blood Groups A, B, O, AB** were discovered; in 1902, **Hormones** were discovered; in 1903, the **Electrocardiograph (ECG)** was invented; in 1906, first successful **Corneal Transplant**; in 1906, **Vitamins** were discovered; in 1909, the causes of **Typhus** were discovered; in 1921, **Insulin for Diabetes** was discovered; in 1928, **Penicillin** was discovered; in 1937, the first **Blood Bank** was established; in 1944, the first **Open Heart Surgery**; in 1943, a cure for **TB**; in 1953, the structure of **DNA**; in 1953, first successful use of **Heart–Lung Machine**; in 1954, **Polio Vaccine** was developed; in 1957, **Ultrasound Scanning** of pregnant women; in 1959, first disposable diaper, **Pampers**.

In 1959, the discovery of the first drug to fight **Leukemia**; in 1967, the **Cat Scan** was developed; in 1967, the first human **Heart Transplant**; in 1973, **DNA Cloning,** or the birth of Genetic engineering, leading to the development of **Synthetic Insulin** for diabetics, a **Clot-Dissolving Agent** for heart attack, and a **Growth Hormone** for underdeveloped children; in 1981, the first use of **Artificial Skin** to treat 3rd degree burns.

It is fair to ask, how well humanity would have fared in the advancements in the medical field without American and European contributions. Life expectancy has almost doubled, quality of life has much improved, infant deaths have radically declined and many challenges from the health perspective are being explored: HIV/AIDS, cancer, diabetes, infections, neurological disorders, genetics and so on. The impact of vaccines, antiseptics, anesthetics, antibiotics, antivirals, organ transplantation, prosthetic advancement, etc. has been unprecedented.

In classical Rome, life expectancy at birth was *"28 years"* [13], and in medieval Britain, it was *"31 years"* [14] *"In 1900, global average lifespan was just 31 years, and below 50 years in even the richest countries. By early 20th century it was 31 years…, in 2005, average lifespan reached 65.6 years; over 80 years in some countries."* [15]

In the early 1900s, the Rockefeller Foundation got involved in treating infectious diseases, and now Bill and Melinda Gates are at the forefront of fighting diseases in developing countries and finding new health solutions. America and Europe offer the best healthcare facilities, where Muslim rulers often come to be cured.

The advances in medicine by the West have produced many positive results worldwide. For example, people are living healthier and longer with cures for diseases once thought to be impossible to cure. Therefore, there should be no argument that all of these improvements in human life through medicine owe credit to the West. No doubt, the continued research and improvements in technology will one day help humans to eradicate all known diseases that exist today.

AMERICAN REVOLUTION

The American Revolution was a political separation wherein the original thirteen colonies jointly broke away from the British Empire, creating a new country: the United States of America. American society, from its inception, gradually had become different from the royal British society. Through their ingenuity, they had created bustling communities in the boonies with hard work and perseverance. They overcame the long travel from Europe to America, they subdued Indians, they starved, they cleared land, they farmed, and they supplied raw materials to or acted as a market for the finished goods from England. The odds were not in their favor, but they prospered and became fearless and independence-minded. They rejected the authority of the British Parliament to govern them without representation

The American Revolution was the result of an Exceptional Mindset with intellectuals transforming both society and the government. Americans rejected the aristocracies of the British society and placed their faith in republicanism, a novel idea at that time of history. They created democratically elected government responsible to the will of the people. In 1788, they created the Constitution, the most amazing document ever written and established a strong federal government led by a President and not a king, as was common in Europe. In 1791, the Bill of Rights followed with the first ten constitutional amendments guaranteeing "natural rights" with relatively broad personal liberties.

The bold decisions made by the forefathers in the creation of this great country are now serving as a beacon of hope and model for many nations. There is no doubt that the American Revolution was one of the major events in history that totally changed the relationship between the governed and those who govern. Absolutism was exchanged with a free entrepreneurial spirit that has produced boundless potential. The revolution sent a clear message that any government that oppresses its citizens has its root in tyranny and will not survive. We all have inalienable rights, and the fundamental solution is less government intrusions in the affairs of its citizens. *"After the Revolution, genuinely democratic politics became possible."* [16]

The new concepts of liberty, individual rights, equality and respect for law and order became core values of American society. America was not afraid of experimentation; over 100 years after the revolution, women had the right to vote, and after the Civil War, slavery was abolished with black Americans gaining full rights in the 1960s. The strength of America lies in its ideals and can-do spirit. Not everything we did was always right, but the spirit and motivation to make it right is the greatest gift that this country possesses, bar none.

AMERICAN INVENTIONS

The Embargo Act of 1807 and the War of 1812 against the British accelerated the industrial revolution in the USA. The Embargo Act was enacted by the United States Congress against Great Britain and France during the Napoleonic Wars. The USA had stayed neutral, but its merchant ships with cargo were seized by the British and French navies. The Act stopped the export of American goods and effectively ended the import of goods from other nations. The desire to become economically independent of European powers pushed America to rely internally in all commerce matters. This

resulted in three critical developments: inland transportation was expanded, the power of electricity was understood and successfully harnessed, and
industrial processes were improved resulting in higher production.

Cotton and Cloth– Eli Whitney, born in Westborough, Massachusetts,
invented the cotton gin in 1794, making it possible to separate cotton seeds
from fiber much faster. In 1814, Francis Lowell of Lowell, Massachusetts
combined the spinning and weaving processes to produce cloth in one factory. This resulted in an increase in production and development of the textile industry in the Northeast.

Transportation– The 620-mile-long Cumberland Road was the first
major highway built that provided a connection between the Potomac and
Ohio Rivers and was used by settlers headed west. It eventually became part
of Interstate 40. The New York to Great Lakes route was opened after the
creation of the Erie Canal. This was a major boon to the New York City
economy.

Railroad tracks expanded from a modest 2,808 miles in 1840 to 254,000
miles by 1916, connecting the Atlantic coast to the Pacific and extreme
fringes of the North to the South. The railroads managed virtually 100% of
all interstate traffic, both passenger and freight. Railroads were taking raw
materials to factories and finished goods to markets and consumers.

Thomas Edison– Thomas Edison and his workshop patented 1,093 inventions. These included the phonograph, the incandescent light bulb and
the motion picture. He was the most famous inventor of his time, and his
inventions had a huge impact on America's growth and history. Mr. Edison
said, *"We will make electricity so cheap that only the rich will burn candles".* [17]

Samuel F. B. Morse– Samuel Morse invented the telegraph, which
greatly increased the ability of information to move from one location to
another. Along with the creation of the telegraph, he invented Morse code,
which is still used today.

Alexander Graham Bell– Alexander Graham Bell invented the telephone in 1876. This invention allowed communication to extend to individuals. Before the telephone, businesses had to rely on the telegraph.

Elias Howe/Isaac Singer– Both Howe and Singer were involved in the
invention of the sewing machine. This revolutionized the garment industry
and made the Singer Corporation one of the first modern industries.

Cyrus McCormick– Cyrus McCormick invented the mechanical reaper, which made the harvesting of grain more efficient and faster. This helped farmers have more time to devote to other chores.

George Eastman– George Eastman invented the Kodak camera. This inexpensive box camera allowed the consumer to take black and white pictures to preserve their memories and historical events.

Charles Goodyear– Charles Goodyear invented vulcanized rubber. This technique allowed rubber to have many more uses due to its ability to stand up to bad weather. Rubber could withstand large amounts of pressure, making it an important industry.

Nikola Tesla– Nikola Tesla invented many important items, including fluorescent lighting and the alternating current (AC) electrical power system. He also is credited with inventing the radio. The Tesla Coil is used in many items today, including modern radio and television.

George Westinghouse– George Westinghouse held the patent for many inventions. Two of his most important inventions were the transformer, which allowed electricity to be sent over long distances, and the air brake. The latter invention allowed conductors to have the ability to stop a train. Prior to the invention, each car had its own brakeman who manually put on the brakes for that car.

Life would be rather dull and boring without the following inventions for which Americans are overwhelmingly responsible:

The Mobile Phone, Search Engines (Google, Bing, Yahoo), Computers, Software, the Internet, Facebook, YouTube, Television, 3-D film, Video Games, DVD, CD, Bubblegum, Credit Cards, Ballpoint Pens, Word Processors, Barcodes, Zippers, Airplanes, Air-Conditioners, Heating Systems, Barbie Dolls, Shopping Malls, Grocery Stores, Skyscrapers and instant coffee.

Today, we use all of these inventions without stopping to think: how did they come into being? How many hours of research and development did the inventors put into their creations? How many sacrifices did each inventor make? We are ever in the debt of these great people with Exceptional Mindsets. All of these individuals were of European descent, giving further credence to the fact that while most of humanity was asleep these people were wide awake and eager to improve the lot of humanity. With globalization today, knowledge is available to the rest of the people of the world.

In conclusion, the Violent and Normal Mindsets must reject hatred and laziness, and then participate in the rewarding process of advancing humanity by pursuing science, research, investigation and experimentation. It is never too late, and it must be done.

Muslim World Asleep At The Helm

There were numerous reasons for the Industrial Revolution in the Western world, which would lead one to wonder why it did not occur in other parts of the world, particularly China or the Muslim world.

The Renaissance led to Enlightenment thus laying the foundation for the industrial revolution. Scholars point out many factors, including the emphasis on free spirit, spread of education, advancement in technology, emerging democracies, capitalism with a supporting financial infrastructure, work ethic, individual empowerment, tolerant religion practices, changes in culture and upward economic mobility. The entrepreneurial spirit and essence of self-worth allowed for the achievements of status and wealth to be possible.

While Europe had figured out the essentials for the successful maturation through industrial revolution leading to economic growth, educational and technological advancements, the rest of the world had neither the capacity nor the systems in place to do so themselves. The classical argument put forth by the Muslim world is that the fault lies with Western Europe, which had colonized their territories. This, they say, did not allow them to progress forward. Europe colonized the Muslim world in the late 1800s and early 1900s; therefore, this useless argument does not hold. It is common among the defeatist nations to think of illogical answers to steady their hearts and fool their populations.

It is important for these nations to take a good hard look at this to truly understand the causes of their stagnation. The Moors in Spain, the Ottomans in the Balkan, the Middle Easterners and the Mughals in India were mainly interested in capturing more land and building beautiful palaces and Harems for their own comfort and pleasure. They were unable to comprehend the subtle changes occurring in Europe. The internal strife in the Muslim world, continuous imposition of self-created religious doctrines, suffocation of free spirit, illiteracy of the masses and branding science as an invention of the heretic mind had sucked all the life out of innovative thinking and zapped the human spirit.

In 1801, the first census occurred in Great Britain, and its population was 8.3 million. In 1857, the Mughal Empire fell and the Indian sub-continent became a part of the British colonial empire. *"In 1861, the British population was 18.8 million"* [18]. Furthermore, the United Kingdom has a total area of approximately *"94,060 sq. mi."* [19]

Now, contrast this *"with the Mughal Empire, which controlled a landmass of 1.93 million sq. mi and had population of 175 million."* [20] Moreover, it is interesting to note that the British government was not directly involved in Mughal India. It was the British East India Company chartered by Queen Elizabeth I that developed trade in Asia to counter balance the Dutch. It is difficult to fathom how such a small country could capture a large empire in Asia. However, the question that we need to ponder is how it was possible for a trading company to become so powerful with less than 50,000 soldiers and was able to capture all of the Indian sub-continent after defeating the last Mughal Emperor so thoroughly.

In 1611, the British East India Company established its first factory in Andhra Pardesh (Machilipatnam) in the Indian sub-continent. From this humble beginning, the Company gained influence over Mughal emperors, created an army and started collecting taxes. *"The East India Company is, or rather was, an anomaly without a parallel in the history of the world. It originated from sub-scriptions, trifling in amount, of a few private individuals. It gradually became a commercial body with gigantic resources, and by the force of unforeseen circumstances assumed the form of a sovereign power, while those by whom its affairs were directed continued, in their individual capacities, to be without power or political influence. — Bentley's Miscellany 43 (1858)."* [21]

The Europeans, due to their inherent curiosity, were more interested in learning about the Islamic world than vice versa. The emphasis on gaining knowledge led to the establishment of Arabic chairs at the French and Dutch universities followed by Cambridge University in 1632 and Oxford in 1636. Europeans were on a binge of exploration of the planet and in science, literature and art, which was truly remarkable. *"By the eighteenth century Europe boasted a considerable body of scholarly literature regarding the Islamic world—editions of texts and translations of historical and literary and theological works, as well as histories of literature and religion and even general histories of Islamic countries, with descriptions of their people and their ways. Grammars and dictionaries of Arabic, Persian, and Turkish were available to European scholars from the sixteenth century onward."* [22]

There is no precise answer as to why the Muslim world was no longer thirsty for the pursuit of knowledge. Muslims controlled vast lands (Ottomans and Mughals), they ruled over several hundreds of millions and overall, they were wealthy nations. Bernard Lewis tackles this puzzling question: *"The Islamic world, with no comparable incentives, displayed a total lack of interest in Christian civilization. An initially understandable, even justifiable, contempt for the barbarians beyond the frontier continued long after that characterization ceased to be accurate, and even into a time when it became preposterously inaccurate."* [23]

The Top Countries In All Fields
(Scientific Papers and Citations)
As of August 31, 2011 [24]

According to the bi-monthly update of Essential Science indicators, the annual "Top 20" listings of countries which have achieved particular distinction based on their papers published in Thomson Reuters-indexed journals from January 2001 through August 31, 2011 are listed by three measures: number of citations, total papers and cites per paper. (*Note: For articles with multiple authors representing different countries, each listed country receives full, not fractional, citation credit for the given paper.*)

RANK	COUNTRY	PAPERS	CITATIONS	CITES PER PAPER
1	USA	3,049,662	48,862,100	16.02
2	PEOPLES R CHINA	836,255	5,191,358	6.21
3	GERMANY	784,316	10,518,133	13.41
4	JAPAN	771,548	8,084,145	10.48
5	ENGLAND	697,763	10,508,202	15.06
6	FRANCE	557,322	7,007,693	12.57
7	CANADA	451,588	6,019,195	13.33
8	ITALY	429,301	5,151,675	12.00
9	SPAIN	339,164	3,588,655	10.58
10	AUSTRALIA	304,160	3,681,695	12.10
11	INDIA	293,049	1,727,973	5.90
12	SOUTH KOREA	282,328	2,024,609	7.17
13	RUSSIA	265,721	1,282,281	4.83
14	NETHERLANDS	252,242	3,974,719	15.76
15	BRAZIL	212,243	1,360,097	6.41
16	SWITZERLAND	181,636	3,070,458	16.9
17	SWEDEN	179,126	2,686,304	15.00
18	TAIWAN	177,929	1,273,682	7.16
19	TURKEY	155,276	819,071	5.27
20	POLAND	154,016	1,036,062	6.73

Source: *Essential Science Indicators*[SM] from Thomson Reuters, time period: 2001–August 31, 2011 (fourth bimonthly period of 2011).

Notice, Turkey stands at number 19. Out of the 47 Muslim countries, Turkey is the most progressive. There is no denial that this ranking at number 19 is a sad affair, affirming the low standing of Muslims in the world of sciences and technology. The Muslim scientists publish a miniscule amount of original science research papers. Edgar Choueiri, Professor at Princeton University states that, *"Only 370 patents were issued to people in Arab countries between 1980 and 2000. In South Korea, which has a population one tenth that of the Arab world, there were 16,000 patents issued in that same period."*[(25)] According to the United Nations, presently no Arab country spends more than 0.2% of its gross national product on scientific research. By contrast, the United States spends more than 10 times that fraction.

Since the 1300s, Muslims have contributed very little to the world of science or technology, and the numbers speak loud and clear. With the suppression of individual freedoms, lack of good educational systems and the use of distorted religious practices, all efforts and importance are placed on the illustrious past instead of the here and now and the future, which has harshly impacted the growth of technology and science advancements in the Muslim world. As human beings, they are endowed with the same capacities and capabilities as Americans, Europeans and Chinese. But why they have fallen behind? Is the answer the religion practices, culture or heritage? This book has attempted to explore in detail the reasons, and hopefully, the reader will have many options to make up his or her own mind.

Another set of data that we can examine is **Noble Prize** winners. Muslims fall way short despite their population of 1.6 billion. Muslims have received only 12, or 1.1%, whereas Europeans received 971, or 93%, of the total Nobel Prize awarded as of 2012. On the science front, out of 500 Nobel Prizes awarded so far the Muslims have scored only two and one of the recipients is an Egyptian American. In other words, today the Muslim world has no Nobel Prize recipient in Science living in their midst.

Dr. Saleem H. Ali, an associate professor of environmental planning at the University of Vermont, states in his article dated February 14, 2010:

> *"The reason for the paucity of Muslim laureates in the sciences is perhaps the relative intellectual inertia in the educational institutions in many Muslim countries. There is a tendency for many Muslims to atavistically celebrate the accomplishments of tenth-century Muslim mathematicians, while investing little in developing contemporary educational capacity. Far too often we hear from imams about the etymology of algebra coming from Arabic and the pharmaceutical accomplishments of Avicenna but do we ask why more of such great scholars have not been seen for a thousand years in Islamic countries? Furthermore, it is important to remember that the golden age of Islam was also its most pluralistic and even then there were fundamentalist forces who constantly threatened these scientists. Let us not forget the ruins of Madinat-al-Zahra, once a show-piece of Islamic art and learning, just outside Cordoba, which was destroyed not by any "kuffar" but instead by radical and retrogressive Muslim factions."*[26]

The word "kuffar" above refers to non-Muslims. Dr. Saleem further states that Muslim scientists are more interested in making money than doing research.

> "Those Muslims who are educated and proceed to develop successful professional careers are often sanguine with a comfortable job but would rather not invest in cutting-edge creativity. An interesting example is the medical profession in which many Muslims, and indeed Pakistani Muslims, have excelled considerably. However, most of these brilliant doctors are focused on making money in clinical practice rather than in creative research which would lead to laurels such as the Nobel Prize. There is cultural complacence that leads to a mindset where success is marked by simply making a good living for the family, contributing some earnings to charity and then living a lavish life." (27)

It would be prudent for Muslims to evaluate the notion of what they have done to Islam rather than what Islam has done to them, and then take concrete steps in moving forward in science, commerce and tolerance. *"It is He Who sendeth the winds like heralds of glad tidings, going before His mercy: when they have carried the heavy-laden clouds, We drive them to a land that is dead, make rain to descend thereon, and produce every kind of harvest therewith: thus shall We raise up the dead: perchance ye may remember"*(28) (Quran 7:57).

THE AGE OF EXPLORATION – NEW LANDS

In the late 1400s, Europeans were not seeking to find new lands but instead to find better routes to the Indies (India, China, Japan and Ceylon). There are three main reasons that accelerated the "Age of Exploration."

Firstly, Europeans sought "Direct Access." The tales of Marco Polo and his visit to China (1271–1295) had introduced the Europeans to the riches that were gained by traveling to the East and by the Silk Road. The Europeans had no direct access to the markets of the East and were dependent upon traders for the transportation of goods. The 5,000-mile Silk Road was a treacherous journey through hills, deserts and plains. It took about a year for the caravans to bring goods to the Mediterranean ports, where they could then be shipped to the European coastal cities. Merchants wanted direct access.

Secondly, "the Fall of Constantinople" in the hands of the Ottomans and the loss of land routes to Asia all but dried up the traffic carrying goods for Europe through the Silk Road, impacting the merchants and their livelihood. This created a strong desire to find new ways to the Indies.

Thirdly, "the Renaissance" had ushered in the era of knowledge and allowed people to read and share new ideas. With the invention of the printing press, books were translated and new books were published. At this time, scholars believed that there were only three continents: Europe, Asia and Africa. No one knew of North and South America, Australia, New Zealand or Antarctica. The Renaissance allowed people to read and share new ideas. Books about astronomy were read with great interest, and map making became popular, giving merchants and explorers hope of other possibilities to reach the Indies.

Prince Henry of Portugal (1394–1460), known as "the Navigator," had the vision and the Exceptional Mindset to lend a hand in the search of routes to the Indies for spices and silk. He understood the value of trade and supported the merchants in the exploration of the coast of South Africa. He set up a school on the Atlantic Ocean and assembled experts and scholars in such critical fields as astronomy, geography, mathematics, navigation, map making and ship building. He provided the necessary funds to find riches and convert pagans to Christianity.

Christopher Columbus (1451–1506), born in Genoa, Northwestern Italy, had been following his dream of sailing to the Indies by going west through the Atlantic Ocean. The expeditions were expensive and needed the support and funds from a monarch. After many failed attempts, the capitulations of Muslim rule in Spain brought about the opportunity that Columbus had been waiting for. King Ferdinand and Queen Isabella of Spain decided to finance the voyage in 1492. Amazingly, instead of reaching the Indies, Columbus landed at San Salvador in the Caribbean. Eventually, using the knowledge gained by Columbus, the Spanish, French, British and Dutch discovered all of the Americas (North, Central and South).

In 1498, a Portuguese expedition led by Vasco da Gama reached Calicut, India by sailing around Africa and eventually landing in China in 1513. In

1522, the Portuguese navigator Ferdinand Magellan led a Spanish expedition west, achieving the first circumnavigation of the world. This opened up the gates of discovery to both the East and West.

Europe had finally reached the Indies and discovered other unknown lands along with the Indian and Pacific oceans. The British, French and Dutch all challenged the mastery of the Spanish and Portuguese and embarked on their own voyages of discovery, taking them to Australia in 1606, New Zealand in 1642, and Hawaii in 1778. The Russians explored and conquered almost all of Siberia in the 1640s.

The Spanish reached the Americas first and set up a colony in Florida in 1513. With the involvement of the British, French and Dutch, many wars ensued. The British set up their first colony at James Town in 1607. The British became dominant in North America, the Spanish in Central and South America and the Portuguese ended up taking Brazil. The French and Dutch gained the least.

These discoveries opened up a new route for trade and the transfer of goods. Cattle, sheep, and horses were sent to the new world, and tea, tobacco, corn, potatoes and slaves were brought back. Some will call this the Age of Imperialism, as it led to the colonization of 70% of the world by the Europeans. The indigenous people of the Americas and Australia could not compete with the superior technology and Exceptional Mindset of the Europeans and unfortunately lost their heritage and lands.

The Chinese, Indians, Mughals, Ottomans, and many other nations did not explore, reach far-fetched places or discover new lands. The Ming and Qing dynasties of China were rich and prosperous, as were the Mughals of India. Were the Muslims only interested in capturing more lands nearby, as shown by the Ottomans and Mughals? There are no simple answers; however, it does lead one to surmise that Europe, which had just came out of the dark ages, must have been hungrier than the powers of Asia, who were marching slowly to their own dark age. Today, China is rushing towards becoming a superpower and an industrial giant and is well on its way surpassing its glorious past. On the other hand, the majority of the Muslim world is mired in ignorance and falling into a deep slumber of its own choosing.

The desire for trade and better access to lands in faraway places turned out to be a bonanza for the Europeans. The emphasis on learning and gaining knowledge opened many new doors. In spite of all the suppositions that existed in that era, including that one could fall off the oceans' horizon because the earth was flat, that beyond the equator was hot and fiery, and that sea monsters existed not far off the coast, one must be truly thankful to the fearless explorers who, with their zeal, determination, adventurism, sacrifices and hard work, discovered new lands that are now home to over a billion people, all mostly having thriving economies and providing opportunities to immigrants from all other lands.

CAPITALISM

According to Merriam-Webster, the definition of capitalism is: "an economic system characterized by private or corporate ownership of capital goods, by investments that are determined by private decision, and by prices, production, and the distribution of goods that are determined mainly by competition in a free market." In Ayn Rand's book *Capitalism: The Unknown Ideal*, she states: *"The moral justification of capitalism lies in the fact that it is the only system consonant with man's rational nature, that it protects man's survival qua man, and that its ruling principle is: justice."* [29]

Capitalism has resulted in improving the standard of living and providing a means to enjoy life. After the Renaissance period in Europe, there was a gradual shift to improve the overall economic sector. There was a reduction in trade barriers, weights and measures were standardized, restrictions on production and labor were diminished and the formation of new businesses was made easier. Two parallel doctrines emerged that accelerated the rise of capitalism. First was the "Property Right" or "legal doctrine" that allowed the legal owner of land to make the best economic use for gain. This principle was reflected by the property laws.

The second was the political doctrine of "Laissez-faire" economics, or "let (them) do." This thinking rejected intrusive governmental regulation as petulant meddling. It cried out for the government to ensure the orderly operations of the free market as that was necessary for the economy to grow.

In capitalism, the processes to create production are privately owned, assembly lines are closely watched and the distribution of income is dependent upon the markets. Together with Reformation, it sanctified thriftiness and hard work. The rise of the English textile industry (16th–18th centuries) also contributed to the early success of capitalism. Capitalism promoted individual efforts to increase productive capacity to meet the additional demand of masses as they moved from rural to urban areas. The surplus cash was invested in additional factories instead of economically unproductive schemes such as palaces or cathedrals.

The rise in production and increasing demand for products in the 18th century generated large amounts of capital for industrialists which could be ploughed back in the factories or used for inventing new machinery. New systems of manufacturing were developed leading to the division of labor by tasks and the standardization of all work related to tasks. These profound changes led to the world-wide dominance of capitalism and its methods of operations.

In the 19th century with the invention of banking, financing and corporation, capitalism started to blossom and the globalization of production and markets started to take hold. The industrialists understood that in order to achieve growth it would be necessary to secure the markets and resources used by aligning the productive capacity of the capital sectors. The role of state slowly shifted to improving business conditions, securing foreign markets and gaining access to raw materials.

Across the Atlantic Ocean, American businessmen were closely watching the developments in Great Britain and quickly learned the value of competitive spirit and innovations. They understood the value of cutting costs and decreasing prices in order to become a dominant player in the market. Congress enacted the Sherman Act (1890) antitrust laws to regulate unjustified decreases in the cost and the pricing of goods. It was the belief of Congress and many businessmen that the economic engine is driven by the small businessman and their entrepreneurial spirit. Therefore, the foundation of this law was that an economy which relies on a few large firms will be worse than one that relies on hundreds of small companies.

The advantages of capitalism became obvious over time. Luxury items became more affordable to the masses, including milk, bread, meat, and clothes. With the passage of time the progress continued with sewing machines, sporting goods, washing machines, dishwashers, ovens, refrigerators, freezers, automobiles, hair dryers, radio, movies, telephones, air conditioners, heating systems, planes, and recently the Internet, smart phones, digital cameras and sporting events.

The genius of capitalism is making basic amenities available to most people. It holds out the guarantee of what Adam Smith called "universal opulence." Capitalism does not solve every human issue nor does it provide equality for all. Instead, a capitalist society provides a constant supply of new goods, gadgets, appliances, and luxuries to the masses.

Since the end of the Second World War, capitalism has proven that it is a better ideology and system than communism or socialism. Capitalism provides more choices than ever before. One can enjoy any type of food or good that they can afford. Generally, there is an equal opportunity for all to improve their life both economically and socially. A person can change his or her fortune within one generation. Steven Jobs, a Syrian immigrant's son who was adopted by a kind American family, went from nothing to becoming a multi-billionaire all the while helping humanity.

Capitalism encourages competition and pushes human beings to discover and create new things that may benefit them individually or as a collective part of humanity. Thanks to the stiff competition in the marketplace today, we have plenty of quality choices in all consumer goods.

Capitalism and democracy go hand-in-hand. Today, there is a greater acceptance of each other among the citizenry, although discrimination has not been completely eliminated. Only in America can a child born into a poor family become a President (Lincoln, Regan, Clinton and Obama) or an immigrant can become governor of the largest state, California (Arnold Schwarzenegger). Capitalism leads to innovation. Free-thinking allows for the germination of new ideas and gives innovators the freedom to cross boundaries that normally are not possible within repressed societies.

The Muslim Extremists' assertion that their solution includes a rebirth of Islam to overthrow the secular regimes that capitalism promotes is totally absurd. Their dogma of total reliance on God without using the brainpower given to us by the same God shows a lack of intellect and borders on ignorance. How can these Extremists ignore the basic fact that most of the people living in the West are much happier and seem to enjoy their lives, while the terrorists are busy killing themselves and the innocent in search of 72 virgins? Terrorism has resulted in lost lives, destruction and fear. Life is too short, and it is the basic right of each individual to live the life as he or she sees fit as long as they are not harming others by stealing, cheating, lying, raping, killing or imposing their lifestyle and beliefs.

Since the birth of their movements in the 1990s, the Taliban and al-Qaeda have done nothing good to further the cause of humanity. They have only created mayhem. They use Western innovations, such as guns, phones, bombs, videotapes, Internet and automobiles, proving not only the point that they totally lack the minimal human skill set but also that they belong to the barbaric and uncivilized era, thousand years past.

DEMOCRACY

The word "democracy," which means "rule by the people," originated in Greece (Europe) around the fifth century B.C.E. Greeks are credited with the creation of a new democratic form of government, but this experiment did not include women and slaves as participants. The Romans took some of these ideas from the Greeks, where nobility had a representative in the Senate and the Assembly represented commoners. The power was divided between both bodies, and they voted on issues that were brought forth. Cicero, the famous statesman of the Roman Senate proclaimed that "all people have certain rights that should be preserved," and he believed that political power should come from the people.

Once Christianity reached Europe, the teaching that all men were created equal became compatible with early democratic principles. When the Magna Carta was penned in the 12th century, England and Scotland contributed further to the cause of democracy. Nobility was able to persuade King John to create a law-making body wherein the English Parliament had higher power than the king. This act started the sharing of power between the king and his people, yet another positive step in the evolution of democracy. Next, two important milestones followed: the Petition of Right (1628), whereby the king could no longer impose taxes on his subjects without parliament's approval; and the most important document, The Bill of Rights (1689), which provided freedom of speech and banned cruel or unusual punishment.

The American Revolution can be proclaimed as one of the most significant events in the evolution of democracy. In 1776, the Declaration of

Independence asserted that human beings have "the right to life, liberty and the pursuit of happiness." In Europe, the French overthrew the king and created the "Declaration of the Rights of Man," emphasizing the right to "liberty, property, security, and resistance to oppression." The American and French experiments did not create a full democracy given that women and slaves were excluded. But nonetheless, they opened the doors for increased individual rights and a reduction of the power of monarchies.

The end of Second World War led to a flourishing of democracy in Western Europe where monarchies and dictatorships vanished and the will of the people had begun to feed through the elected representatives. At the same time, East Europe fell under the authoritarian rule of communism, leading to lower standards of living, few economic opportunities and an overall diminished quality of life from which they still have not recovered. In Asia, Japan became the first country to adopt a new constitution giving its people basic rights. India became the world's largest democracy after its independence in 1947. Today, many Far Eastern countries have moved or are moving towards a democratic form of government.

Europeans, through their Exceptional Mindset, were able to mature the concept of democracy over 2,000 years. The right to purse happiness is part of our makeup, and its denial stifles the development, competition and spirit of entrepreneurship. The West understood that the Bible does not provide for a participatory government system, even though it states that all men are equal. They had to go outside religion to find the answers.

So why are the Muslim countries averse to the idea of Democracy? There are only a handful of Muslim countries that can be considered borderline democratic (Turkey, Bangladesh, Indonesia), just three out of 47 Muslim countries. This is rather unfortunate when taking into account that 1.5 billion Muslims constitute an important segment of humanity. Muslims scholars continue to insist that Sharia Law provides the answers to all that is needed to run the government. Sharia Law may be useful in certain aspects, but it is not all encompassing with the modern world. For example, the rights of women are limited in Sharia, and it does not discuss basic human rights. There is no mention of the pursuit of happiness. The Holy Scripture leads to conflicting interpretations by various groups in promotion of their own causes. Muslim scholars will need to think outside the box by accepting doctrines that enhance basic principles of humanity and questioning those that denigrate humanity or promote violence.

THE MELTING POT AND IMMIGRATION

Historian James Truslow Adams popularized the phrase "American Dream" in his 1931 book, *The Epic of America*. He described the American dream as *"that dream of a land in which life should be better and richer and fuller for everyone, with opportunity for each according to ability or achievement. It is a difficult dream for the European upper classes to interpret adequately, and too many of us ourselves have grown weary and mistrustful of it. It is not a dream of motor cars and high wages merely, but a dream of social order in which each man and each woman shall be able to attain to the fullest stature of which they are innately capable, and be recognized by others for what they are, regardless of the fortuitous circumstances of birth or position."*[30]

There is no doubt that America is a land of opportunity and immigrants. The Native Americans crossed the land bridge connecting Siberia and Alaska thousands of years ago. The Spanish were the first to settle Florida in the 16th century, followed by British and French in the 17th century. Indentured labor came from Europe, and slaves were brought from Africa. The English founded their first permanent settlement at Jamestown in the Virginia Colony, followed by the Pilgrims who arrived and established Plymouth, Massachusetts for the pursuit of religious freedom.

A larger share of immigrants came to America seeking economic opportunities of their own free will since they could afford to pay for their trip and had sufficient funds to start a new life. Additionally, there was a large number who could not pay their way, so they came as indentured servants. Thousands were convicts. All of the slaves who came had no choice and were forced to leave their homeland in agony and pain. Whatever the reason—good, bad or ugly—everyone helped with the building of this great country. The immigrants even sacrificed their lives in the Civil War to make this country strong. Many were taken directly from the ship that brought them here to the battlefield. After the Civil War, the influx of newcomers pitted Anglo-Saxon Protestants against Catholics when competing for existing jobs.

From the late 1800s to right after the First World War, masses of people came to America from Eastern and Southern Europe. With the rise of Nazism in Germany, Jews came to America from the 1920s to 1950s. Asian and Latin American immigration started in the late 1950s. The peaceful combining of different religions, customs, and ethnicities led to the coining of the term "melting pot." The immigrant found this opportunity to mix their qualities into the fabric of our nation, thereby making the U.S. a stronger, more diverse country.

"The first American census in 1790, shortly after the formation of the United States, counted nearly 4 million people, of whom at least 20% were of African descent." [(31)] The Native American Indian population was difficult to determine due to the tribal fragmentation but some historians estimate it to be around 15 million.

"The European newcomers, including Catholics and Jews, faced hostility from the American who had arrived earlier. Then when Chinese and Asians started to trickle in the slogan of inherent superiority of the Anglo-Saxon "race" was the battle cry." [(32)] But nothing could stop the continual tide because no walls could be built or doors could be closed. America was the magnet, a beacon of hope, and the end of all miseries, and most of all, it was the Promised Land.

In 1965, Congress passed the Immigration and Nationality Act, which did away with quotas, based on nationality and allowed Americans to sponsor relatives from their countries of origin. As a result of this act and subsequent legislation, the nation experienced a shift in immigration patterns. Today, the majority of U.S. immigrants come from Asia and Latin America rather than Europe.

Immigrants built this country with their blood, sweat and tears, and their tales are forever a part of American lore. By the end of the 19th and early 20th centuries, they were the key players in building America's power and influence. They contributed to the development of popular American culture that after World War II became the envy of the world. No doubt, that the American economic, military and technology advancement have mesmerized the rest of the world but also created jealousies.

SOME INTERESTING LANDMARKS IN IMMIGRATION HISTORY [33]

- *1795–Naturalization Act restricts citizenship to "free white persons" who reside in the United States for five years and renounce their allegiance to their former country.*
- *1808–The importation of slaves into the United States is prohibited.*
- *1840s -Irish Potato Famine; crop failures in Germany; the onset of industrialization; and failed European revolutions begin a period of mass immigration.*
- *1849–California Gold Rush spurs immigration from China.*
- *1870–Naturalization Act limits American citizenship to "white persons and persons of African descent," barring Asians from U.S. citizenship.*
- *1891–Congress makes polygamists and persons with dangerous diseases and misdemeanors ineligible for immigration. The act establishes the Bureau of Immigration within the Treasury Department.*
- *1892–Ellis Island opens, processing 12 million immigrants over the next 30 years.*
- *1917–Congress enacts a literacy requirement for immigrants to read 40 words in some language.*
- *1923–In the landmark case the Supreme Court rules in United States v. Bhaghat Singh Thind that an Asian from the Indian subcontinent could not become naturalized U.S. citizens.*
- *1940–The Alien Registration Act requires the registration and fingerprinting of all aliens in the United States over the age of 14.*
- *1943–The Chinese Exclusion Act is repealed. By the end of the 1940s, all restrictions on Asians acquiring U.S. citizenship are abolished.*
- *1944–In the case of United States v. Korematsu, the Supreme Court upholds the internment of Japanese Americans as constitutional.*
- *1945–The War Brides Act allows foreign-born wives of U.S. citizens who had served in the U.S. armed forces to enter the United States.*
- *1946–The Luce-Cellar Act extends the right to become naturalized citizens to Filipinos and Asian Indians. The immigration quota is 100 people per year.*
- *1948–The Displaced Persons Act permits Europeans displaced by the war to enter the United States outside of immigration quotas.*

- *1950–The Internal Security Act passed, denying admission to any foreigner who is a Communist or who might engage in related activities.*
- *1965–Immigration and Nationality Act repeals the national origins quota system and gives priority to family reunification.*
- *1980–Refugee Act, enacted in response to "the boat people" fleeing Vietnam, grants asylum to politically oppressed refugees.*
- *1986–The Immigration Reform and Control Act gives amnesty to approximately three million undocumented residents and provides punishments for employers who hire undocumented workers.*
- *1988–The Redress Act provides $20,000 compensation to survivors of the World War II internment of Japanese and Japanese Americans.*
- *1996–The Illegal Immigration Reform and Immigrant Responsibility Act strengthens border enforcement and makes it more difficult to gain asylum.*
- *1997–Congress restores benefits for some elderly and indigent immigrants who had previously received them.*
- *1998–The American Competitiveness and Work force Improvement Act increases the numbers of skilled temporary foreign workers U.S. employers are allowed to bring into the country.*

VALUES

I believe values can be personal, moral, ethical, cultural, ideological, religious, aesthetic, business, and social.

The previous pages show that the Americans and Europeans have put humanity on the path of no return through their pursuit of knowledge and by applying the common sense principles. As a result, a body of values has become an integral part of our core values. A human mind, endowed by its Creator, has achieved much in spite of experienced adversity. The world is designed to move forward instead of standing still or moving backward.

"The mind of the superior man is conversant with righteousness; the mind of the mean man is conversant with gain."

—CONFUCIUS, 551 B.C. [34]

"We do not act rightly because we have virtue or excellence, but we rather have those because we have acted rightly."

—Aristotle, 384 B.C. [35]

"For what profit is to a man if he gains the whole world, and loses his own soul? Or what will a man give in in exchange for his soul?"

—Mathew, 60–100. [36]

"But to those who believe and do deeds of righteousness, He will give their (due) rewards,–and more, out of His bounty."

—Quran, 612 – 632. [37]

"To you is granted the power of degrading yourself into the lower forms of life, the beasts, and to you is the granted the power, contained in your intellect and judgment, to be reborn into the higher forms, the divine."

—Giovanni Pico della Mirandola, 1463–1494. [38]

"You cannot teach a man anything; you can only help him to discover it in himself."

—Galileo Galilei, 1564-162. [39]

"Religion must be destroyed among respectable people and left to the canaille large and small, for whom it was made."

—Voltaire, 1694–1778 [40]

"I believe in one God, and no more. I do not believe in the creed professed by the Jewish Church, by the Roman Church, by the Greek Church, by the Turkish Church, by the Protestant Church, not by any Church that I know of. My own mind is my own Church."

—Thomas Paine, 1737–1809. [41]

I am sure there is no agreement on the basic set of human values, but let me try to define a few which I believe more people will agree than disagree with.

1. Respect all human life

2. Treat others as you would like to be treated

3. Speak the truth

4. Help others

5. Honesty

6. Justice

7. Work hard

Almost all of us learn these values at an early stage of our formative lives irrespective of race, religion, country and gender. Then what causes some nations or groups to cling, hone and add to these values while others go the opposite way? Is this is due to "Dissociative Identity Disorder" as explained by the Scottish author Robert Louis Stevenson in his classic tale "The Strange Case of Dr. Jekyll and Mr. Hyde," where Dr. Jekyll is good and Hyde is evil? It makes sense to infer that all humans have a "split personality" with different sets of values and opposite morals.

Considering that this argument is able to define the "good" and "evil," Hyde has risen within the terrorist Muslim population. In addition to the increasing violence, there is a breakdown of moral and ethical values, giving rise to corruption, dishonesty and laziness in the society. The religion is used to create chaos and fear among the masses. It has become common to turn a blind eye towards basic human rights and the freedom of speech.

THE AMERICAN AND EUROPEAN IMPACT ON HUMANITY

Today, it is intriguing to watch how the USA, UK, Germany, France and other European nations have become a beacon of hope for millions from Asia, the Middle-East and Africa, as large numbers of people have been migrating to the West since the end of World War II. One can easily conclude that if there were no visa requirements or restrictions on entry, billions would pack up and move to the West in spite of their hate, bigotry, biases and prejudices against the West and Christianity.

The West provides economic upward mobility and individual freedoms that are so lacking for billions of inhabitants of this earth. In the Western environment, everyone has the opportunity to become enlightened, become rich, get a better education, learn the value of consensus and practice his or her religion of choice freely. The West is not perfect but still presents immigrants with the best choice, so they willingly leave the land of their birth.

So what makes America and Europe so attractive to millions, and what are the reasons for their dominance for the past 500 years? America and Europe have been successful in creating an infrastructure that is of the highest level in human civilization history. There were several steps taken intentionally or un-intentionally by kings, queens, presidents, rulers, governors, businessmen, industrialists, academicians, scientists, scholars, clergy and citizens jointly or individually over the span of a few hundred years that no other country can lay claim to. From the dark ages, it started with the Renaissance (14th–17th century), the Age of Exploration (1492–1800), the Scientific Revolution (1550–1700), Enlightenment (17th–18th century), and Industrial Revolution (1760 forward). Add to this mix the other critical ingredients: Capitalism, Democracy, Consumers, Modern Medicine, Constitution, Law and Order, Property Rights, Individual Rights and Religious Tolerance, and you have the most powerful concoction directly benefiting humanity that was ever created.

The infrastructure that the West created has allowed people to think freely, raised living standards, created new jobs in industries that did not exist 10, 30 or 50 years ago, and provided a better understanding of different cultures due to the increased travel and observance. The pursuit of new knowledge created higher learning institutions. As people learned, they asked questions, some of which could be answered and others that could not, which resulted in further research and investigation.

No doubt that the road to Western dominance involved wars, imperialism, suffering, death and misery, but in spite of all those negative events, human beings are better off today than they could have been otherwise.

The Poem

AMERICA,
THE GREATEST COUNTRY THAT GOD EVER CREATED

There is an Atlantic Ocean, Pacific Ocean,
And this is the greatest country ever created.
There are Rocky Mountains, sycamore trees,
There is the Grand Canyon, the Redwood Forest,
And this is the greatest country ever created.
There are brave soldiers, the freedom to speak,
There are gleaming skyscrapers, pristine prairies,
There is American know how, American can do,
And this is the greatest country ever created.
There is Disneyland and Civil War Battlefields,
There is the Wild West and the Deep South,
Washington, Jefferson, Lincoln, Roosevelt and Reagan,
Edison, Bell, Dale Carnegie, Ford, Gates, Jobs,
And this is the greatest country ever created.
New York, Los Angeles, Washington, Chicago, Atlanta,
Christians, Mormons, Jews, Muslims, Atheists,
Native Americans, Whites, Blacks, Hispanics, others,
Innovations, freedom, individual rights, democracy,
And this is the greatest country ever created.
Science, technology, capitalism,
Baseball, football, basketball,
Internet, YouTube, Facebook, IPhone,
And this, this America, is the greatest country ever created.

—Mubarak Chouhdry

PART III

CHAPTER 4

THE PAKISTAN THAT WAS!

"A perfect Muslim is one from whose tongue and hands mankind is safe"

—PROPHET MOHAMMAD

ONCE UPON A TIME

IT IS HARD TO COMPREHEND what has become of Pakistan of today. There is daily violence, sectarian killings, bomb explosions and a strong Taliban and al-Qaeda presence. Their terrorist menace combined with rampant corruption, increasing illiteracy, out of control population, and poor economic conditions is leading Pakistan towards becoming a failed state.

I realize that it sounds strange to say that I grew up in a very different Pakistan that was tolerant, progressive and offered hope not only to its citizens but also to the international community. Even though I left Pakistan many years ago and am now a proud and loyal citizen of the United States of America, I still wonder that if Pakistan had continued on the path of economic prosperity and respect for all, today, just like all other immigrants, I would feel good about the land of my birth. Instead, I am embarrassed and saddened by its current state.

In the next few pages, you will see pictures that illustrate the life and culture in which I grew up. Suffice to say that Pakistan was not America or Europe, but there was a palpable hope. Pakistan was carved out of India in

1947 as the British left, and for its first 23 years or so, it was mainly on the right track as a civilized society.

PROGRESSIVE AND TOLERANT PAKISTAN

The Pakistan that I see today is not the same land where I spent my first nineteen years full of happiness and hope. The fanatics do not practice the Islam that I grew up with, and they certainly do not behave as I remember good Muslims around me behaving. I was taught to do good deeds for others before myself and strive for excellence in everything I did. God was merciful and killing anyone, unless in the purest example of self-defense, was a most heinous crime. I was taught to respect my neighbors and help everyone regardless of religion, ethnicity, or gender. I was taught that the life of the Prophet Mohammad was full of compassion and charity. I was taught that the jihad of the sword was dead, and the jihad of knowledge was alive and was the shining beacon for the future. And just as important, I was taught to gain knowledge from everyone, especially those in foreign lands, and then use what I learned to contribute to the betterment of society.

I grew up in Pakistan in the late 1950s to early 1970s. Obviously, everything changes with time. However, the country that I see today in the news has become more violent, less tolerant, more illiterate and worse economically. When I grew up, it was progressive, peaceful and well on its way to becoming a respected player on the world stage. By the late 1960s, Pakistan was on track to become an economic power in Asia with an average growth rate of well above 6%. *"When it gained independence in 1947 from UK, Pakistan's average economic growth rate since independence has been higher than the average growth rate of the world economy during the period. Average annual real GDP growth rates were 6.8% in the 1960s, 4.8% in the 1970s, and 6.5% in the 1980s."* [1]

In the early 1960s, South Korea, whose per capita income was less than half that of Pakistan, based their *"Second Five Year Plan of 1960–65 on the Pakistani model."* [2]

Eastern and Western values mingled, and people talked openly about any number of ideas without fear or prejudice. The emphasis in school and in society was on knowledge, competition, and getting ahead as an individual and together as a nation. The British had left a solid infrastructure of education, law and order, transportation, justice, and trade, and these systems were well taken care of and managed by everyone. English was the national language, the West and America were admired and religious fanatics weren't given any credit to their name.

The decline of Pakistan began when it attacked India in 1965 and lost the war. In order to save their credibility, the Pakistani leaders promoted that "Muslim Pakistan had won the war." This lie gave rise to the so-called "glorious" Arab past (Pakistanis are Indian not Arabs), and the gradual shift in the wind started to manifest. The selfish leaders used the Arab–Israeli conflict, which is over 1,000 miles away, to inflame the citizens' passion. The street riots against India and Israel sanctioned by the government were used to distract from the local issues on hand. The closeted fanatic Mullahs slowly began to take advantage of this political and cultural shift, as domestic woes were interpreted as problems that could only be solved through fanatical religious adherence. The political agendas that leaders advocated brainwashed millions of Pakistanis to support the idea of defeating mother country of India. Overnight, the leaders became dictators and lied to the population in the government-controlled media, and personal agendas superseded that of national interest. In this reckless process, fear was used to silence all that was gained through the 1960s.

These tactics used by the self-righteous leaders and Mullahs gave rise to chaos, violence, and corruption resulting in economic despair for everyone. Today, the literacy rate is below 40%, corrupt leaders stash their loot in foreign lands and the growth rate of less than 3.5% is barely meeting the needs of the rapid population growth.

The military continues to siphon money from the national coffers in the hopes of fighting mother India, while 90% of the population move closer and closer to complete poverty and hunger. To make matters even worse, Pakistan has between 100–200 nuclear weapons, and if it were to become a failed state, these weapons of mass destruction could easily fall in the wrong hands, causing undue harm to the world.

I, like many other immigrants, have no desire to go back to Pakistan and live. My only hope is that one day Pakistan will make peace with India, realize that her culture and history is more Indian than Arab, promote the education of science and technology, separate religion from state, embark on the path of economic growth and create prosperity for her citizens to become a promoter of peace in the world.

In the next few pages, you will see several photos from the Pakistan of 1950s and 1960s attesting to the open and tolerant culture of the past.

These photos show Americans being welcomed with open arms, girls in a pool wearing western swimwear, a Pakistani woman riding motorbike, local Christians worshiping openly, Western tourists visiting without fear, Western music mingled with the Eastern music, the presence of a Jewish synagogue in Karachi, and many more.

These photos will not repeat themselves in the near future. There is a clamp down by the fanatics to control the mind and soul of the individuals in the name of God. The ignorant Mullahs have only one goal: to manipulate the masses by spreading their dictatorial and autocratic form of Islam. They believe that only they fully understand the true Islam, and they must whip everyone to get them in line.

PHOTOS FROM THE YESTERYEARS

The First Lady Jacqueline Kennedy visited Pakistan in 1962 riding in open car with President Ayub Khan in Karachi. Americans were welcome with open arms by the masses.

A 1963 brochure printed by the government of Pakistan to assist the influx of western tourists. It contained maps, famous tourist spots, beaches, resorts, hotels, nightclubs and bars in the country.

A 1966 Pakistani ad announcing the launch of the Chrysler Australia car, Valiant. It was one of the first cars to be assembled in Pakistan. —Picture courtesy of DAWN.

Girls taking part in a swimming competition at a sports complex in Karachi in 1970.

Students celebrating elections at the Karachi University
in 1969. —Picture courtesy of Tarek Fateh.

Astronauts Neil Armstrong and Buzz Aldrin during their tour of South Asia being greeted
by an enthusiastic crowd outside the Karachi Airport. —Picture courtesy of LIFE.

A young Pakistani woman sitting on her motorbike in the Soldier Bazzar area of Karachi. —Picture courtesy of Zarmeena P.

A 1972 picture showing European visitors and local Christians seen during a Church ceremony at a Catholic school in Rawalpindi. —Picture courtesy of John Meacham.

Pakistan International Airlines (PIA) ad. PIA was considered one of best airlines in the world in the 1960's serving excellent cuisine and a wide selection of whiskey, wine and beer.

A European tourist with students of the Peshawar University without fear of being tortured and killed.

A European tourist family outside a rest house at the
mountain resort of Murree near Islamabad.

Western tourists enjoy a buggy ride outside Peshawar's Hotel Intercontinental.

Western tourists jam with a Pakistani tabla player in Karachi (1975).

A group of young European tourists travelling and enjoying a cup of tea on a Pakistani train.

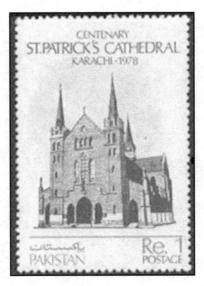

A special stamp released by the government of Pakistan to mark
the centenary of St. Patrick's Cathedral in Karachi (1978).

An American Christian evangelist addressing Pakistani Christians and converts
in a village near Abbottabad in 1977. -Picture courtesy of Williamson.

Visiting American President, Dwight Eisenhower, being introduced to the
Pakistan cricket team at Karachi's National Stadium in 1959.

The Jewish synagogue that was situated in Karachi's Ranchore Lines area.
The small Jewish community eventually moved to Israel and the USA.

A 1960 brochure announcing the founding of a Methodist
Church in Karachi's Garden Road area.

Pakistani Prime Minister, Hussain S. Suhrawardy, in Karachi in a cowboy hat (1956).

Pakistani Prime Minister, Liquat Ali Khan (left), having a chat with
famous Hollywood star Jimmy Stewart in Lahore (1951).

Famous American mystic, Samuel Lewis visited the Sufi
shrine of Data Ganj Baksh's in Lahore (1962).

A coaster depicting Pakistani Murree beer from the bar at Karachi's
Excelsior Club that was forced to close down in 1977.

A 1968 press ad of Coca-Cola. This ad also appeared in American newspapers.

A bar band performing at the Hotel Metropole in the 1960s.

A 1965 brochure for tourists interested in visiting the historic Gandhara site for ancient Buddhist art.

A Pakistani family waiting for their car after attending a
function at Karachi's Beach Luxury Hotel in 1973.

THE ERA OF EXTREMISM STARTED IN 1977

Mohammad Ali Jinnah, founder of Pakistan, and his companions created
Pakistan as a secular state with equal rights for all religions. This practiced
continued until 1974 when socialist Prime Minister Zulfiqar Bhutto fell under the spell of religious parties while trying to save his government and
agreed to put Pakistan on the religious path. Zia-ul-Haq over threw Bhutto
in a military coup in 1977 and started the Islamization of Pakistan.

ARMED FORCES SET UP INTERIM RULE

MARTIAL LAW IS PROCLAIMED: ELECTIONS IN OCTOBER NEXT

Gen Zia is CMLA: President stays

Top PPP, PNA leaders in protective custody

Sections of constitution under suspension

From M. A. MANSURI

ISLAMABAD, JULY 5: IN A LIGHTNING OPERA-TION LED BY ARMY CHIEF GENERAL MOHAMMAD ZIA-UL-HAQ, THE ARMED FORCES OF PAKISTAN HAVE TAKEN OVER THE COUNTRY'S ADMINISTRA-TION.

Mr Zulfikar Ali Bhutto, former Prime Minister, his Cabinet colleagues and top PNA leaders, except Begum Nasim Wali Khan, have been placed under protective custody temporarily.

Proclamation by Chief ML Administrator

Four-man Military Council at Centre

ML Administrators for provinces

Political activities banned in country

RAWALPINDI, July 5: The Chief of the Army Staff, General Mohammed Zia-ul-Haq announced this evening

News gets wide coverage in US media

Lahoris welcome Zia's speech

DAWN newspaper proclaimed the take-over by the dictator General Zia-ul- Haq (July 1977). Zia ruled for 11 years and was responsible for starting Pakistan on the road to Extremism from which it has yet to recover.

The Los Angeles Times' a cartoon of the Pakistani dictator Zia, who executed former Prime Minister Bhutto, is shown doing ballet over Bhutto's disembodied head.

Women organizations were at the forefront of the many movements that took place against the brutal dictatorship of Zia-ul-Haq. This 1980 photograph is from a violent protest held by female college students (in Lahore) against the Zia regime's 'masochistic attitude' towards women.

A BRIEF HISTORY OF PAKISTAN

Pakistan's history is fraught with violence and corruption. It is a country carved out of India for Muslims with two geographically separate parts: West Pakistan and East Pakistan, which never got its footing. Due to its poor economic state and unstable government, it now poses a real danger to world peace with its nuclear arsenal of 100–200 warheads.

The founder of Pakistan, Mohammad Ali Jinnah, had a western education and was a moderate Muslim who died within a year of Pakistan's birth. West Pakistan (currently Pakistan) and East Pakistan (currently Bangladesh) were separated by 1,000 miles. The culturally different Bengali population was dominated by the West Pakistani bureaucrats, who allowed the local Bengali politicians little say in the matters of running governmental affairs.

The generals and political hawks quickly pushed the new country into a brawl with India over Kashmir. Liaquat Ali Khan (Oxford educated), who took over after Jinnah, was shot dead in 1951. No one has been able to pin-point the reason for the assassination, but Mr. Khan was guiding Pakistan on the path of becoming a vibrant democratic state. The next seven years saw many governments come and go, which created considerable instability and corruption. In 1958, the army strong-man, Mohammad Ayub Kahn led a coup d'état and became the Chief Martial Law Administrator.

General Ayub was trained at the prestigious British Royal Military Academy (Sandhurst) and had fought alongside Allied forces on the Burma front World War II. Economic growth under his government was in double digits. There was peace, the middle-class was on the rise and signs of general prosperity had started to blossom. However, being a military man, he attacked India under the excuse of liberating Kashmir. The war was lost, but he was able to turn the defeat to victory through the government-controlled media. Slowly and gradually, the facts started to leak out with the public turning against his government.

In 1969, General Ayub transferred the power to another military strong-man, General Yahya Khan, who assumed the role of Chief Martial Law Administrator. Soon, he lost interest in running the nations' affairs and busied himself with booze and women. In 1971, elections were held, and the Awami League Party led by Mujib-ur-Rahman from East Pakistan (now Bangladesh) won a majority of seats in the parliament. The Peoples Party, led by Zulfiqar Ali Bhutto, won majority of seats in West Pakistan. Bhutto refused to let the Awami League form the next government. This became contentious on the streets. To make matters worse, General Yahya sent in the army to East Pakistan to subdue riots. India took the side of Bangladesh and the ignorant Pakistani generals took India's bait and attacked, widening the war with India on the Pakistani front.

Within two weeks, India overwhelmed the Pakistani army on the eastern front. East Pakistan became Bangladesh, and 90,000 Pakistani soldiers surrendered to the Indian army. The Pakistani generals' foolish promise to the masses of achieving the old "glory days of Islam" never materialized. The Nixon government had to persuade India to halt its further march into Pakistan on the western front. General Yahya, more interested in partying than running the government, handed power over to Bhutto.

Bhutto, a Berkley educated man, tried to experiment with socialism with the slogan "bread, clothing, house [for everyone]." Bhutto, who was well adept as a politician, showed little interest in learning and managing economics or monetary policies for the country on the brink of bankruptcy. Within two years, riots started against Bhutto. I remember very well since I had just been admitted to the Engineering University in Lahore. The demonstrations and strikes led to violence, loss of life, destruction of property and the closing of schools. My university and all other educational institutions were closed for 9 months. Just imagine the loss of intellectual property. With the treasury empty and the economic development of the Ayub era stalled, the masses started to feel the pinch with both high unemployment and inflation. Hoping to avoid a military coup, Bhutto took a gamble and promoted lower ranking General Zia-ul-Haq as Chief of Staff over six senior generals.

The gamble did not pay off, and Zia overthrew Bhutto in 1977, imprisoning him under trumped up murder charges and finally hanging him in 1979.

Zia was a shrewd man; he realized the danger from rising Islamists and the empty treasury and was looking for an opportunity. It quickly came his way when the Soviet Union captured Afghanistan under the pre-text of helping their stooge President Najibullah of Afghanistan. The United States, which had basically cut off all ties with Pakistan upon learning that it was developing a nuclear weapon, felt that it was in their strategic interests to challenge the Soviet Union. Saudi Arabia, rich with petrodollars after the 1973 oil embargo and coffers flushed with billions, entered the Afghani Theater. The troika was formed with the USA (CIA) supplying arms, Saudi Arabia supplying the cash and jihadi recruited to fight against the communist infidels. Pakistan provided training for the jihadi and recruited more from the tribal Pushtun. The Pakistan army and the ISI (Inter-Services Intelligence) provided management, training and logistical support to Afghani fighters.

The operation went smoothly. U.S. Congressman Charlie Wilson of Texas became a champion of the Afghani fighters, known as Mujahidin, and worked closely with the Regan administration in supplying arms that could not be traced back to the Americans in order to avoid Soviet complaints. After eight years, the Soviet Union lost the will and zeal to continue fighting, just like we Americans have after 11 years in our current wars. Alexander the Great also had difficulty in subduing people of this desolate region, and the British learned their lesson in the late 1800s.

Since the war against the Soviets was promoted as jihad against "Infidels," Zia used Mullahs and religious parties in Pakistan embarked upon turning Pakistan into an Islamic state, implementing Sharia laws. The good days were over, floggings and hangings in public became common, bars and night clubs were closed, TV announcers had to wear a hijab and blasphemy laws were passed to take away the rights of the minorities. Zia ruled with an iron fist. Americans did not object to his autocratic rule, as our policy was to work with the dictators in faraway lands rather than against them.

Zia did not have much time to celebrate. After watching an American M1Abrams tank demonstration, he boarded a C130B Hercules with the American Ambassador Arnold Lewis Raphel and General Herbert Wassom, the head of the American military aid mission to Pakistan. Soon after take-off, the plane crashed and exploded on impact, killing all 32 on board. There are many conspiracies theories but investigation could not pinpoint to real cause.

With the Soviets gone, the Americans also left the region in 1989, having felt that their mission was achieved. Saudi Arabia decided to continue to fund the Madrassas (religious schools) and jihadis. The Pakistani Army and ISI (Inter-Services Intelligence, a Pakistani spy agency), having inherited hundreds of thousands of jihadi, came up with new a scheme to use them as proxy to control Afghanistan and one day fight against India to liberate Kashmir.

After Zia, the successive governments of Benazir Bhutto and Nawaz Sharif were weak and corrupt. Pakistan detonated a nuclear weapon in 1999. Under pressure on the street and fearful of another coup, Nawaz Sharif tried to remove General Pervez Musharraf from his post of Chief of Staff; however, General Musharraf was quicker in dealing his hand. He arrested Nawaz Sharif and exiled him to Saudi Arabia. Now the fourth military dictator had seized the power.

The USA government under Clinton had cooled off the relationship with Pakistan after the nuclear explosion and removal of the elected civilian government of Nawaz Sharif. The jihadi movements combined under the banner of Taliban (word Taliban means student) took over Afghanistan to experiment with the new Sharia government. Taliban decimated the Afghani culture and ignored the universal condemnation of their atrocities. Pakistan looked the other way thinking that as long as it was across the border in Afghanistan, all was well on their side. Osama bin Laden had settled in Afghanistan and was considered a guest under the Pushtun Taliban protection.

Then, the evil act of terror on 9/11 occurred. President Bush's doctrine "that you are with us or against us" quickly brought Pakistan into the fold. General Musharraf saw an opportunity to cozy up to the Americans, legitimize his military coup and bilk dollars to support bankrupt Pakistan. Once again, we ended up working with the dictator. General Musharraf negotiated billions of dollars for land routes and support while willingly providing safe havens for the Taliban.

General Musharraf resigned in 2009. To avoid prison or the same fate as Bhutto, he went into self-exile and now is living abroad. Benazir Bhutto (twice Prime Minister of Pakistan, daughter of Ali Bhutto, Harvard graduate) returned to Pakistan from exile but was killed supposedly by the Taliban in 2008. Her husband, who was famous for corruption when she was Prime Minister in the 1990s, then became President of Pakistan.

The readers may have noticed that Pakistani leaders are exiled, killed or tried in court so that they can be sidelined until their death. As a matter of fact, this is the reality all over Muslim countries. Historically, Muslim leaders hang on to power until they are disgraced and pushed out. Mubarak of Egypt, Gaddafi of Libya and Saddam of Iraq are a few examples. With the exception of a few, Muslim leaders rule like dictators with absolute power. Unless they can learn from the western example of term limits with the intention of leaving gracefully, their countries and citizens will stay mired in uncertainty, leading to violence and upheaval.

RELIGION IN PAKISTAN

There is no agreement on the structure of the ideal Islamic state. There is no historical proof that the Islamic state that the Mullahs want to create ever existed. Soon after the passing of Prophet Mohammad and the four Caliphs, the Muslims only had Kings, Sultans, Emirs and Emperors who ruled with all the worldly trappings of intrigue, greed, women, lust, land, gold, wars, conspiracies, deceit, etc. So in reality, this longing for an Islamic state or Caliphate represents a new fantasy dreamed up by the Mullahs.

The Pakistani founder Mr. Jinnah had always promoted a vision of a secular and democratic state for all the people, regardless of their religious affiliation. Religion got shoved into Pakistani culture first by Prime Minister Bhutto to buy the Mullah allegiance, and then by General Zia-ul-Haq to lead the war against the Soviets in Afghanistan as a jihad (holy war). From the 1980s onward, the intellectuals and western-educated found themselves in a minority. The majority, illiterate and agrarian, bet with the Mullahs, as they controlled the mosques and Madrassas. John Esposito of Georgetown University writes, *"Pakistanis have found it easier to rally under the umbrella of Islam in opposition movements, e.g., against the British and Hindu rule or, more recently, against the Bhutto regime, than to agree upon what Islam and an Islamic state are."* [3]

Zia-ul-Haq, the Sunni military dictator, created the Sharia courts, put women behind the veil and treated minorities as third class citizens. According to M. Ilyas Khan and Zaigham Khan, two political Pakistani thinkers, Zia was able to change the political landscape along dictatorial and fundamentalist lines. *"He rendered politics unworkable in Pakistan by blurring the distinction between politics and terrorism. By raising the bogey of Al-Zulfikar (Bhutto) and conducting a massive propaganda campaign against terrorism, he hanged, flogged, and imprisoned pro-democracy political activists.*

In the order (created by Zia), anything that was democratic was branded as un-Islamic which in effect meant that all political parties agitating for democracy found themselves battling a holy warrior instead of military dictator." [4]

Zia wanted to leave a legacy of conceiving an Islamic state, but for all practical purposes, he ended up creating a police state with no rights for women and minorities and limited freedom of expression for the citizens. *"Zia-ul-Haq used Islam to perpetuate his autocratic rule but left behind a legacy of division, disruption, contradiction and conflicts."* [5]

Hina Jilani, an eminent Pakistani commentator, writes, *"A survey of laws and policies instituted by Zia reveals that Islam was invariably employed where rights were to be cur-tailed, and not for the expansion thereof."* [6]

Zia destroyed the political infrastructure and manifested a division that still permeates in all facets of Pakistani society. In the September 13, 2012 article "Be Critical," Nadeem F. Paracha, a columnist for the Pakistani English newspaper Dawn, writes, *"Zia in his zeal to turn into a political Islamic country is responsible for creating an environment for "monsters" like Al-Qaeda and Taliban. The impact this process had on society was catastrophic. The dividing lines between various Muslim sects in Pakistan had for decades remained blurred due to a vague consensus of tolerance between the sects. But these divides became politicized when they were exploited to put forward a prejudiced line of thought. This thought now propagated 'real Islam' to mean violent jihad, xenophobia, isolationism, coercion, and at times sheer barbarism that was proudly explained as acts replicating the mythical ways of ancient Muslim heroes."* [7]

The religious indoctrination in Pakistan has been so deeply rooted in the purposely distorted history books that, according to Mr. Paracha, *"Pakistanis eventually gobbled up a myopic and unthinking brand of religious logic. So much so, that today the overall intellectual faculties of critique in the society have been overpowered by loud discourses that are incapable of ever venturing outside about the faith that has been fed to us since the 1980s."* [8]

Most human beings are endowed by the creator to think, evaluate and investigate prior to rendering an opinion. However, the majority of Pakistanis are unable to follow this logic and go on to blame everyone else except themselves. As stated by Mr. Paracha, *"In such a distorted scenario, when certain disturbing events start taking place in the name of faith, how can one expect*

Pakistanis to react accordingly? Most of us just distract ourselves by blaming the 'enemies of Islam." [9]

Today, Pakistan is lacking a strong civilian government, as it was never allowed to flourish. The strong military continues to drain all economic resources. One can easily argue that the USA, China and Russia need large armies to fulfill their roles as world powers through their strong economies. However, countries like Pakistan and Egypt, which are totally dependent on hand-outs from the USA, IMF or the World Bank, are devoid of leadership that can logically comprehend the cost of their military. The resources it sucks out of the economy could be used to address the basic needs of citizens by building roads, increasing manufacturing, and bolstering the economy to lift the nation out of poverty.

A Few Solutions For Pakistan

Pakistan needs to learn that they have to stand on their own feet. They can start this process by building a basic infrastructure that is driven by their economy. Listed below are a few recommendations:

1. Let democracy take hold.
2. Get rid of corruption from the lowest to the highest level.
3. Collect taxes due instead of taking bribes and making deals.
4. Close all Madrassas and develop a comprehensive educational system that promotes knowledge, learning and harmony.
5. Stop distorting the history that is taught and is based on the hatred of others.
6. Quit aligning with all the causes of Muslims on the planet and let them learn to resolve their own issues.
7. Resolve all issues with India and form a federation to improve economy and commerce.
8. Let Kashmir go, as it has caused so much devastation in the region already.
9. Separate state from religion and regulate the Mullah Community.

10. Repeal the blasphemy laws and provide equal rights to all minorities, religions and genders.

11. Reduce the size of the military each year until it disappears.

12. Follow the Korean and Chinese examples and work on becoming an industrial powerhouse.

13. Foster the return of the qualified and educated Pakistanis from overseas to help with the re-building.

In summation, there is no doubt that both Pakistan and Afghanistan are incubators for terrorists and jihadi organizations alike, with a host of others joining from Arabia, Egypt, Chechnya, Uzbekistan, Yemen, Sudan and Algeria. We cannot leave Pakistan and Afghanistan alone. We will have to respond by creating an International Alliance, as discussed on page 196, and providing institutional support that will allow for these countries to become prosperous so terrorism is eliminated.

PART IV

CHAPTER 5

THE HISTORY OF ISLAM

"If you are irritated by every rub, how will your mirror be polished?"

—RUMI, 12TH CENTURY PERSIAN POET AND SUFI

THE START – 610 TO 661

MUSLIMS BELIEVE THAT ISLAM CAME to Arabia to root out the era of Ignorance known in Arabic as "Jahiliyyah." Prior to Islam, most Arabs were idol worshippers with 360 idols in Kaaba (the cubed building considered most sacred) in Mecca, and a smaller number of citizens followed Judaism and Christianity. Pagan Arabia lacked a political structure or government. Society was based on tribal lines, and the chief managed his tribe through the acknowledgement of his authority. If a crime was committed against an individual, the injured party took the law in its own hand and, with the help of other tribal members, tried to even the score with the offending party. In the absence of police, court, judges and lawyers, the desire to avenge the loss led to battles among tribes that could last for years. There was permanent anarchy, and achieving peace through negotiations was frowned upon. In the desert land, long feuds provided relief from the desert monotony.

Since the desert was not suitable for agriculture, most Arabs depended upon looting traveling caravans or extracting money from them in exchange for safe passage. Mecca was an important city whose citizens were mostly merchants who took goods to Syria in the summer and to Yemen in winter.

The male dominated society accorded few rights to women and no rights for slaves. A man could have as many wives as he could support. Daughters sometimes were buried alive in the name of "honor." Drinking and gambling were the main pastimes. Usury and prostitution were accepted.

According to Islamic traditions, God sent Prophet Mohammad to rid Arabs of their vices and moral decay. He was born around 570 to the high-ranking tribe of Quresh in Mecca, now in Saudi Arabia. His father died few months prior to his birth, and his mother passed away when he was about a year old. His grandfather raised him till the age of five, and upon the grandfather's death, Uncle Talib took over this responsibility.

Very little is known about his early childhood except that he worked as a shepherd for his uncle. At the age of twenty-five, he married the respected and wealthy widow Khadija, fifteen years his senior. Khadija was impressed with his honesty, fairness, and high moral character. She offered him a job managing her trade affairs on a trip to Syria, which turned out to be a profitable venture for the lady.

At age 40, while meditating in a cave near Mecca, Prophet Mohammad received his first revelation of God when Angel Gabriel asked of him (Quran 96:1-5), *"Proclaim! (or read!) in the name of thy Lord and Cherisher, Who created–Created man, out of a (mere) clot of congealed blood: Proclaim! And thy Lord is Most Bountiful,–He Who taught (the use of) the pen,–Taught man that which he knew not."* [1]. In Arabic, the term "Islam" means "submission to the will of God," and a "Muslim" is one who makes that submission. The Muslims believe that the basic message of Islam is similar to the Old Testament, with the emphasis on one powerful God who is the creator of universe. There is a judgment day with rewards for good deeds and punishment for straying away from the path. Islam is a monotheistic faith, and Muslims see the Quran as a continuation of the earlier teachings revealed to Noah, Abraham, Jacob, Moses and Jesus, along with other prophets of both the Old Testament and New Testament.

After 10 years in Mecca, Prophet Mohammad was forced to migrate to Medina, located 270 miles north of Mecca, thus starting the Islamic calendar of Emigration (Hijra). Meccans did not like his message of upholding moral values, treating all beings equal and giving up drinking, gambling and unfair usury practices. When the Meccans could not stop Islam from gaining converts, they decided to kill Prophet Mohammad, and upon learning of this plot, the Prophet decided to migrate.

Muslims prospered in Medina, and the religion slowly started to spread. Prophet Mohammad's message was of peace, and he spoke of fighting only in the case of self-defense. Jews had welcomed him in Medina as a wise man. The religious structure was established: Friday was declared a holy day, daily prayers were prescribed, the call to prayer from the minaret was decreed, the direction of the prayer was changed from Jerusalem to Mecca, Ramadan was declared as a month of fasting, Zakat or alms for the poor was established and the pilgrimage to the Kaaba, Mecca was endorsed.

In 630, Muslims captured the city of Mecca. Meccans were afraid that they would face retribution for their crimes of the past against innocent Muslims. Prophet Mohammad responded with clemency for everyone who no longer wished to fight. Meccans were surprised with this gesture of kindness, and some decided to become Muslim. Thus, the conquest of Mecca ended the years of warfare and violence between both groups.

Prophet Mohammad died in 632. He lived a modest life in an earthen home consisting of few rooms. He ate simple foods, mended his own clothes and was easily accessible to his followers. He promoted the cause of orphans and considered all human beings to be equal, especially women who were looked down upon in the Arab culture. He left little wealth, and his two sons died at young ages. He was survived by four daughters, and the most famous, Fatimah, married his cousin Ali, who later became the Fourth Caliph (Caliphs were successors of Prophet Mohammad. The first four Caliphs were his companions. The later caliphs Umayyad, Abbasid and Ottomans ruled as kings are discussed later in this book).

Prophet Mohammad did not set up a succession structure, and there is no historical record describing whom he would have liked to take over the growing Muslim community. However, the issue of succession did lead to a schism that is discussed later. Furthermore, there is no tangible evidence that the Prophet set up an Islamic state with Sharia during his lifetime.

At this time in history, Arabs had not advanced either socially or intellectually due to their nomadic environment. Their loyalties were still bound to their respective tribe. The Prophet must have been an excellent preacher and communicator to win over the most barbaric people of his time. His brilliance lies in bringing together both rich and poor under the banner of Islam by breaking down the tribal loyalties and creating a social order where religion superseded the emphasis on the blood lines of the past. In principle, no one was superior and all Muslims were now joined in the new brotherhood. The words of the Prophet emphasizing this brotherhood at his last sermon were: *"All mankind is from Adam and Eve, an Arab has no superiority over a non-Arab nor a non-Arab has any superiority over an Arab; also a white has no superiority over black nor a black has any superiority over white except by piety and good action. Learn that every Muslim is a brother to every Muslim and that the Muslims constitute one brotherhood. Nothing shall be legitimate to a Muslim which belongs to a fellow Muslim unless it was given freely and willingly. Do not, therefore, do injustice to yourselves.* [2]

These words of "brotherhood" were forgotten shortly after his death, and the question of succession quickly became contentious. The followers quickly reverted to their old ways of tribal loyalties and bloodlines. Islam did not get to build the strong foundation and infrastructure that is essential for a new organization. The Muslim numbers grew rapidly, and there were some elements that joined Islam only to ride the wind of power.

Today, there is nothing wrong with Islam; the fault lies with the Muslims who have changed the doctrines over the years both consciously and unconsciously to fulfill their agendas. As a result, there are over 70 Muslim sects practicing varied elucidations of the simple doctrines brought by the Prophet Mohammad. The rise in violence of the last 60–70 years teamed with the lack of viable economic progress, illiteracy, denigration of women's rights and insignificant contributions to science and technology do not paint a good picture of Muslims in this ever shrinking world in which we live. Though other religions were not immune to the violence and mayhem in their past, somehow they have managed to overcome the senseless violence committed by Muslims in the name of God.

The Schism – Sunni & Shia – 632 to Present

The companions of the Prophet gathered in 632 in Medina to mourn the loss of their leader and then agreed on a successor in the absence of clear directives. After much debate, a compromise was reached to accept Abu Bakar, giving him the tile of Caliph (successor, spiritual leader and head of state). Abu Bakar was the first adult who accepted Islam and was a close friend of the Prophet.

The first four Caliphs (Abu Bakar, Omar, Usman, Ali) were companions of Prophet Mohammad and ruled from 632 to 661. They are called the Rightly Guided Caliphs by Sunnis but not by Shias, which was the underlying reason for schism. During this period, the Muslim Empire expanded and conquered the Persian Empire, and also took control of the Eastern Roman Empire, North African and Syrian territories. The Muslims controlled much of the Arabian Peninsula and were well on their way to becoming a major world empire, extending from Spain in the West to India in the East.

The caliph Abu Bakr was successful in maintaining a sense of peace and unity for the two short years of his reign. Upon his natural death, Omar succeeded in 634 as the second Caliph. Under his reign, Islam expanded rapidly and captured the Sassanid Persian Empire (Bactria, Azerbaijan, Armenia, Caucasus and Makran), Jerusalem, Damascus and Egypt. Omar is considered one of the most influential leaders in Sunni Islam. He lived a simple life and did not adopt pomp as practiced by the contemporary rulers of the time. In 644, he was assassinated by a Persian known as Abu Lulu in response to the Muslim conquest of Persia. Omar was stabbed six times in the stomach while leading the morning prayers and died three days afterward. His unfortunate death established violence as a norm among Muslims.

Caliph Usman succeeded Umar and is best known for forming the committee to compile the basic text of the Quran that had been gathered on parchments, bones, rocks and in the memory of the reciters. Usman was 70 when he became Caliph, and he was a soft-hearted and a tender-spirited man. During his reign, the Muslim empire continued to expand in Central Asia. His caliphate was marred by a civil war, which led to the murder of the Caliph himself in 654. Now the second Caliph had died a violent death by the hands of Muslims. No Hindus, Jews, Christians or any other group maligned by Muslims today were involved.

Ali (son-in-law and cousin of Prophet Mohammad) became the fourth Caliph. He was the wisest among many cotemporaries of his time. The civil unrest started under Usman's caliphate continued during Ali's reign. Muawiyah (considered a horrible person by some Sunni and most Shias) was a kinsman of Usman and governor of Syria. He disputed the succession of Ali, and a civil war ensued.

Kindling the tribal loyalties once again, the powerful Umayyad (described later in the book) clan, with Muawiyah as their leader, demanded revenge for the death of their relative Usman. Consequently, Muawiyah fought a protracted war against Ali while refusing to acknowledge his caliphate. Ali marched to Syria, and a clash occurred between two Muslim armies at the Battle of Siffin. Neither side won a victory, nor did they opt for arbitration and resolution through peaceful talks. However, the talks produced no fruitful results. Ali came back to Medina, Muawiyah continued to rule Syria, and the stalemate continued.

Ali was assassinated in 661 during morning prayers in Kufa, present day Iraq. Imagine: three companions of Prophet Mohammad were assassinated by Muslims. There were no Americans, Europeans or any other nationalities involved in these killings except Muslims. It is ironic, however, that Muslims have learned to ignore these historical facts as a path of convenience and, today, are open to blame everything on non-Muslims or Jews for all that ails them.

Ali's son, Hasan, signed a truce with Muawiyah and retired to private life in Medina. Muawiyah declared himself caliph (actually king) and thus set up the foundation for broader political and theological divisions in Islam. As a result, two Muslims sects, Sunni and Shia, were born, and they have fought for the past 1400 years for the supremacy and claim to the righteousness of Islam.

Mainstream Sunni consider the first four Caliphs "Rightly Guided." The Sunni claim that they are the righteous Muslims since their doctrines are based on the Quran, Hadith (sayings of the Prophet) and Sunnah (traditions of the Prophet). However, the interpretation of these three has created conflicts within Islam in answering the needs of religion, state and citizens.

Shia believes that Prophet Mohammad had in reality designated Ali and do not consider first three Caliphs as rightly guided. Ali was the first rightful Imam (leader and currently practiced in Iran). Therefore, leadership and authority rests with the Imam (just like Ayatollah Khomeini), who has the special characteristics of having divine guidance and is the descendant of the Prophet. Even though the Quran is the same for both Sunni and Shia, there are subtle difference in the offerings of Prayers and interpretation of Hadith and Sunnah (described in the next chapter).

Forlornly, the division between Sunni and Shia Islam was further exacerbated in 680 when Hussain, Ali's son and the Prophet's grandson, was killed along with 72 of his supporters by an Umayyad army under the leadership of Yazid (considered to be the worst person by many Muslims) son of Muawiyah at Karbala (in present day Iraq). Shias considered the martyrdom of Hussain as an icon for the cause of righteous Islam. The death of Hussain is celebrated each year by Shia Muslims, keeping the flame of Hussain's tragic death alive for over 1300 years.

THE UMAYYAD DYNASTY – 661 TO 750

The Umayyad dynasty ruled from 661 to 750 after Muawiyah proclaimed himself Caliph and consolidated his power. He declared Damascus his capital instead of Medina, leading to fundamental changes within the religion and the expansion of the Muslim Empire.

Religiously, Umayyad viewed Islam exclusively for Arabs. Non-Arabs were discouraged from conversion to Islam until they first became a subject of an Arab tribe. Therefore, conversions of non-Arabs (Mawali) during this era were minimal. The major non-Muslim groups were called Dhimmis and included Christians, Jews, Zoroastrians and Hindus. They were required to pay taxes to the state for their legally protected status as second-class citizens as long as they accepted and acknowledged the Muslim political power. They could not hold high public office but held many bureaucratic positions within the government.

Umayyads made Arabic the language of the realm. They constructed two famous buildings still used today: the Dome of the Rock in Jerusalem and the Umayyad Mosque in Damascus. They transformed the religious Caliphate to Imperial Caliphate, making succession hereditary. The Umayyad set up court at Damascus, rivaling that of Byzantine Constantinople.

The Umayyads continued the Muslim conquests, incorporating present day Uzbekistan, Tajikistan, Kyrgyzstan and Kazakhstan, the Iberian Peninsula, Sind in India, and present day Tunisia, Libya, Algeria and

Morocco. *"At its greatest extent, the Umayyad Caliphate "covered 5.79 million square miles making it the largest empire the world had yet seen."* [(3)]

By the early 7th century, the sheer size of the empire became difficult to manage, and a series of palace coups added to the looming downfall. Civil wars between Sunni and Shia and constant campaigning to conquer new territories drained the treasury. The Berbers of North Africa rebelled due to discrimination by the Arabs. Persia became a haven for the splinter Muslim group of Kharijites. The great wealth acquired was mostly reserved for the Umayyads to support their lavish lifestyle while the majority faced poverty and misery.

Finally, the opposition led by the descendants of Prophet Muhammad's uncle, Abbas, succeeded in overthrowing the Umayyads in 750. Abbas claimed the mantle of Caliphate and the throne, thus starting the era of third Caliphate in Sunni Islam: the Abbasid Dynasty.

THE ABBASID DYNASTY – 750 TO 1258

Islamic civilization flourished under the Abbasids, who ruled from 750 to 1258 with a total of 37 successive caliphs. The famous "Golden Age" of Islam occurred during the reign of the first seven Abbasid Caliphs, who made Baghdad the center of power and culture of the Muslim world. It would be here that Muslim enlightenment reached its apex in science, philosophy, medicine, education, commerce, arts and poetry. Baghdad attracted immigrants from Greece, Jerusalem, India and Spain and was home to Muslims, Christians, Jews, Hindus and Zoroastrians.

The expansion of the Muslim world continued by both peacefully proselytizing and by force. The areas from the inner Asian frontiers of China to the Ganges River in India and the sub-Saharan West Africa had become parts of the Muslim world. The Caliphate evolved into a true monarchy fashioned after the imperial systems of Persia and Rome. The Persians became dominant in the court bureaucracy, and Abbasid appreciated their rich history and intellect. The Caliphs not known for their piety were nonetheless accepted by the Sunni majority as the successors to the Prophet. After 150 years of continuous reign, the Caliphs in Baghdad became weaker due to internal politics that was originally dominated by the Persians and then Turks. They were forced to relinquish power in their large empire to a local ruler known as Emir, Malik or Sultan, who only nominally acknowledged the Caliphs' authority.

The Mongol started their invasion of Central Asia in 1219. This resulted in a colossal loss of human life and unprecedented economic ruin. The Mongols spread throughout Central Asia and Persia. Helagu Khan, the grandson of Genghis Khan, destroyed Baghdad, the largest city in the Islamic world, in 1258. The last Abbasid Caliph, Al-Mustasim, was captured and killed. Baghdad was ransacked and devastated with looting, massacre and rape. The Grand Library of Baghdad containing precious historical books and documents along with libraries, hospitals and palaces were burned. Finally, the Mongol army was stopped by Muslim Egyptian (Mamluk) army north of Jerusalem in the battle of Ain Jalut. The Crusaders, who were no friends of Muslims, considered Mongol as a greater threat. They allowed the Mamluk forces to use their territory in order to defeat the Mongols.

Ironically, it is important to note that three of the Mongol Khanates, the successors of Genghis Khan, later embraced Islam:

- The Il khanate was established by Helagu Khan. The seventh ruler in his line, Mahmud of Ghazni, accepted Islam in 1295.
- The Golden Horde was established by Batu Khan. Tode Mongke, the ruler from his line, accepted Islam in 1281.
- The Chagatai Khanate was established by Chagatai Khan. Baraq, great grandson of Chagatai, converted to Islam during his rule from 1266–71.

The Golden Age under Abbasid started in 800 and lasted until 1100. Abbasids promoted the pursuit of knowledge in Baghdad for both Muslim and non-Muslim scholars alike. They translated Greek literature and philosophy into Arabic which later was translated into Turkish, Hebrew and Latin. Baghdad then became the translation capital of the world. The Persians, with their rich cultural heritage, led the charge with other immigrants translating Greek, Persian and Sanskrit literature into Arabic to expand knowledge. The exchange of ideas for the sake of gaining knowledge became the norm. Haroon Rashid, the caliph of the Arabian Nights, and Mamoon Rashid, who followed him, actively supported intellectual pursuits in science, art and philosophy, giving rise to the mini-Renaissance. Mamoon founded an academy called the "House of Wisdom".

This religious freedom allowed both Muslim and non-Muslim scholars to push the limits and converse openly without the fear of the Mullah. Arts and poetry blossomed, and the legendary book *One Thousand and One Nights*, with its characters Ali Baba, Sindbad and Aladdin, became famous all over the world. Learning from the works of the Greeks and Hindus, the Muslim scholars of Baghdad made advances in the fields of philosophy, medicine, science and math. During the reign of Abbasids, classic works of antiquity were saved through translation into Arabic. This work was later adopted by the Europeans during the Renaissance. *"During this period the Muslim world was a cauldron of cultures which collected, synthesized and significantly advanced the knowledge gained from the ancient Roman, Chinese, Indian, Persian, Egyptian, North African, Greek and Byzantine civilizations".* [4]

Al-Khwarizmi (780–850), the Persian scholar, was a mathematician and astronomer. He introduced Hindu-Arabic numerals and the concept of Algebra. Hindus developed the numbering system, and scholars of Baghdad popularized their usage. He wrote a book entitled *al-Kitab al-Mukhtasar fi Hisab al-Jebrwal Muqabla*, or *The Compendious Book on Calculation by Completion or Restoring and Balancing*. The book describes the explanation and the solution to quadratic and linear equations. The word Jebrwal in Arabic translates to modern day "Algebra."

Ibn Sina, or Avicenna in the West, advanced medical science though his books *The Canon of Medicine* and *The Book of Healing*, which were used by many European scientists during Renaissance. During this era, over 800 doctors practicing in Bagdad made discoveries in anatomy and in the identification of diseases. Following the Quran's teaching *"For every disease, God has given a cure,"* Muslims broadened the art of surgery, progressed pharmacology and compiled medical knowledge into encyclopedias. Muslims named hundreds of stars due to their advanced learning of astronomy: Aldebaran, the Andromeda galaxy, Betelgeuse, Deneb, Rigel, Vega and hundreds more. Other notable contributions include distillation techniques by Alchemists, advanced paper and linen making from China, sugar cultivation and production, citrus farming, maps for navigation, rope making, matting, etc.

The Abbasids were influenced by the Quranic injunctions and hadith such as" the ink of a scholar is more holy than the blood of a martyr" that stressed the value of knowledge. [5]

Then, yearning for knowledge suddenly stopped in the Muslim world. According to the New Atlantis Journal dated September 2, 2011, *"By the thirteenth century, Arabic science was the most advanced in the world. Advances in optics, astronomy, medicine, architecture, and more had brought a golden age of science and technology. Today, however, the scientific contribution of Muslim countries pales in comparison. Since 1901, only two scientists from Muslim countries have won Nobel Prizes in science. In total, forty-six Muslim countries contribute just one percent of the world's scientific literature. Out of approximately 1,800 universities in Muslim countries, only 312 of those universities have scholars who have published journal articles. Muslim countries have only nine scientists, engineers, and technicians per thousand people, compared with a world average of forty-one. What happened?"* [6]

Prominent Pakistani physicist Pervez Hoodbhoy notes, *"Since the end of the Golden Age, not a single major invention or discovery has come from the Muslim world."* [7]

Some Muslim scholars consider Al-Ghazali, or Algazel (1058–1111), a Muslim philosopher of Persian descent, responsible for the damage to Islamic scientific progress because of his writings. He wrote against following the Hellenistic philosophy of Plato and Aristotle: *"We must therefore reckon as unbelievers both these philosopher themselves and their followers among the Islamic philosopher, such as Ibn Sina, Al-Farabi, and others, in transmitting the philosophy of Aristotle."* [8]

Hoodbhoy further states that Al-Ghazali warned young scholars of science, *"O youth, how many nights have you remained awake repeating science and poring over books and have denied yourself sleep. I do not know what the purpose of it was. If it was attaining worldly ends and securing its vanities and acquiring its dignities and surpassing your contemporaries and such like, woe to you and again woe."* [9]

The codification and rise of Sharia led to the suffocation of scientific research, as Mullahs were successful in associating it to the work of the devil and contrary to the teachings of Islam. One can only wonder what the world may look like today if the Exceptional Mindset that flourished in the

Golden Age had continued to follow the path of innovation and progress. There is no doubt that Islam could have been truly called the "Religion of Peace," and "9/11" would not have occurred.

Islam In The Sub-Continet India – 712 to 1857

Arabs were trading with the merchants of Malabar, in today's Kerala state of India, prior to the birth of Islam. Did this merchant relationship lead to the first appearance of Islam in the sub-continent, or is Will Durant's claim that Islam came to India via conquest valid? In his famous book, *Oriental Heritage*, published in 1935 Durant writes, *"The Mohammedan Conquest of India is probably the bloodiest story in history. It is a discouraging tale, for its evident moral is that civilization is a precarious thing, whose delicate complex of order and liberty, culture and peace may at any time be overthrown by barbarians invading from without or multiplying within."* [10].

Whatever the causes, the sub-continent of India was ripe for the taking due to its wealth, vast territorial divisions and rule by many local Rajas and Maharajas. Durant further argues that the internal conflicts and the basic teachings of the Hindu religion allowed the conquest by Muslims: *"The Hindus had allowed their strength to be wasted in internal division and war; they had adopted religions like Buddhism and Jainism, which unnerved them for the tasks of life; they had failed to organize their forces for the protection of their frontiers and their capitals, their wealth and their freedom, from the hordes of Scythians, Huns, Afghans and Turks hovering about India's boundaries and waiting for national weakness to let them in. For four hundred years (600-1000), India invited conquest; and at last it came."* [11].

The Islamic conquest started when Mohammad bin Qasim, a young Arab General, was sent on a mission by Hajjaj, his uncle and Governor of Iraq. At the time, the local Indian population practiced Hinduism, Buddhism or Jainism. He defeated Raja Dahir in 712 and captured Sindh, in present day Pakistan, expanding the dominion of the Umayyad Dynasty. Unfortunately, upon the sudden death of the Caliph and his uncle, Qasim was recalled, imprisoned, tortured and killed by orders of the new Caliph due to personal animosity with his uncle.

Mahmud of Ghazni (present day Afghanistan) launched 17 attacks on India, starting with the defeat of Raja Jayapala in 1001 at the Battle of Peshawar (present day Pakistan). The Ghaznavid rule in India lasted from 1010 to 1087 with Lahore (present day Pakistan) being the capital. Mahmud also fought with the Shia Ismaili Fatimid of Multan and thus continuing the sad feud between Sunni and Shia. His empire extended from the Caspian Sea to Punjab. Mahmud is worshipped by the Muslims and reviled by the Hindus. Hindus accuse him of looting temples, burning monasteries and killing hundreds of thousands of their people. Mahmud believed in waging jihad against Hindus. Sir Henry Miers Elliot, a famous scholar writes:

"Mahmud utterly ruined the prosperity of the country, and performed their wonderful exploits, by which the Hindus became like atoms of dust scattered in all directions, and like a tale of old in the mouth of the people." [12]

THE MUGHAL EMPIRE – 1526 TO 1857

The Mughal Prince Babur was descended from Timur (Tamerlane) on his father's side and Genghis Khan on his mother's side. He defeated and killed Ibrahim Lodhi, the last of the Delhi Sultanate, in 1526. The Mongols, who had sacked Baghdad and fought with the Muslims for decades, had accepted Islam, intermarried with Turkic and Persian peoples and assimilated into the local culture. They used Persian as their official court language, and most favored the tolerant Sufism, which is the most tolerant branch of Islam as preached by the famous philosopher Rumi.

Babur (born in Andijan, present day Uzbekistan) was able to capture Kabul from where he turned south and conquered much of the Indian Sub-Continent. Babur followed a rather loose interpretation of the Islamic doctrines and enjoyed wine and smoking hashish.

Humayun (son of Babur) succeeded his father in 1530. He was inexperienced and regarded as an ineffective ruler and lost his reign from 1540 to 1556 to the Afghani strongman Sher Shah. Humayun recovered the lost territories before his death and left a stable empire to his teenage son Akbar who later became known as "Akbar the Great."

Akbar succeeded to the throne in 1556. Akbar was a tolerant and gifted soul who followed the Sufi concept of Sulh-e-Kuhl, or "Peace to All." Hindus, Buddhists, Zoroastrians, Jains and Christians graced the royal court of the Emperor. He respected his Hindu subjects and their religion. His first marriage was with Princess Jodha Bai, a Rajput, in pursuit of cementing and enhancing his relationship with the Hindu majority. He repealed the non-Muslim tax (Jaziya) and the special tax required from Hindus for visiting sacred sites. He supported religious freedom; he allowed Hindus to build their own temples, organize their own public worship and gave them important positions in the government. All these positive policies led to an increase in his standing as a just ruler among the majority of his subjects, especially the Hindus.

In 1582, his open and curious mind concerning religion led him to send a letter to King Philip II of Spain chiding him for the Spanish policy of expelling and forcibly converting Jews, Muslims and Protestants to Catholicism. Akbar wrote: *"As most men are fettered by bonds of tradition, and by imitating ways followed by their fathers... everyone continues, without investigating their arguments and reasons, to follow the religion in which he was born and educated, thus excluding himself from the possibility of ascertaining the truth, which is the noblest aim of the human intellect. Therefore we associate at convenient seasons with learned men of all religions, thus deriving profit from their exquisite discourses and exalted aspirations."* [13].

It is not known if Philip II received the letter calling for religious tolerance; however, it shows Akbar's Exceptional Mindset towards the followers of other faiths. During his reign, the Mughal Empire became such a rich and vital trading partner that several emissaries were sent by European rulers, including Elizabeth I of England and Henry IV of France.

Akbar's legacy of religious tolerance and liberal tax policies gave most of his subjects a chance to prosper. He was famous for his love and support of the arts and sciences. It is no wonder that he is honored as one of the greatest rulers in human history. He died in 1605.

Jahangir succeeded Akbar in 1605. He used the strong kingdom inherited from his father to continue building upon its strong economy and cultural achievements. He practiced freedom of religion and did not favor forced conversions. Sir Thomas Roe was the first ambassador of Queen Elizabeth I of England to the court of Jahangir. The emperor enjoyed wine, opium and women. The tale of his romance with courtesan Anarkali has been adapted to Bollywood movies as well as Indian art and literature.

After the death of Jahangir in 1627, Shah Jahan inherited a farfetched empire. Four years into the reign, his beloved wife Mumtaz Mahal died during the birth of their fourteenth child. The emperor went into deep mourning and ended up building a lovers' monument in her honor known as the Taj Mahal. Sadly, Shah Jahan's third son, Aurangzeb, seized the throne, had all of his brothers executed in in 1658 and imprisoned his father at the Agra Fort. Shah Jahan spent his declining years gazing out at the Taj Mahal until his death in 1666.

Emperor Aurangzeb is considered to be the last of the "Great Mughals." He ruled for 49 years, had over 100 million subjects and claimed a landmass of 1.92 million square miles. He left a mixed legacy; he rejected the religious tolerance of his predecessors and thus remains a controversial figure in the sub-continent. He banned the usage of music, directly impacting Hindu worship. *"He learnt that at Sindh, Multan, Thatta and particularly at Varanasi, the Hindu Brahmins attracted large numbers of indigenous local Muslims to their discourses. He ordered the Subahdars of these provinces to demolish the schools and the temples of non-Muslims."* [14]. On the other hand, he lived a simple life and did not use the royal treasury for personal use. He made caps and copied the Quran to earn money to support himself. However, he wasted millions in fighting the Marathas of Deccan and spent 26 years of his life toward the cause, which led to the quick decline of the Mughal Empire.

The Portuguese were early traders who reached India 100 years prior to the arrival of the British. The British East India Company (founded in 1600) started trading with India during the reign of Akbar. Sir Thomas Roe became close to the Mughal Emperor Jahangir thus allowing the British a fast track to gaining a strong foothold, which led to profits in Indian silks, cottons and other rich textiles. Highly skilled artisans, dyers and weavers in India produced cloth with beautiful designs and eye pleasing colors. These were already being exported throughout Asia and became popular with British.

The Mughals ruled most of present-day India, Pakistan, Bangladesh and Afghanistan for several centuries. By late 1700s, the Mughal Empire was in a state of decline, and many smaller states were vying for power. The British East India Company began to get involved in power politics by raising its own army and playing one state against another. In 1857, the infamous

"War of Mutiny" as British called it or "War of Independence" as Indians called it, occurred when the Indian Army rose up against the British East India Company.

The British monarchy intervened to protect its financial interest in the Company, and the rebellion was put down successfully. Ironically, with the help of Indian soldiers, there were only 50,000 British soldiers who helped add the Jewel of India to their expanding empire, which gave rise to the saying that the "Sun Never Sets in the British Empire."

The last Mughal Emperor, Bahadur Shah Zafar, was arrested, tried for treason and exiled to Burma, ending the Great Mughal Empire.

The Moors In Spain – 711 to 1492

Spain was conquered mainly by the Berbers of North Africa, who were originally conquered by the Muslims of Arabia. In 711, the Berber general Tariq bin Ziyad and an army of 7,000 troops landed at Gibraltar, and by 712, the Muslims had defeated the Visigoth army and their King Roderick, who was killed in battle. By 720, the Muslims had conquered most of Spain and Portugal with little opposition and thus started the reign of the Moors. The Islamic rulers gave the Iberian Peninsula the name of "Al-Andalus," which is the root name for the present-day southern regions of Spain, Andalusia.

The Muslims created a thriving multi-cultural society with the followers of three monotheistic religions: the Jews, Christians, and Muslims. One can debate whether or not Muslims treated the other two religions equally in every aspect of daily life, which included a non-Muslim Dhimmis tax; nevertheless, Spain provides the best example of these three religions managing to create a better understanding of each other and benefitting well from each other in that period.

The Muslim community of Spain was diverse and faced social tensions among the Moors of North Africa and the Arab leadership from Arabia. In spite of this, Granada and Cordoba flourished. Cordoba became the largest and richest city in Western Europe. Muslims, Christians and Jewish intellectuals revitalized and magnified classical Greek learning in Europe.

Islamic control of Spain was gradually eroded by the Spanish Reconquista (Re-conquest) as the divisions among the Muslim rulers continued to manifest. The Catholic Kingdoms of northern Spain eventually managed to succeed in defeating and conquering most of the Muslim states. The Granada War began in 1482, and Muslim defeat was complete in 1492 by the forces of Catholics led by Queen Isabella and King Ferdinand II. This ended the 781-year Muslim rule in Spain. This was the same year Christopher Columbus started his voyage to the New World. The Treaty of Granada guaranteed religious tolerance toward Muslims and Jews. This did not last for long, however, as both were ordered to convert to Catholicism or face expulsion from Spanish territories during the Spanish Inquisition.

THE OTTOMAN EMPIRE – 1301 TO 1922

After the Mongols destroyed Baghdad, the Seljuks founded Sultanate in the East and in Central Asia Minor. In 1301, Usman Bey, an Uzbek of the Osman clan, overthrew the Seljuk Sultanate and declared himself the Sultan of Asia Minor. Thus the Ottoman Empire was born in northwestern Anatolia. The conquest of Constantinople, the last stronghold of the Byzantine Empire, was completed by Mehmed II in 1453. He renamed the city Istanbul, meaning "the City of Islam."

The capture of Constantinople ended the 1100-year-old Byzantine Empire. This had an enormous effect on Christian Europe. In Rome, the Pope demanded a crusade against the infidels to recapture the city, but memories of the disastrous crusade that took place earlier easily dissuaded the Kings of the West. The loss of Constantinople to Muslims suffocated the Eastern trade routes and accelerated the efforts by the Western nations to explore new routes to the East. This gave rise to the "Discovery Stage" of finding new routes by going west to reach the East.

Istanbul became more than a political and military capital. Because of its central location at the cross road to Asia, Africa and Europe, it became a great trading junction of the world. The new Ottoman Empire reached its peak at 1590 while covering territories in Asia, Europe and Africa. The long reign of the Ottomans lasted for 621 years, from 1301 to 1922. In 1922, the Caliphate was abolished, and the new state of Turkey was born from the remnants of the old Ottoman Empire.

During the reign of Suleiman the Magnificent (1520–1566), the Ottoman Empire reached its zenith and became one of the most powerful in the world — a true cosmopolitan empire. The Sultan encouraged the migration of Jewish intellectuals and traders from Europe and specifically Spain to migrate to the Ottoman Empire. The empire stretched from the Holy Roman Empire to the outskirts of Vienna, Royal Hungary (modern Slovakia), from the Polish–Lithuanian Commonwealth in the north to Yemen and Eritrea in the south, and from Algeria in the west to Azerbaijan in the east.

The Harem (many women as wives and concubines) was at the Sultan's command and was considered to be a part of normal life for his pleasure. The number of concubines was in the hundreds, and the capture of new territory added to this treasure regularly. To protect the Sultan's booty, only eunuchs were allowed as permanent male staff in the palace. With Islam's maximum allowance of only four legitimate wives and their offspring, the harem added further confusion by adding countless births of brothers and half-brothers, creating chaos at the time of succession. Therefore, to avoid bloodshed, Sultan Selim introduced the policy of Fratricide. Under these new rules, after the new Sultan had been selected, his brothers were locked up in an apartment. Once a son was born to the new Sultan, all of the brothers and their sons were killed. The new Sultan's sons would then be confined to an apartment until their father's death, whereupon a son would follow his father's reign with his own.

These strange rules were not Islamic but were freely used by the Sultan to keep his hold onto the throne. As noted by Alan Palmer, this policy led to chaos in the hereditary succession: *"In January 1595, the killing of a record eighteen brothers of Mehmed III left the dynasty so short of males that religious leaders began to question the morality and wisdom of mass fratricide. It was accordingly decided that close male relatives should henceforth be confined to a kafe (cage), one of several small apartments in the Fourth Courtyard of the Sultan's principal palace, the Topkapi."* (15)

From time to time, the Sultan had to face a religious fatwa. Until 1922, when the reign ended, 13 Sultans or Caliphs were deposed under the Fatwa by the *"Chief Mufti in response to questions framed by political enemies on the Sultan's observance of Holy Law."* (16)

The Ottoman Empire had gradually declined by the end of the 19th century. In World War I, the Ottoman Empire chose the wrong side and aligned with Germany. The ensuing defeat of the Central Powers led to the capitulation of the Ottoman rule that lasted from 1299-1923. Mustafa Kemal, who became known as Atatürk or "Father of the Turks" was the first democratic president of new nation called Turkey.

Mustafa Kemal Atatürk had an exceptional mindset and began to modernize Turkey. He declared Turkey a secular state and embarked upon ambitious economic development programs. He viewed Turkey as a Muslim state that must aligned itself with Europe. He implemented European laws, promoted European dress, and emancipated women— making Turkey the first in the Muslim world by allowing women to vote. The modern countries that gained independence after the demise of Ottoman Empire include Albania, Bosnia and Herzegovina, Bulgaria, Egypt, Greece, Iraq, Lebanon, Romania, Saudi Arabia, Serbia, Syria, Jordan, Turkey, Balkan states and North Africa countries.

CHAPTER 6

ISLAMIC
DOCTRINES

"There is no capital more useful than intellect and wisdom, and there is no indigence more injurious than ignorance and unawareness."

—ALI BIN TALIB (FOURTH CALIPH)

ANALYSIS

MUSLIMS RELY ON VARIOUS SOURCES to practice their religion, including the Quran (revealed to Prophet Mohammad), Hadith (Sayings of the Prophet), and Sunnah (Actions of the Prophet). These sources and related material are described in this chapter for the reader to get a better understanding of Muslims.

Over the years, the various interpretations have mingled with different cultures, giving birth to over 70 sects in Islam (discussed later). The differences in how these sects practice Islam range from minor to major. The debate among various sects on the true meaning of certain verses of Quran, validity of certain Hadith and reliability of certain actions attributed to the Prophet Mohammad has resulted in violence and destruction. Most sects fiercely protect their understanding of religious doctrines even to the point of declaring other sects as heretics and infidels.

Christianity went through a similar debate when Martin Luther was declared heretic after he hurled insults at the Pope. Luther's actions led to the Thirty Years' War, which pitted Catholics against Protestants in Europe from 1618 to 1648. In the 12ᵗʰ century, Catholic Church had embarked upon the "Inquisition" against heretics, resulting in loss of life and destruction of property in Europe. Despite this turmoil, Christianity went through its motions and now is at peace within itself.

The Muslim world is getting warmed up on its own path of violence between various Muslim sects, as well as with non-Muslims, in the name of God and to protect His doctrines as each sees fit. The times now are much different than 500 years ago when schism in Christianity started. With the availability of lethal weapons, including nukes, the potential for shear destruction is unimaginable. Peace-loving Muslims derive their understanding of these doctrines in a totally different way than terrorists do.

THE QURAN

Muslims consider the Quran a book of God, and they consider its message valid until the Day of Judgment. According to Muslim traditions, God revealed the Quran to Prophet Mohammad through Angel Gabriel over a period of 23 years: 13 years in Mecca and 10 years in Medina. Since paper had not been invented yet, the Muslims wrote it on stones, leaves and whatever else was available. After the Prophet's death, Usman the Third Caliph compiled the Quran into its present form. It consists of 30 Chapters and 114 Suras (verses) of varying lengths.

The fundamentalists believe that the Quran has an answer for everything, including all aspects of daily life, government structure and sciences. This absolute belief has led to division and confusion among Muslims. For clarification, some sects of Islam use the Hadith (sayings of Prophet) in order to support their understanding. There is no mention of Sharia Law in the Quran, but fundamental Muslims justify its use through interpretations from the Hadith. The traditional Burqa is not mandated in the Quran, but Muslims will find a Hadith supporting their manifestation.

The Quran is in Arabic, and 80% of Muslims are non-Arabic with little or no understanding of the language, which leaves plenty of room for a lack of the clear grasp of understanding among the masses. They end up relying upon a Mullah at the pulpit to do the interpretation. The Majority of the Mullahs are laden with cultural and ethnic biases that add or subtract from meaning of the Arabic text. The Quran is also poetic and allegoric, making it difficult to understand without a scholar of the Quran who has good understanding of Arabic. Education in the meaning of the Quran is voluntary even though all Muslim families do their best to have children read the Quran at early age. However, the young mind is not fully ready to comprehend the meanings of these complex reflections. The best example of this is the Taliban teaching the Quran in Pakistani Madrassas to brainwash children into following violence.

The challenge that Muslims face today is how to interpret the Quran and then have the ability to ask questions without fear of being declared an infidel. The Quran does not provide answers to many anomalies that Muslims face today. With changing times, Muslim scholars are unwilling to develop answers that are relevant for the present times. Mullahs forbid intellectual dialogue that could enhance knowledge; however, the open discussion could promote a better understanding of the Quran. The terrorist groups use verses from the Quran to justify the killing of innocent people and the destruction of property, whereas the majority of Muslims do not agree with their logic.

Christianity was spared this fate even though there are many interpretations of the Bible. The Reformation movement, printing press and the availability of the Bible in many languages other than Latin has lessened the dependence on the pastor. The open debate in Christianity has allowed followers to ask questions in order to enhance the understanding of verses that were difficult to comprehend without being declared a heretic.

Until Muslim scholars are able to accept that God is not close-minded and the variations embedded in this universe are of His virtues, they will continue to swim aimlessly in the ocean of ignorance. In order to get out of this predicament, Muslims must first attain an Exceptional Mindset and then collectively figure out the best way to teach the Quran so that it is compatible with modern times and its true meaning is made easily accessible for the masses, not the chosen few. By looking around, one can easily see that God's creations are not constant. This is evident in the fact that the Muslims themselves have not stayed constant; there are now more than 70 sects when Prophet Mohammad had only one sect, called "Muslim."

THE HADITH

Hadith refers to examples, rituals, actions and sayings of the Prophet Mohammad and serves as a basis for better understanding of Islam. The fundamentalists use Hadith to propagate the implementation of Sharia, to treat women unequally and to control the masses.

Interestingly, Hadiths were compiled and gathered during the 8th and 9th centuries, long after the death of Prophet Mohammad (632) and mostly by the Persian scholars.

There is an irony and madness to the method of compilation, which most Muslims conveniently ignore. The Hadith writers travelled to Arabia 175 years after the death of Prophet Mohammad to write his "sayings" by first locating and then interviewing the relatives of many deceased companions of the Prophet. How these relatives of the relatives remembered verbatim what the Prophet had said, and how he had said it, has resulted in a debate among Muslims. Different sects accept some Hadith and reject others. In those primitive days, it would not have been possible to completely write everything that the Prophet communicated, resulting in various interpretations of what he actually said. Even in today's modern environment with numerous technological gadgets at our disposal, a statement made by anyone on TV can be interpreted in many ways by TV pundits or commentators.

Muslims will be best served by exploring how the Hadith that contributed to primitive Arabia can best be applied in modern times. The purpose is not to denigrate the message of the Prophet but to investigate the best path for the here and now. For example, an automobile's purpose is to take a person from point A to B. The Ford Model T accomplished this objective over 100 years ago and so does the Ford Taurus today; however, a side-by-side comparison will clearly show that these two cars are both different and dissimilar but in essence accomplish the same goal.

The two largest denominations of Islam, Shia and Sunni, have different sets of Hadith. Some Muslims believe that Hadith provide answers for every aspect of life, including work, marriage, prayers, sex, dealing with others, business, etc. In a similar fashion, al-Qaeda, Taliban and other terrorists fully justify jihad, suicide killing and a host of other violent acts though various Hadiths. The six Hadith compliers/scholars are listed below:

Muhammad al-Bukhari was born in 810 in the city of Bukhara (now in Uzbekistan). He traveled to Mecca for pilgrimage and then visited important Islamic centers of his time. He talked with over 1,000 men and learned of over 700,000 Hadiths, ultimately choosing only 7,275 due to authentication issues.

Muslim ibn al-Hajjaj was born in 817 in Nishapur (now in Iran). He traveled to Iraq, the Arabian Peninsula, Syria and Egypt. He evaluated 300,000 Hadiths and selected between 3,033 and 12,000. The variation in range is dependent upon different Muslim sects.

Abu Ibn Mājah was born in Qazwin, the modern-day Iranian province of Qazvin, in 824. He visited Iraq, Mecca, the Levant and Egypt. There is no consensus but his compilation of Hadith, known as "The Sunan," includes about 4,000 Hadith.

Ahmad Al-Nasai was born in Khorasan, Iran in 829. His collection is known as Sunan al-Sughra. He traveled to the Arabian Peninsula, Iraq, Syria and Egypt. He collected 1,800 Hadith.

Abu Dawood Suleman was commonly known as Abu Dawood and was born in Sistan Iran. He traveled to Hejaz, Iraq, Egypt and Syria in order to collect Hadith. Out of about 500,000 Hadith, he chose 4,800 for inclusion in his work.

Abu Isa Mohammad Termezi was born in Termez (now Uzbekistan) in 824. He was a Persian collector of Hadith known as Jami al-Tirmidhi in Sunni Islam.

SUNNAH AND HADITH

Sunnah, which consists of what the Prophet did, believed, implied, or tacitly approved, was noted by his companions in Hadith. In the context of biographical records of Prophet Muhammad, Sunnah often stands synonymous with Hadith since most of the personality traits of the Prophet are known from descriptions of him through his sayings and his actions. How far Hadith contributes to Sunnah is disputed and highly dependent on the context.

Sunni and Shia Hadith collections differ because scholars from the two traditions do not agree on the reliability of the narrators and writers. Narrators who took the side of Abu Bakr, Omar and Usman (first three

Caliphs) rather than Ali (4th Caliph) in the disputes over leadership that followed the Prophet's death are seen as unreliable by the Shia.

Differences in Hadith collections have contributed to differences in worship practices and sharia law, hardening the dividing line between the two major groups. Sunni and Shia Muslims accept the authenticity of the majority of Hadith, though they often disagree over the authenticity of certain Hadith or how others might be interpreted and have different canonical collections.

The unquestioned following of Hadith by most Muslims underscores the power of faith. However, there is no denial that the majority of Hadith became available after the compilers' deaths. Criticism of Hadith revolves primarily around the question of the authenticity of Hadith reporters and whether they are attributable to the Prophet.

Muslims who refute the authority of the Hadith and follow the Quran alone are referred to as Quranist Muslims. They reject the authority of Hadith on theological grounds, pointing to verses in the Quran itself (6-38): *"Nothing have We omitted from the Book."* [1]. They declare that all the necessary instruction can be found within the Quran, without reference to the Hadith. They argue that following the Hadith has led people to stray from the original purpose of God's revelation to the Prophet in the form of Quran.

Sir Syed Ahmed Khan (1817–1898), an Indian Muslim scholar often considered the founder of the modernist movement within Islam asserted that Hadith were not binding and suggested using "rational science" to both Hadith and Quran.

There are questions about the authenticity of the Hadith attributed to the Prophet Muhammad written much later after his death. The majority of Hadith are not the words and actions of the Prophet but invented and fictional material of the Mullah community.

Could this be the reason that the total reliance on Hadiths has left Muslims lagging behind in the critical thinking, reasoning and discovery?

SHARIA

Sharia is the Muslim code of conduct that pretty much attempts to control the follower's life from sunrise to sunset. Sharia divides all Muslim acts into permitted (Halal) or forbidden (Haram). The Sharia deals with prayers, fasting, law, politics, crimes, economics, marriage, sexual intercourse, personal hygiene, diet, death, dealings with non-Muslims and division of property. The fundamentalists consider it to be the "infallible law of God," which all must follow.

Today's Muslims differ considerably among themselves as to what exactly it entails. The debate among modernists, fundamentalists and terrorists leads to many different interpretations of Sharia. Shia and Sunni have entirely different views, as do the other 70 sects. Muslims living in different countries and cultures have varying interpretations of Sharia as well.

Fundamentalist Muslim scholars have failed to rationalize that the God they follow so fervently does not live frozen in time. His message must be looked at through the prism of present time, thus allowing for improvements while keeping basic tenants the same.

Neither the Prophet nor the first four Caliphs implemented Sharia in Medina. Sharia law can be attributed to the five Islamic scholars noted below during the reign of Umayyad of Damascus and Abbasid of Baghdad. They are the ones who led the charge in developing Sharia 100 years or more after Prophet Mohammad's death. Muslims largely rely on these scholars for the interpretation of Sharia:

Jafar ibn Muhammad (702–765), a great-grandson of Ali, was respected by both Sunni and Shia. He advocated a limited predestination and rejection of Hadith that were contrary to the Quran.

Abu Hanifa (699–767) was of Persian heritage and from Kabul. He promoted the use of logic when faced with questions based on the Quran and Sunnah. He is considered liberal and practical, and his teaching became popular among the masses. He relied on analogy for deducing law. Sadly, he died after he was imprisoned by the second Abbasid Caliph, Al-Mansur, over a minor misunderstanding.

Malik ibn Anas (711–795) is one of the most respected scholars in Sunni Islam and was of Yemeni origin. He is considered conservative in legal doctrines.

Al-Shafi (767–820) was of Arab descent. He promoted unity for all Muslims but prevented the growth of autonomous and local-based legal systems. In religious decisions, he advocated equal weight to the Quran and Hadith.

Ahmad ibn Hanbal (780–855) was of Arab descent and born in Baghdad. He became a leading scholar of Hadith and Sunnah. His Sharia Law promotes orthodox Sunni dogma.

These men in Islam created Sharia to meet the needs of their times, as the Muslim Empire was expanding and absorbing new converts and different cultures. Therefore, the Sharia that was developed by them was a work-in-progress. The Muslim scholars of today completely ignore this fact to avoid looking outside the box. This has caused the biggest confusion among various sects of Muslims. The debate that is now raging involves a few who insist on keeping Islam in the dark ages of antiquity and others who promote the use of logic and common sense to create a Renaissance, aiming for positive changes that can truly benefit Islam.

Today, it is difficult to have an open dialogue with Extremist Muslims on the topic of Sharia due to its inelasticity and the insistence of its divinity, hence requiring no improvement. With this attitude, the debate for reformation, which is needed to get Muslims on the path of peace, can never start.

Despite the scare tactics used by some, a few Muslim scholars are quietly examining the Quran that was revealed during the first 13 years in Mecca, rather than that revealed in the last 10 years in Medina. They argue that the Meccan Quran provided equality for all citizens regardless of their faith, race and gender. Abdullahi Ahmed An-Na'im is the Charles Howard Candler Professor of Law at Emory University School of Law, Atlanta, Georgia, and he argues *"That message was characterized by equality between men and women and complete freedom of choice in matters of religion and faith. Both the substance of the message of Islam and the manner of its propagation during the Mecca period were predicated on ismah, freedom of choice without any form or shade of compulsion or coercion."* [2]

Furthermore, An-Na'im promotes a secular state and separation of state and religion so that one can practice their faith freely without fear of persecution. A Sharia run state will run an autocratic form of government with no rights for minorities, as it is evident in Iran, Saudi Arabia, etc.

An-Na'im suggests that Muslim scholars start by changing Sharia in three areas first: *"male guardianship of women (qawama,"* *"sovereignty of Muslims over non-Muslims (dhimma),"* and *"violently aggressive jihad."* [3]

Fazlur Rahman Malik, professor of Islamic Studies, taught at the University of Chicago and McGill University. He has objected to the literal interpretation of the Quran while emphasizing the importance of interpretation through historical context instead. He argues that intellectual dynamism is essential to the Islamic revival. He promotes the understanding of law over ethics and feels that *"moral values"* [4] require constant interpretation.

These scholars are few in number, and it is disheartening to find very few Muslim organizations that are openly against terrorism or jihad. Generally, there is a fear among the moderate Muslims that by condemning terrorists they may become targets of violence through fatwa or other irrational acts. However, liberal Muslims must unite, collaborate and act through positive dealings to rid themselves of the cancer within Islam in the form of terrorism and violence in order to become thriving and productive citizens of this world.

MUSLIM SECTS OR DENOMINATIONS

After schisms and disagreements that began centuries ago, Islam now has more than 70 sects leading to varying interpretations of Islamic doctrines. Each sect believes that they are the only ones following the true Islam and that others are on the wrong path. One must then ask an important question: since Prophet Mohammad brought only one message, how did it get divided into so many shards? The consensus that would have provided Islam a few hundred years of peace never materialized. Most Muslim rulers continued to lust after land and gold and used either violence or jihad as a weapon not only against non-Muslims but against Muslims too.

Sunni– 80% of Muslims belong to Sunni, claiming direct continuation of their doctrine as defined by the Prophet. The Sunni derive their name through the "Action" (Sunnah).

Sufi (Dervish or Fakir) – These are the mystics within the Sunni and Shia sect, a liberal religious order that follows mystical interpretations of Islamic doctrines and practices. Sufism started in Central Asian Muslim countries and is now popular in India, Uzbekistan, Turkey, Morocco, Senegal, Bosnia and Pakistan. Ottoman and Mughal Empires followed the Sufi traditions, as did the Muslims of Spain. The famous Sufi Rumi played a critical role in spreading tolerant Islam in the Muslim countries of Central Asia and Indian Sub-Continent. The whirling Dervish belongs to Sufism.

Salafi or Wahhabi– Mohammad ibn Abd al-Wahhab began a campaign of spiritual renewal in the 1700s in present day Saudi Arabia. The Wahhabi theology focuses on the literal interpretation of the Quran. It is quite strong in Saudi Arabia and Afghanistan. It demands punishment for those who enjoy music and severe punishment for drinking alcohol, sexual transgressions and missing daily prayers. It condemns those who do not pray as unbelievers, a view that never previously existed in mainstream Islam. Jihad with a sword or gun is promoted and was an inspiration to Osama bin Laden. Salafi growth began in the 1970s when Saudi, rich with petro dollars, started funding Wahhabi schools (madrassas) and mosques from Indonesia to USA. The 1980 Afghanistan invasion by the Soviet Union provided Saudi Arabia with a golden opportunity to spread Salafism in Pakistan and Afghanistan by helping to open thousands of Madrassas with cooperation from the Pakistani military dictator General Zia-ul-Haq.

Ahl al-Hadith– A conservative Sunni group that emphasizes the use of Hadith while interpreting Islam. The term is often used to describe Salafi or Wahhabis. They are mostly located in India, Pakistan, Yemen and Bangladesh.

Deobandi– A conservative Sunni group located mainly in India, Pakistan, Afghanistan and Bangladesh. The founders of the Deobandi movement were influenced by the Wahhabi movement.

Barelvi– A liberal Sunni-Sufi group that was founded in the Indian Sub-Continent in opposition to the Deobandi group.

Shiite– The second largest sect after Sunni is Shia, which accounts for 20 percent of all Muslims. They believed that, after Prophet Mohammad, Ali (cousin and son-in-law) should have been chosen to succeed. Ali finally became the Fourth Caliph, and the raging civil war among Muslims led to his murder. Ali's son and the Prophet's grandson, Hussein, was also killed near Karbala (now in Iraq), thus starting the total separation between Sunni and Shia.

Kharijis– Accounting for less than 1 percent of all Muslims, the Kharijis were the first major schism within Islam. They broke away in 658 when they rejected the use of arbitrators who were empowered to decide major issues within the faith.

Druze– An Islamic sect found mostly in Lebanon and Syria that emerged during the 11th century from Shia Islam. The Druze are known for their loyalties to the country of their residence, and they try to blend in. Conversions are not allowed and intermarriages forbidden. Their religious structure is based on secrecy, and they are permitted to deny their faith when facing a life threat.

Alawi– Followers of Ali (Fourth Caliph), also known as Alawites, is a sect of Islam that broke away from the Shiite in the Ninth Century. For the most part, they live in Syria. Their holidays include some Islamic and some Christian, and many practices are kept secret. Alawi believe in a system of divine incarnation and regard Ali as divine.

Ismaili– A Shiite sect that believes the succession of spiritual leadership should have continued through Ali, who was the first spiritual leader also known as Imam. The current Imam Prince Karim Aga Khan is the 49th Imam of the Ismaili Muslims. He attended Le Rosey School in Switzerland for nine years and graduated from Harvard in 1959 with a BA (Honors) in Islamic History.

Ahmadiyya– Founded in Qadian, India, by Mirza Ghulam Ahmad. The Ahmadis (named after Ahmad, another name for Prophet Mohammad) believe their founder was a renovator of Islam. He claimed to have fulfilled the prophecies of the world's reformer as promised Messiah and Mahdi and awaited by Muslims. The Ahmadis believe in ending religious wars and jihad with pen, not sword. Many mainstream Muslims do not consider Ahmadis to be Muslims, resulting in severe persecution or death.

PART V

Chapter 7

The Muslim World Since World War II

"By three methods we may learn wisdom: First, by reflection, which is noblest; Second, by imitation, which is easiest; and third by experience, which is the bitterest."

—Confucius

Analysis

As soon as World War I ended, the British and French gained full control the over the Muslim world. The last of the Muslim Caliphates of the Ottoman Empire had ended and was replaced by a secularist republic. The Qajar dynasty in Iran was overthrown and replaced by the secularist Reza Shah Pahlavi. The end of World War II ushered in the launching of a new era in the Muslim world. The Mughal Empire had died in 1857, and the numbers of Muslims unwilling to stay with the Hindu majority pushed the British to carve Pakistan out of India. Arabia and North Africa became home to many monarchies. The old Levant was now divided into Syria, Lebanon, Israel, Jordan and Palestinian Territories.

The new era in the Muslim world also brought a new beginning to the Western world and the Far East. After centuries of warfare, the European powers found themselves totally exhausted, and they finally started to put their animosities to rest. This only came after millions of people were either maimed or perished and billions of dollars in property destruction occurred.

For a very short period, it seemed that humanity had finally learned from the mistakes of the past and given up on violence and bloodshed. The advancement of science, medicine and economics would lead to a utopian society romanticized by Sir Thomas More in his 1516 book *Utopia*. However, the hope for everlasting peace faded quickly. The USA and USSR locked horns in the name of capitalism vs. communism. China turned communist in search of its glorious past. The people of Africa once again started decimating each other on disputes over tribal lines.

The Muslim countries, which totaled around 47 countries in comparison to less than ten in the past, were now ruled by either absolute monarchs or dictators. The rulers were totally unprepared to deal with individual freedom, had no skill set in running government both politically and economically and failed to understand the new realities of the 20th century. *"Oil aside, the 260 million people of the Muslim Middle East exported less than the 5 million people of Finland—so much the better. Genuine economic development in that region is long overdue, and the world hardly owes anyone a living for being lucky enough to sit on top of so much its oil..."* [1]

Most of the rulers, intoxicated with absolute power and devoid of intellect, have kept a majority of the citizenry both illiterate and unemployed. Among this bedlam, they have been successful in promoting a mythical glorious past and brainwashing the masses into believing that Islam once again should dominate the world through militaristic means. As a result, these policies have led them to paths of illiteracy, violence and bloodshed. If only they had become masters of economics and science, some of these Muslim countries had the potential of becoming a power through peaceful means and contributing immensely to the betterment of humanity.

MUSLIM WORLD AFTER WORLD WAR II

The Muslim movements after World War II were generally established in the context of either nationalism or secular radicalism. Indian Muslims began to define their communal identity, which led to the partition of India or in terms of Indian nationalism, those who wanted to stay in India. This thinking by the Muslims was instrumental in the creation of the independent country of Pakistan in 1947. Pakistan, which quickly surpassed India economically, fell into the trap of trying to humiliate India under the pretext of helping people of Kashmir in order to become a dominant Muslim Empire (in 1947, the Rajah of Kashmir decided to join India, whereas Pakistan believes that the majority of Kashmiri, who are Muslims, wanted to join Pakistan). The controversial division of India resulted in three wars between India and Pakistan (1948, 1965, and 1971). However, today it is India that has become an economic giant, and Pakistan is floundering economically.

The emergence of Wahhabi religious and political customs and traditions occurred in the Arabian Desert led by Abd al-Aziz Ibn Saud (1888–1953). He was also successful in conceiving Saudi Arabia which is the only country in the world named after a specific family, the Saud family. The Saudi country was neither nationalist nor modernist, but it was a distinctive endeavor, creating a Sharia state with the strict interpretation of traditional Islam. Since the 1970s, Saudis have used their petrodollars to promote their rigid brand of Islam.

Other movements similar to the Saudi approach include the Muslim Brotherhood, established in Egypt in 1928 by Hasan al-Banna (1906–1949) and the Jamat-i Islami (Islamic Society), founded in India in 1941 by Abu Ala Maududi (1903–1979). They claimed that only Islam defines a complete way of life, therefore it should be adopted by the country and applied to each Muslim. These fundamentalist movements abhor Western values and reject the Western economic and political systems but offer no concrete solutions or productive replacement systems.

The Israeli–Palestinian conflict started with the rise of nationalist movements within the Jews and Arabs. After World War I, relations between Jews and Arabs were friendly, and the "Faisal-Weizmann" agreement created an outline for both to live peacefully. After World War II, a large number of European Jews moved to Palestine as a result of the Hitler led Nazi's crimes and the Holocaust. This migration led to a displacement of many Palestinian both Muslim and Christian. The three Arab–Israeli wars (1948, 1967, and 1973) that followed resulted in Muslim defeats. The Muslim rulers were not willing to blame themselves but were happy to sing "O' glorious past," and the Muslim Mullahs called for the "Caliphate to the rescue."

In Iran, the monarchy was overthrown in 1979 by an Islamic revolution, a major indication of the resurgence of political Islam in the late twentieth century. In other areas, older elites were also overthrown or displaced by newer and frequently more ideologically radical groups.

Movements with primarily Islamic identification existed but with less political influence. Pakistan, as an explicitly Islamic state, was unable to develop a clear constitutional self-definition. Internal divisions led to a civil war in 1971 and the creation of East Pakistan as independent Bangladesh.

AL-QAEDA

The Arabic word al-Qaeda means "base." The roots of Osama bin Laden's al-Qaeda network stem from the decade-long conflict that plagued Afghanistan from 1979–1989 after the invasion by the Soviet Union. The United States, along with Pakistan, wanted to defeat the Soviets to contain the "domino effect." Under President Ronald Regan, the USA did not want to be seen as directly involved and so started the war of proxy. Pakistan was selected to manage the manpower, training and logistics; Saudi Arabia was to provide the funds and raise the flag of jihad; and the USA supplied guns and ammo along with strategic and military direction through the CIA. The Afghans had not yet turned into extremists and were organized by the Pakistani military in the common cause of expelling the Soviets.

The war quickly became a rallying call for jihad against the communist "infidel," drawing young Muslims from around the world, including Osama bin Laden. Osama was the 17th of 20 sons of a multi-millionaire Saudi construction industrialist of Yemeni origin. He was well trained in conservative Wahhabi Islam at the King Abdul Aziz University in Jeddah, Saudi Arabia by Muhammad Qutb and Abdullah Azzam, both of the Muslim Brotherhood.

Osama made his first visit to Afghanistan a few years after the December 1979 Soviet invasion and then relocated to Pakistan near the border with Afghanistan. He reportedly used some of his personal fortune to establish himself as a donor to the Afghan Mujahedin and as a recruiter of Arab and other volunteers for the war under the banner of jihad. He set up a complex international organization with the support of financiers from Saudi Arabia and Persian Gulf states.

Saudi Arabia and the United States poured billions of dollars secretly to the Afghani freedom fighter (Mujahedin) in cooperation with Pakistani dictator Zia-ul-Haq, the Pakistani military and its spy agency the ISI (Inter-Services Intelligence). The "Holy War" against infidel communist was on track to creating a Soviet equivalent to the U.S.–Vietnam conflict. The USA considered jihadi movements to be positive contributors to defeat the Soviet, and U.S. officials made no effort to stop the recruitment of the Pakistani, Arabs, Chechens, Uzbeks, etc. for the war.

Congressman Charlie Wilson of Texas became a champion in leading the United States to covertly finance the war, which amounted to $3 billion and the supply of arms, Stinger anti-aircraft missiles and paramilitary officers for training. There was jubilation all around when the Soviets pulled out in 1989.

After the Soviet Union withdrew, the Americans left the arena believing the mission was accomplished. At the end of the war, there were around 5 million Afghani refugees in Pakistan, millions of arms in Afghani hands and Osama had successfully established Al-Qaeda (The Base) as a potential force for the future jihad ventures. Ayman al-Zawahiri, who had been imprisoned for the assassination of Egyptian Anwar Sadat, was acquitted and joined Bin Laden as his second in command.

Al-Qaeda follows a Sunni Wahhabi Islam, promotes jihad, adheres to a strict interpretation of Sharia Law and uses acts of terrorism, including suicide bombings, to achieve its goals. Al-Qaeda regards Shia, Sufi and liberal Muslims as infidels and believes in their elimination by force.

With the Iraqi invasion of Kuwait in 1990 and subsequent U.S. military landing in Saudi Arabia, Bin Laden turned from a de-facto U.S. ally against the Soviets into one of its most vigorous antagonists. Bin Laden had returned home to Saudi Arabia in 1989 after the completion of the Soviet withdrawal from Afghanistan. Once Operation Desert Storm was successfully completed, the U.S. withdrew most of its military except for 6,000 U.S. troops left in military bases in Saudi Arabia. Bin Laden used these remaining forces as a pretext and successfully painted U.S. forces as occupiers of the scared land.

In 1991, he moved to Sudan, recruiting and training al-Qaeda radicals to support jihadi movements in Bosnia, Chechnya, the Philippines and Kashmir. He was expelled from Sudan under Egyptian and U.S. pressure, and then returned to Afghanistan as a guest of Mullah Omar and the Taliban. Afghanistan was now controlled by a majority of the old Mujahedin, now turned ruthless Taliban, with the help of the Pakistani military in their wider interest of keeping India out of northwest politics.

Al-Qaeda had become a coalition of fanatic groups with cells operating throughout the Muslim world, most with the goal of overthrowing their own government. Bin Laden had transformed al-Qaeda into a global threat to U.S. security. In 1998, the U.S. embassies in Kenya and Tanzania were attacked by al-Qaeda terrorists. In 2000, al-Qaeda struck the ship U.S.S. Cole in Yemen, leaving 17 American sailors dead.

On September 11, 2001, al-Qaeda executed its most lethal strike, taking out both the North and South towers of the World Trade Center in the New York City, demolishing part of the Pentagon and crashing a commercial airliner into a field in Shankstown, Pennsylvania. In all, approximately 3,000 civilians were killed.

The U.S. military response in Afghanistan crippled al-Qaeda and dislodged the Taliban from power. Finally, bin Laden was killed by U.S. Navy Seals on May 2, 2011 in the military garrison town of Abbottabad, Pakistan. Al-Qaeda operatives are in disarray but not totally eliminated, bidding their time in Pakistan, Yemen and North African countries.

It is suffice to say that the USA, the West and civilized nations cannot rest on their laurels until the terrorist threat from al-Qaeda and like are completely eliminated. The civilized world cannot ignore this threat since it would ultimately result in peril.

The Taliban

The Taliban and its disciples belong to the Wahhabi Sunni sect of Muslim and come mostly from the Afghanistan's Pashtun tribes. The Taliban-Pashtun dominates large swaths of Afghanistan and a big area of Pakistan's Federally Administered Tribal Areas (FATA), covering most of Waziristan.

The Taliban are a by-product of the Soviet invasion of Afghanistan and the civil war that ensued after the withdrawal of Soviet troops. The Soviets withdrew in February 1989, and America, having achieved its goal of a Soviet defeat, left in the hope that Afghans would settle their affairs amicably. The ten-year war with the Soviets had devastated the poor country of Afghanistan. It was left in ruins mired in social and economic shards, around 2 million dead, millions of refugees in Pakistan and Iran, and hundreds of thousands of orphans living in refugee camps in Pakistan. Saudi Arabia had poured billions into the war but also had taken the lead in spreading Wahhabi Islam by building thousands of Madrassas, which became a sanctuary for the orphan Afghani children. They were taught a perverted form of Islam with emphasis on jihad and Islamic dominance by force.

Afghanistan is an ancient land famous for the Silk Road, which has witnessed many military campaigns, including those of Alexander the Great, Genghis Khan, the Mughals, British, Soviets and Americans. It is a landlocked mountainous country where archaeologists have found evidence of human habitation dating prior to 2000 B.C.E. *"Urban civilization is believed to have begun as early as 3000 B.C.E., and the early city of Mundigak (near Kandahar in the south of the country) may have been a colony of the nearby Indus Valley Civilization."* (2)

King Amanullah Khan took over the reign in 1919 after the Anglo–Afghan War. Following a tour of Turkey and Europe in the 1920s, he decided to modernize and educate women. The Burqa was abolished, elementary education became compulsory and numbers of co-educational schools were opened. Mohammad Zahir Shah became king in 1933 and continued with the implementation of liberal policies. In 1973, Daud Kahn, the king's cousin and brother-in-law, engineered a coup and became the first President of Afghanistan.

In 1978, the Afghani communist party seized power, leading to a civil war among various factions. Babrak Karmal became a Soviet stooge and asked for their intervention to prop up his government. This started the chaos, suffering and violence that has drained two superpowers and, after 40 years of struggle, still has not produced a viable solution.

After the Soviets left, Najibullah took over the power for a brief period that ended in 1992. Afghan warlords substituted their war with the Soviets with a civil war among themselves. While the civil war was raging, Pakistan decided to fill the gaping political vacuum left by the Soviets. Afghanistan expert Neamatollah Nojumi writes, *"These new political and military developments in Afghanistan forced the Pakistani intelligence agency ISI to organize a military plan with forces belonging to Hekmatyar's Hezb-i Islami... This militaristic plan aimed to capture Kabul and was in full force when... the rest of the Muhajideen leaders in Pakistan agreed to the UN peace plan. On the eve of the successful implementation of the UN peace plan in Afghanistan the ISI, through Hekmatyar and non-Afghan volunteers, led hundreds of trucks loaded with weapons and fighters to the southern part of Kabul.*"[3]

Afghan orphans numbering in the thousands grew up in Pakistani refugee camps never knowing Afghanistan and were schooled in Pakistani madrassas, most of them manufacturing terrorists. They were nurtured by the Pakistani military and eventually rose up, overwhelming the warlords and all other factions. They had only few goals; they wanted to establish a Sharia Caliphate that would neither tolerate nor recognize all other sects of Islam. Democracy, equal rights, secular governments were the evil ways of infidels with no place in their brainwashed Islam. Women were to be locked up or hidden behind a Burqa with the total abandonment of education for their gender.

The Taliban turned to Mohammed Omar, a Mullah from Kandahar in southeastern Afghanistan. He had fought the Soviets and had lost one eye in the process. The Pakistani intelligence agency (the ISI), Pakistani military and Benazir Bhutto, the Pakistani prime minister, all supported the Taliban in hopes to control Afghanistan and use this proxy army against India in Kashmir. Initially the Clinton administration supported the Taliban. No one could have seen the future monster that was being created because everyone saw only a solution to end of the chaos in Afghanistan.

According to New York Times article published on October 23, 1996, Glyn Davies, a State Department spokesman said that the Taliban *"will move quickly to restore order and security and to form a representative interim government that can begin the process of reconciliation nationwide."*[4] The Clinton administration stopped its support of Taliban in 1997, after Secretary of State Madeleine Albright saw the Taliban cruelties used on citizens and the barbaric treatment of its women.

The Taliban used fabricated Sharia law where they held misogynistic opinions of women. Women were treated worse than animals and not allowed to leave the four walls of their homes without permission or unless accompanied by an adult male person. All western clothing was prohibited along with the use of make-up, nail polish, lipstick, etc. Women were forced to hide behind a head-to-toe Burqa with only a few holes for the eyes to find their way around. Music, movies, dancing, drinking, parties and gatherings of opposite sexes were totally banned. A Taliban Mullah, regardless of his age, could forcibly marry a young girl 30–40 years his junior. At times, a father would sell his daughter for the loan and other obligation that he owed. Women not following the Taliban rules were stoned or shot to death. In March 2001, the Taliban demolished the two-century-old Buddha statues of Bamiyan, totally forgetting that their ancestors at one time had been adherents of this peaceful religion.

The Taliban's ruthless rule lasted for five years. They created mayhem under the guise of perverted interpretations, forcing inaccurate and contradictory Islamic practices. The Violent Mindset pretty much destroyed all that was good and beautiful. The Taliban were overthrown in the 2001 with the NATO-American backed invasion of Afghanistan after Mullah Omar (Taliban leader) refused to hand over Osama bin Laden. They were never defeated completely, as they retreated and hid in the remote areas of Afghanistan and Pakistan. They are on the rise, and no one can see what the future holds for the people of Afghanistan.

The Pakistani Taliban hails from the Pakistani side of the border regions of Afghanistan and commit their terrors under the umbrella of Tehirk-i-Taliban Pakistan or TTP. They have been successful in establishing control in the Federally Administered Tribal Area (FATA). The Mehsud tribe provides de-facto leadership to the TTP, which is a coalition of about 13 terrorist groups.

The Pakistani Taliban goals are to establish Sharia Law initially in the Pashtun area then in Pakistan, leading to the overthrow of the Pakistan government and control of Pakistan's nuclear weapons. Their tactics include suicide bombings against Pakistani citizens and other Islamic sects, including Shia and Sufi.

The Pakistani military, which covertly supports Afghani Taliban, has been fighting with the Pakistani Taliban since 2002. According to a BBC article published in 2004,

> "The military offensive had been part of the overall war against Al-Qaeda... Since the start of the operation, the [Pakistani] military

authorities have firmly established that a large number of Uzbek, Chechen and Arab militants were in the area... It was in July 2002 that Pakistani troops, for the first time in 55 years, entered the Tirah Valley in Khyber tribal agency. Soon they were in Shawal valley of North Waziristan, and later in South Waziristan... This was made possible after long negotiations with various tribes, who reluctantly agreed to allow the military's presence on the assurance that it would bring in funds and development work. But once the military action started in South Waziristan a number of Waziri sub-tribes took it as an attempt to subjugate them. Attempts to persuade them into handing over the foreign militants failed, and with an apparently mishandling by the authorities, the security campaign against suspected Al-Qaeda militants turned into an undeclared war between the Pakistani military and the rebel tribesmen. [5]

The Pakistani Taliban is responsible for hundreds of suicide bombings in Pakistan, sectarian violence, attacks on Pakistan military bases, and the shooting of a 15-year-old Pakistan girl named Malala Yousufzai in 2012, whose only fault was the promotion of the right to an education. Their terroristic activities have resulted in the deaths of over 40,000 Pakistani Muslims, which undoubtedly proves that they are not following Islam or Quran but only their barbaric, inhumane and evil ways.

The tide is slowly turning against the Pakistan Taliban, but their indiscriminate killing raises fear among many. Will they ever part with their barbaric ways? The solution is rather complex, requiring the closing of thousands of Madrassas responsible for promoting jihad and the creation of job opportunities for many young Pakistanis who, without any hope for the future, are easy prey for the seasoned terrorists.

CHAPTER 8

EXTREMISM IN THE MUSLIM WORLD

"At least two thirds of our miseries spring from human stupidity, human malice and those great motivators and justifiers of malice and stupidity, idealism, dogmatism and proselytizing zeal on behalf of religious or political idols."

—ALDOUS HUXLEY, ENGLISH WRITER

ANALYSIS

A MAJORITY OF MUSLIMS TODAY still hold onto a liberal interpretation of the faith and still have hope that the intellectual engine will take over someday soon. This change must come from within the Muslim world while the outside world can only create the environment that will lead to this process. The natural order of the universe is designed to move forward, and the Muslim world must take its rightful place on the world stage through peaceful means. The pendulum is slowly shifting out of sheer human desire to be free and enjoy the short life we have on this earth. Hopefully, it is only a matter of time before the terrorists realize this phenomenon. However, there is still much more to accomplish.

The events of September 11, 2011 were a rude awakening for Americans and the West. We all watched in horror as the planes crashed into the towers which then tragically collapsed. The world has not been the same since then, and most nations still have not fully recovered both from the collective fear of extremism and the economic devastation.

It is difficult for us to understand the reasons behind the anger within the radical Muslim world. The terrorists' desire to destroy everything that we see as full of life and beautiful is hard to comprehend. The usage of the words "infidel," "jihad," and "blasphemy" and their glorification in the name of religion by the terrorists is unfathomable. The prevalence of violence by the Extremists is not only directed against the West but also against the peaceful Muslims who have suffered greatly.

So what do these terrorists want? Their wishes include the dominance of the distorted Islam conjured through their Violent Mindset. Out with normal human behavior and in with the changing of the human behavior by a few with force. Out with the natural beauty and in with hiding all that is beautiful. Out with individual rights and in with the bearded Mullah dictatorship. Out with economic growth and in with poverty. Out with intellect and in with ignorance. Out with the consensus and in with totalitarianism. Out with a God that is merciful and in with a God that is violent. Out with equality and in with discrimination. Out with the progress and in with stagnation. Out with sovereign nations and in with the Caliphate. Out with democracy and in with the despotism.

The terrorists got a chance in Afghanistan to create their dream society, and it was an utter failure from human, economic and religious perspectives. Obviously, their Violent Mindset does not have the capacity to clearly see the shortcomings of their proposed un-Islamic ideology and the devastation that it caused for the people they were supposed to lead.

The Rise Of Petro Dollars

"The lifeblood of terrorism is money, and if we cut off the money we cut the blood supply."

—Michael Chertoff. [1]

There is a plethora of books and articles analyzing Islam and the proposed solutions to the issue of terrorism. One of the causes of terrorism that is mentioned is "The Rise of Petrodollars" starting around 1970 and specifically after the 1973 Arab–Israeli war.

The term "Petrodollars" was coined in 1973 by Ibrahim Oweiss, a professor of economics at Georgetown University. Oweiss felt that OPEC countries of the Middle East (Saudi Arabia, Kuwait, Qatar, Bahrain and UAE) were amassing large surpluses of Petrodollars. These countries with small populations were unable to invest all of the surpluses into their own land. Saudi Arabia used their Petrodollars over the years not only to enrich their land but also to support extremism through the spread of their conservative Wahhabi doctrines. Since 2009, net oil export revenues for the members of OPEC (Organization of Petroleum Exporting Countries) have nearly doubled to $1.03 trillion, reaching $1.17 trillion in 2012.

In the 1950's and 1960's, the citizens of the Arab OPEC nations were living wealthy lives. The 1967 war with Israel ended in a devastating loss for the Muslim world. Shia Iran, having no quarrel with Israel, was on the road to modernization. There was anxiety in Saudi Arabia as their status and power was considerably lower than Iran.

That all changed. The oil crisis of 1973 brought unprecedented power to the people of Arabia. This level of influence hadn't been seen in history since the early rise of Islam. The Saudi Petrodollars financed the Afghan war against Soviets. The Saudis used the Petrodollars to build Madrassas, Mosques, and Charities in the third world Muslim countries that did not have the oil and were happy to have the dollars from a brotherly Muslim nation.

In his 2004 article entitled "When Petro-Dollar Speaks "Mohammad Sageer writes, *"The leaders of the third world countries have been so naive that none of them suspected the hidden agenda behind the Arab generosity. The local dawa groups, mostly comprising unemployed youth ran relentless campaigns inviting people, to religion or persuading liberal Muslims into strict compliance of the Islamic rituals. They targeted mostly poor and middle-class Muslim women who were not really mindful about observing Islamic dress code, forcing them into all encompassing Arabian Burkha (A black cloak- like shroud that covers from head to toe)."* [2]

In its race with Saudi Arabia to protect Shia interests, Iran has been using its Petrodollars to build nuclear weapons, helping the Syrian regime and providing material to support to both Hamas and Hezbollah in Southern Lebanon.

Since 9/11, the Petrodollars have continued to play their devastating role. According to International Monetary Fund, Arab OPEC countries generated a $1.3 trillion surplus from 2000–2008. Their windfall came after paying for the domestic boom, billions of dollars in purchases of military hardware from the USA and luxury goods from all over the world. Some of these funds were used for legitimate purposes, and some funds cannot be traced according to Middle East Research and Information Project. In "Petrodollars at Work and in Play in the Post-September 11 Decade," Karen Pfeifer writes: *"The cumulative value of the Gulf countries' current account surpluses was almost $912 billion in the period 2003-2008, of which $544 billion could be traced to external destinations and $368 billion could not... But where might the $368 billion worth of untraceable surpluses have gone? Two economists for Global Financial Integrity project in a January 2011 report reasoned "that the main destination was most likely private accounts overseas, drained out of current account surpluses via "illicit financial flows," more commonly referred to as capital flight."* [3]

These funds are not illegal but considered "illicit" in a sense that they can be used to avoid taxes, to promote drug trafficking or to support terrorism. The four richest Arab Petrodollar countries, "Saudi Arabia, the UAE, Kuwait and Qatar, placed fourth, sixth, seventh and ninth, respectively, among all developing countries ranked by the amount of "illicit" funds lost from 2000 to 2008." In this period, the cumulative capital flight was a total of $957 billion. How much of this amount went to hide the wealth or in support of Extremists' activities cannot be verified in this complex financial world despite efforts by the U.S.

Projected Petrodollars Arab OPEC Nations - 2012

COUNTRY	CRUDE OIL RESERVES*	% OF OPEC SHARE	DAILY CRUDE OIL PRODUCTION **	PROJECTED DAILY REVENUE ***	PROJECTED YEARLY REVENUE	POPULATION ****
Saudia Arabia	265,400,000,000	22.1%	9,854,000	$1,872,260,000	$683,374,900,000	28,705,000
Kuwait	101,500,000,000	8.5%	2,821,000	$535,990,000	$195,636,350,000	2,892,000
UAE	97,800,000,000	8.2%	2,626,000	$498,940,000	$182,113,100,000	8,106,000
Qatar	25,400,000,000	2.1%	743,000	$141,170,000	$51,527,050,000	1,939,000
Iraq	141,400,000,000	11.8%	3,129,000	$594,510,000	$219,996,150,000	33,703,000
Iran	154,600,000,000	12.9%	2,723,000	$517,370,000	$188,840,050,000	75,612,000
Totals	786,100,000,000	65.6%	21,896,000	$4,160,240,000	$1,518,487,600,000	150,957,000

*Proven Crude Oil Reserves, End 2011 from the 2012 Organization of the Petroleum Exporting Countries
**Daily Crude Oil Production, September 2012 Reporting from the Organization of the Petroleum Exporting Countries
***Calculated at $190 per barrel
****UN Estimates 2012

It is important to note that all of the countries above are autocratic except Iraq. Moreover, we can infer now that there is no indication that the Shia government in Iraq will follow the aspirations of democracy that President Bush had hoped for and that over 4,400 brave Americans gave their lives for.

EXTREMISM

There are two schools of thought in the Muslim world: the Progressive Group and the Extremist Group. The Progressives believe in enhancing knowledge through education in economics, science and technology. This group had the upper hand until the early 1980s.

Unfortunately, the Palestinian issues and the Soviet invasion of Afghanistan gave rise to modern terrorist groups who have diminished the voice of the Progressive Muslims through the indiscriminate use of violence. Consequently, the Muslim majority suffers from a widespread anxiety circulated by the terrorist groups' use of violence. Their Violent Mindset found solace in the teachings of Salafism. The word Salaf, meaning predecessors or ancestors, emphasized that the earliest Muslims were model examples of Islam.

By forcing Muslims to follow their brand of Islam, Extremists believe that they can bring back the Islamic dominance of the past and successfully force non-Muslims into submission. As seen in the earlier chapters describing Islamic history, however, the Umayyads, Abbasids, Moors, Ottomans and Mughals mostly practiced progressive Islam. They were liberal in their manners, and most of them followed the Sufi order of Islam. So when Extremists talk about their inflexible form of religion, it is not only hard for Westerners to understand but it is also shocking for the majority of Muslims too. The Extremist teachings include:

1. Using the Quran as the source of all education, including modern science

2. Following the Hadith (sayings of the Prophet Mohammad) literally, as it provides guidance for every aspect of life from birth to death

3. Practicing their form of Islam so that God will reward them with dominance

4. Believing that Americans, European and Jews have conspired together and must be defeated by all means

5. Promoting that all Muslim societies must follow the Sharia (Islamic Laws)

After World War I and II, a progressive Islamic society made considerable gains in Turkey, Iran, Pakistan, Egypt and even Afghanistan. Most of these countries were considered secular, and progressive concepts took root both in culture and in their day-to-day lives. Kemal Ataturk even outlawed hijabs and beards. Most of the Muslim world adopted western education, customs, and clothing (as shown earlier in photos from Pakistan). There was tolerance among various sects and an emphasis on education, specifically science and math.

Secular Progressive Muslim intellectuals were respected for pursuing the modernization of their societies. Mohammad Ali Jinnah led the creation of Pakistan on the basis of secularism. His parents sent him to study at the prestigious Christian Missionary School in India. He then went to London and joined Lincoln's Inn (established in 1422), a renowned legal association that helped law students study for the bar exam. Mr. Jinnah passed his legal exam at age 20 in 1896 and was the youngest ever to have been accepted to the bar.

Mustafa Kemal Ataturk, the founder of modern Turkey, attended a private school with a secular curriculum at the direction of his father. He joined the army and later graduated from the Ottoman Military College in Constantinople in 1905. He led in abolishing the Sunni Caliphate that had existed for over 400 years. Mustafa Kemal Ataturk said, *"The religion of Islam will be elevated if it will cease to be a political instrument, as had been the case in the past."* [4]

Syed Qutb of Egypt is idolized by both Osama bin Laden and Ayman al-Zawahiri of al-Qaeda. He was imprisoned, convicted and executed by the Egyptian government for plotting the assassination of Egyptian President Gamal Nasser in 1966. He also blames the Jews for the downfall of the Muslims and accuses them of plotting to conquer the whole world by proclaiming the famous "Protocols of the Elders of Zion." Qutb is also known for his intense disapproval of the society and culture of the West, which he saw as obsessed with materialism, violence and sexual pleasures. Qutb wrote the Islamic manifesto *Ma'alim fi-l-Tariq* (Milestones) in which he emphasized, *"True Islam would transform every aspect of society, eliminating everything non-Muslim."* [5]

The establishment of Israel has given rise to the Arab–Israeli conflict spanning a century of political tensions and open hostilities. In the mid-19th century, the persecution of Jews in Europe led to the creation of the Zionist movement. The tragic events of the Holocaust hastened the creation of Israel for the Jewish people. Israeli independence in 1948 was marked by massive migrations of Jews from both Europe and the Islamic world to Israel and by the subsequent displacement of the Palestinian people. These events resulted in an adverse relationship between the Arab nations and Israel.

The Extremists have successfully exploited this situation. Initially, the animosity involved only the adjacent Arab nations bordering Israel; however, the tensions against Israel have gradually spread to the other non-Arab Muslims. The defeat of Arab armies in the Six-Day War and the Yom Kippur War of 1973 provided Extremists with a trump card, which they have been exploiting in the cause of jihad.

The educational curriculum of many Muslim nations demonizes Christians, Jews, Hindus and other religions of the world. The mushrooming growth of Madrassas teaches only the one subject, Islam, while leaving out Math, Science, History, Art and Technology. In the Saudiwoman's Weblog published in the May-June 2012 issue of Foreign Policy magazine, Eman Al Nafjan writes, *"A 2011 study published by religious scholar Abdulaziz al-Qasim found that Saudi religion textbooks have focused far too much on the lowest educational and skill objectives, such as rote memorization and classification, and neglected entirely the objectives of analysis, problem-solving, and critical thinking,"* leading to *"passiveness and negativity."* [6]

CURRICULUM OF INTOLERANCE

A Freedom House Study published in 2006 analyzed Saudi Arabian religion textbooks used in that academic year. These books were provided by teachers, administrators and families with children in Saudi schools. Freedom House had them translated by two independent Arabic speakers. Listed below are excerpts from the books taught from 1st grade to the 12th grade: [7]

- *"Condemn and denigrate the majority of Sunni Muslims who do not follow the Wahhabi understanding of Islam, and call them deviants and descendants of polytheists."*
- *"Condemn and denigrate Shiite and Sufi Muslims' beliefs and practices as heretical and call them 'polytheists.'"*
- *"Command Muslims to "hate" Christians, Jews, "polytheists" and other "unbelievers," including non-Wahhabi Muslims, though, incongruously, not to treat them 'unjustly.'"*
- *"Teach the infamous forgeries, The Protocols of the Elders of Zion, as historical fact."*
- *"Teach other conspiracy theories accusing Freemasons, Lions Clubs and Rotary Clubs of plotting to undermine Muslims."*
- *"Teach that "Jews and the Christians are enemies of the [Muslim] believers" and that "the clash" between the two realms is perpetual."*
- *"Instruct students not to "greet," "befriend," "imitate," "show loyalty to," "be courteous to," or "respect" non-believers."*
- *"Assert that the spread of Islam through jihad is a 'religious duty.'"*
- *"Instruct that "fighting between Muslims and Jews" will continue until Judgment Day, and that the Muslims are promised victory over the Jews in the end."*

AL-QAEDA DECLARATION OF JIHAD

On February 23, 1998, Osama bin Laden and Ayman al-Zawahiri issued their "Declaration of Jihad against the Crusaders and the Jews," which was a declaration of all-out holy war against the U.S. and its allies.

JIHAD AGAINST JEWS AND CRUSADERS [8]

World Islamic Front Statement–23 February 1998
Shaykh Usamah Bin-Muhammad Bin-Ladin
Ayman al-Zawahiri, amir of the Jihad Group in Egypt
Abu-Yasir Rifa'i Ahmad Taha, Egyptian Islamic Group
Shaykh Mir Hamzah, secretary of the Jamiat-ul-Ulema-e-Pakistan
Fazlur Rahman, amir of the Jihad Movement in Bangladesh

Praise be to Allah, who revealed the Book, controls the clouds, defeats factionalism, and says in His Book: "But when the forbidden months are past, then fight and slay the pagans wherever ye find them, seize them, beleaguer them, and lie in wait for them in every stratagem (of war)"; and peace be upon our Prophet, Muhammad Bin-'Abdallah, who said: I have been sent with the sword between my hands to ensure that no one but Allah is worshipped, Allah who put my livelihood under the shadow of my spear and who inflicts humiliation and scorn on those who disobey my orders.

The Arabian Peninsula has never — since Allah made it flat, created its desert, and encircled it with seas — been stormed by any forces like the crusader armies spreading in it like locusts, eating its riches and wiping out its plantations. All this is happening at a time in which nations are attacking Muslims like people fighting over a plate of food. In the light of the grave situation and the lack of support, we and you are obliged to discuss current events, and we should all agree on how to settle the matter.

No one argues today about three facts that are known to everyone; we will list them, in order to remind everyone:

First, for over seven years the United States has been occupying the lands of Islam in the holiest of places, the Arabian Peninsula, plundering its riches, dictating to its rulers, humiliating its people, terrorizing its neighbors, and turning its bases in the Peninsula into a spearhead through which to fight the neighboring Muslim peoples.

If some people have in the past argued about the fact of the occupation, all the people of the Peninsula have now acknowledged it. The best proof of this is the Americans' continuing aggression against the Iraqi people using the Peninsula as a staging post, even though all its rulers are against their territories being used to that end, but they are helpless.

Second, despite the great devastation inflicted on the Iraqi people by the crusader-Zionist alliance, and despite the huge number of those killed, which has exceeded 1 million... despite all this, the Americans are once against trying to repeat the horrific massacres, as though they are not content with the protracted blockade imposed after the ferocious war or the fragmentation and devastation.

So here they come to annihilate what is left of this people and to humiliate their Muslim neighbors.

Third, if the Americans' aims behind these wars are religious and economic, the aim is also to serve the Jews' petty state and divert attention from its occupation of Jerusalem and murder of Muslims there. The best proof of this is their eagerness to destroy Iraq, the strongest neighboring Arab state, and their endeavor to fragment all the states of the region such as Iraq, Saudi Arabia, Egypt, and Sudan into paper statelets and through their disunion and weakness to guarantee Israel's survival and the continuation of the brutal crusade occupation of the Peninsula.

All these crimes and sins committed by the Americans are a clear declaration of war on Allah, his messenger, and Muslims. And ulema have throughout Islamic history unanimously agreed that the jihad is an individual duty if the enemy destroys the Muslim countries. This was revealed by Imam Bin-Qadamah in "Al- Mughni," Imam al-Kisa'i in "Al-Bada'i," al-Qurtubi in his interpretation, and the shaykh of al-Islam in his books, where he said: "As for the fighting to repulse [an enemy], it is aimed at defending sanctity and religion, and it is a duty as agreed [by the ulema]. Nothing is more sacred than belief except repulsing an enemy who is attacking religion and life."

On that basis, and in compliance with Allah's order, we issue the following fatwa to all Muslims:

The ruling to kill the Americans and their allies — civilians and military — is an individual duty for every Muslim who can do it in any country in which it is possible to do it, in order to liberate the al-Aqsa Mosque and the holy mosque [Mecca] from their grip, and in order for their armies to move out of all the lands of Islam, defeated and unable to threaten any Muslim. This is in accordance with the words of Almighty Allah, "and fight the pagans all together as they fight you all together," and "fight them until there is no more tumult or oppression, and there prevail justice and faith in Allah."

This is in addition to the words of Almighty Allah: "And why should ye not fight in the cause of Allah and of those who, being weak, are ill-treated (and oppressed)? — women and children, whose cry is: 'Our Lord, rescue us from this town, whose people are oppressors; and raise for us from thee one who will help!'"

We — with Allah's help — call on every Muslim who believes in Allah and wishes to be rewarded to comply with Allah's order to kill the Americans and plunder their money wherever and whenever they find it. We also call on Muslim ulema, leaders, youths, and soldiers to launch the raid on Satan's U.S. troops and *the devil's supporters allying with them, and to displace those who are behind them so that they may learn a lesson.*

Almighty Allah said: "O ye who believe, give your response to Allah and His Apostle, when He calleth you to that which will give you life. And know that Allah cometh between a man and his heart, and that it is He to whom ye shall all be gathered."

Almighty Allah also says: "O ye, who believe, what is the matter with you, that when ye are asked to go forth in the cause of Allah, ye cling so heavily to the earth! Do ye prefer the life of this world to the hereafter? But little is the comfort of this life, as compared with the hereafter. Unless ye go forth, He will punish you with a grievous penalty, and put others in your place; but Him ye would not harm in the least. For Allah hath power over all things."

Almighty Allah also says: "So lose no heart, nor fall into despair. For ye must gain mastery if ye are true in faith."

THE JIHAD DEBATE AMONG MUSLIMS

The Extremists want to achieve two objectives with their jihad against the West. First, they want to overthrow almost all of the Muslim rulers whom they consider "heretic" because their leaders are not following the true Islam. They are commanded by God to fight them, depose of them and establish a truly Islamic Sharia government. The second goal is to wage jihad against the West and Jews, as they are the forces of evil on this earth. Of course, Israel is singled out by extremists because it is occupying the holy city of Jerusalem. For Westerners and Progressive Muslims alike, jihad to kill and destroy is a shocking and utterly incomprehensible phenomenon.

It needs to be clarified that not all Muslims believe in jihad and consider Infidels either "People of Book" or non-Muslims. There is a significant debate between Progressive and Extremist Muslims in the true meaning of jihad:

In Modern Standard Arabic, jihad is a term used for a struggle for any cause with non-violent meanings. It can simply mean striving to live a moral and virtuous life with "duty toward God," with no militaristic connotations. For the Progressive branch of Islam, jihad means:

1. *"A commitment to hard work"* and *"achieving one's goals in life"*

2. *"Struggling to achieve a noble cause"*

3. *"Promoting peace, harmony or cooperation, and assisting others"*

4. *"Living the principles of Islam"*

Some Muslim scholars believe that there are four kinds of jihad. According to Majid Khadduri in *War and Peace in the Law of Islam*, they are: [9]

"Jihad of the Heart" (bil qalb/nafs) is concerned with combatting the devil and in the attempt to escape his persuasion to evil. This type of Jihad was regarded as the greater jihad (al-jihad al-akbar).

1. *"Jihad by the Tongue" (jihad bil lisan) is concerned with speaking the truth and spreading the word of Islam with one's tongue.*

2. *"Jihad by the Hand" (jihad bil yad) refers to choosing to do what is right and to combat injustice and what is wrong with action.*

3. *"Jihad by the Sword" (jihad bis saif) refers to "armed fighting in the way of God, or holy war (qital fi sabilillah). Thus this has become the most common usage by Salafi and Wahhabi Muslims.*

Another tool used by the Extremists is blasphemy, which refers to the act of insulting or showing contempt or lack of reverence for a religious deity or irreverence towards religious or holy persons or things. Insulting anyone is wrong, but the response needs to be balanced with the basic human rights of free speech. The world has shrunk, the Internet allows everyone to express his or her opinions instantly, and no single entity, including the mighty USA, can regulate instant communication. In Muslim countries, Blasphemy Laws are used to persecute minorities.

Drs. Abdullah Saeed and Hassan Saeed in their book, *Freedom of Religion and Apostasy in Islam*, debate the merit and justification for the death penalty for blasphemy, *"The Quran and the Hadith do not mention blasphemy."* [10] According to the Pakistani religious scholar, Javed Ahmed Ghamidi, *"nothing in Islam supports blasphemy law."* [11] A minority group in Saudi Arabia, Pakistan, Afghanistan or Iran is not protected and most often is singled out under the archaic blasphemy laws leading to prison or death.

Muslims are taught many stories about the Prophet Muhammad's compassion and kindness to others. One of the stories goes like this:

When the Prophet started preaching in Mecca, a lot of people became hostile towards him. Meccans threw stones at him, mocked him and made fun of him, but he never became angry or upset. A woman was rather hostile towards him and would throw a basket full of garbage at his head if he walked by her house, yet he never rebuked her. One day as he walked by her house, there was no basket of garbage thrown at him. He turned back and went looking for his tormentor and learned that the woman was sick and could not get out of bed. He visited her and took care of her needs while she lay sick. She was so awestruck by his kindness that she became a Muslim.

Isn't it ironic that the Mullahs exhort Muslims today to get out on the street if there is a cartoon published or a video made by a few ignorant people? A Fatwa is issued, people are killed, property is destroyed and violence is committed all in the name of the Prophet who set an example otherwise. Here are a few recent examples of blasphemy that have resulted in Fatwa for death and violence:

1. Danish Cartoons of the Prophet Mohammad.

2. The Movie "Innocence of Muslims."

3. Salman Rushdie's Book "Satanic Verses."

4. Shahin Najafi, an Iranian rapper, releasing a song in Persian against the 10th Imam Ali al-Hadi.

5. A Shia Bahraini blogger accused of remarks against Aisha (Mohammad's wife) in retaliation for Sunni posting online against Shia figures.

6. Rimsha Masih, a handicap Pakistani Christian girl, for allegedly desecrating pages of the Quran. However, authorities discovered that it was done by a Mullah.

7. Shahid Nadeem, a teacher in a missionary school accused of deliberately burning three pages of the Quran, who is now in hiding.

8. Shahbaz Bhatti, Catholic Pakistan's Federal Minister for Minorities Affairs, was killed while working on reforming Pakistan's blasphemy laws.

9. Asia Bibi, a Christian, was sentenced to death on a charge of blasphemy.

10. Punjab Governor Salman Taseer, a Muslim, was shot dead by his security guard for supporting Asia Bibi and speaking out against Blasphemy laws.

11. Pastor Rashid Emmanuel and his brother Sajid were shot dead in Pakistan while being escorted by the police from a district court. Both had denied the charges of blasphemy.

12. Two Extremist groups, Sipah-e-Sahaba and the International Khatm-e-Nabuwat (IKNM), torched Christian homes and killed Christians in Punjab. They said that a Christian had defiled and spoke against Prophet Mohammad.

13. A physician threw away a pestering pharmaceutical salesman's business card in Pakistan. The pharmaceutical salesman's name was Mohammad. By throwing it in the trash, he was going to be prosecuted under blasphemy laws.

It is time for Muslims to look in the mirror and question why the petty matters described above really play such an important role in their daily lives and why it consumes them so much to the point that it results in destruction and mayhem.

Women In Islam

At least in the Western world, Muslim men have no problem working side by side with women, sitting next to them while traveling, going to the mall and walking near women and having the ability to interact freely. In the Muslim world, however, women are generally separated from men and are allowed very little interaction with the opposite sex. Even though the status of women has improved somewhat, it still lacks considerably in comparison to the West and Far East. In most Muslim countries, women are required to wear a burqa or hijab when venturing outside of their house. In Saudi Arabia, women cannot go out unless they are accompanied by a male guardian who is at least 18 years old.

The atrocities committed by the Taliban against women are well documented. Honor killing is a common event in many Muslim countries. Turkey and Malaysia are the exceptions where women enjoy considerable freedom. The Prophet himself consulted women and weighed their opinions seriously. Women contributed significantly to the canonization of the Quran. Women prayed in mosques unsegregated from men, engaged in commercial transactions, were encouraged to seek knowledge and were both instructors and pupils in the early Islamic period. The Quran mentions the "Modesty of Women," which should be applicable to men also if one thinks logically. There is no proof in the early history of Islamic society that segregation of the sexes was a requirement. Again, these ignorant practices arose from tribal and cultural mores where males generally dominated and made the laws. A few of the reasons that Extremists use to force the wearing of the Hijab or Burqa are listed below:

1. To preserve women from being seen by men in gaudy or showy dress.

2. To preserve men from being seduced by their beauty.

3. To protect a wife's husband from falling for another woman.

4. To safeguard and to protect the whole society from temptation.

5. To secure the stability of marital lives.

6. To protect women from being harassed or from the lusty motives of men.

Interestingly, men and women pray together at the Kaaba's Grand Mosque in Mecca without segregation; however, they are segregated in all other mosques, which simply defies logic. Islam continues to linger in the dark ages, and the centuries-old practices are enforced under the guise of the Quran, Hadith, Sharia culture or pure illiteracy. Obviously, God has been turned into such a small figure in the likeness of a cruel school principal who is quick to punish over items of little importance.

Mohammad Ali Jinnah, founder of Pakistan deplored the women's condition in the Muslim world and exhorted men to consider them as equal partners. *"No nation can rise to the height of glory unless your women are side by side with you. We are victims of evil customs. It is a crime against humanity that our women are shut up within the four walls of their houses as prisoners. There is no sanction anywhere for the deplorable conditions in which our women have to live. You should take your women along with you as comrades in every sphere of life.".*" [12]

—MUHAMMAD ALI JINNAH 1944, FOUNDER OF PAKISTAN

Mustafa Kemal Ataturk, founder of Modern Turkey, another leader with an exceptional mindset, questioned a society progressing without the equal participation of women. *"Human kind is made up of two sexes, women and men. Is it possible that a mass is improved by the improvement of only one part and the other part is ignored? Is it possible that if half of a mass is tied to earth with chains and the other half can soar into skies?"* [13]

—MUSTAFA KEMAL ATATÜRK, FOUNDER OF MODERN TURKEY

DEMOCRACY IN ISLAM

It is well established that the four Caliphs (spiritual leaders) who succeeded Prophet Mohammad did not command universal acceptance by all Muslims, resulting in the separation of Islam into the Sunni and Shia sects. The Sunni rulers of the Ottoman Empire called themselves Caliphs, but in reality they ruled as kings. The Shia called their spiritual leaders Imam. Except the first four caliphs, the Muslim rulers assumed royal titles and ruled as autocratic leaders. They used Islam to justify both their civil and religious authority.

As Christianity spread, the Roman Church was able to control the narrative of divine authority. Even after absorbing many pagan traditions for the sake of a wider acceptance, they kept their fundamental doctrines intact. Thus, the Pope provided Christianity with a strong foundation and infrastructure that Islam has not experienced. For almost 1,200 years since its arrival in Rome, Christianity has been able to establish basic rules for the masses under a single authority respected by most people. The schism in Christianity did not start until 1517. The Romans, already endowed with an Exceptional Mindset, gave Christianity legs for it to stand on and prosper.

On the other hand, the schism in Islam started within 32 years after the death of the Prophet Mohammad. The Muslims, lacking religious maturity and an Exceptional Mindset, reverted back to their tribal loyalties and were unable to provide the young religion with the foundation that would have fostered the development of intellect and free thinking scholars. With the lack of a fully established infrastructure, the rapid spread of Islam did more damage than good.

The Umayyad dynasty that followed the first four caliphs became enmeshed in the trappings of royal courts and started to govern in the same fashion of the Persian and Byzantine kings. They acted as both divine and worldly, a lethal combination, thus corrupting many doctrines and the original message of the Prophet Mohammad. The Muslim rulers became absolute monarchs. The non-Arab Muslim rulers did not fully understand Arabic and therefor had to rely on religious scholars for the interpretation of religious doctrines. The Sunni interpretations are different than Shia. Among Sunnis, Salafi interpretations are different than other Sunni sects. Each sect dances to the tune of its own drum while calling other drum beaters "infidels." This inappropriate fixation on the micro-level aspects of the religion has led to the downfall of Muslims and is now keeping them shackled to the mindless doctrines.

In the early history of Islam, the close partnership between Kings and Mullahs became a strong institution where each needed the other for survival. Kings fought the battles and added more lands and converts to the kingdom, and the Mullahs interpreted the religion as they saw fit. Mullahs benefited from the Treasury and acted as a willing partner when Friday prayers were held in the King's name.

After military losses in the 19th century, the Ottoman Empire tried to reform Sharia Law from doctrines to a set of rules that could be consulted and referenced through books when necessary. This may have enabled the military rulers after the First World War to abolish the Caliphate and declare it a secular state. In the modern era, Turkey became the first Islamic country to separate religion from state.

The continued propagation by Muslim scholars of the bygone golden days of Islam (8th to 11th century) has a nostalgic value but does not provide a roadmap for success in the 21st century. Today, they are quick to blame their poor state of affairs on the colonial powers or the Western and Jewish conspiracies while totally ignoring the conspiracies of the Umayyad, Abbasid, Mughal or Ottoman courts. The other fact that they completely ignore is that many Far Eastern countries, including China, at one-time or another were under the control of colonial powers. Today, China, Korea,

Vietnam, Hong Kong and Singapore are thriving societies and economies. Japan was annihilated after the Second World War but is now a major industrial power. Germany lost two world wars but is the strongest economy in Europe. How did the Far East, Japan and Germany find the inner strength to become strong once again? Whatever that Holy Grail may be, it is absent in the Muslim world.

India and Pakistan both gained independence from the British in 1947 after 90 years of colonial rule. Today, India is the largest democracy, well on its way to becoming an industrial powerhouse. On the other hand, Pakistan is languishing behind both politically and economically. It has become a home to terrorist networks and jihadi movements. The corruption is rampant and the civilian government is always facing the threat of a military coup. So, what caused India to move forward and Pakistan backward? These are the questions that Muslim leaders and intellectual needs to evaluate and answer.

The reality is that there is no problem with Islam as a religion but only with the followers who practice Islam to suit their own desires and wishes. In order to achieve their objectives, they have distorted the history and corrupted the doctrines by limiting the vast landscape of the human mind to think, explore and reason. The hardened hearts, the inflexible man-made dogmas and narrow thinking has led to the state of apathy. Dictatorial rule in Muslim countries does not allow for the free exchange of ideas and open debate on religious doctrines. The majority of Muslims is poor, illiterate and can barely afford to provide for their families' daily needs. They are dependent on the Mullahs for the understanding of religion, and the sad results of the indoctrination by Mullah are obvious. The educated and intellectuals are afraid to disturb the beehive and wish to avoid getting stung at all costs. The few brave souls who do talk are unable to get the traction they need and constantly face threats. So this leaves the Extremists and terrorists to carry their violent agenda forward, making life miserable for the citizens of their own country and the rest of us.

Traditional Islam promotes a consultative decision-making body (Shura) and the principles of consensus (Ijma) that can be used to provide a basis for democracy in the Muslim countries. Nonetheless, uneducated Mullahs are unwilling to listen and consider the viable options where citizens can participate. The Mullah argues that Sharia applies to all aspects of political, religious, social and private life. However, their brand of Sharia is outdated and not applicable in this dynamic world. Their Sharia Law stifles the advancement of mankind, provides women with a fewer rights, promotes persecution of minorities and outlaws modern education. The goal is to subjugate the masses, a rather frightening idea when Islam clearly proclaims (Quran 2:256): *"Let there be no compulsion in religion: Truth stands out clear from Error."* [14] This is an obvious example how Mullahs use Islamic doctrines to further their own personal causes.

Democracy In The Muslim Countries

Like any other religion, Islam should not be viewed as an obstacle to democracy; it is the Muslim rulers and fundamentalists who use various means to thwart democracy to hold onto their sphere of influence. The most common tools used by the fundamentalists are outdated doctrines, military power, illiteracy, economic deprivation and division along the lines of tribalism and feudalism. Saudi Arabia and Iran have used religion in establishing autocratic Sharia Law. Afghanistan uses illiteracy, Pakistan uses economic deprivation and Iraq uses tribal loyalties. According to Reza Aslan, an associate professor of creative writing at the University of California, Riverside, *"The truth is no religion either encourages or discourages democracy. Indeed, because religions are in their nature absolutist, all religions reject the principles of liberalism and popular sovereignty that are at the heart of the democratic ideal."* [15]

The autocratic rules in Islamic countries have robbed their citizens of basic human rights, including freedom of speech, the right to vote and ability to voice their opinion openly without fear of persecution. Additionally, if the exercise of election is completed, the elements clinging to power work hard to nullify the results. They use any means within their power to control the outcome in their favor, dissolve the legislative body or take over the government through a coup if there is a strong army. Hosni Mubarak was forced to leave Egypt in 2011 after 30 years of rule; Gadaffi died a terrible death in Libya after ruling for 40 years; Musharraf, who came to power in military coup in Pakistan, was forced out after 10 years; in Syria, the al-Assad family (Bashar and father Hafiz) has been in power for over 40 years; and in Saudi Arabia, the Saud family has been ruling in one form or another since the late 1700s. These are just a few examples.

According to the "Freedom in the World 2011 Report" by Freedom House, out of 115 democratic countries, only 3 Islamic countries can be called democratic: Turkey, Bangladesh and Indonesia.

According to this report, *"The year featured drops in the number of Free countries and the number of electoral democracies, as well as an overall deterioration for freedom in the Middle East and North Africa region." "The Middle East and North Africa remained the region with the lowest level of freedom in 2010, continuing its multiyear decline from an already-low democratic baseline."* [16]

The Freedom House report gives ratings to "political Rights" and "Civil Liberties" from scale 1–7, where 1 = Most Free and 7 = Least Free.

It is no surprise that not a single Islamic country got the rating of "1" while the Western world easily earned the "1" rating. While most stay under the rule of monarchies or dictatorships, few countries are following the path of democracy, namely Turkey, Bangladesh and Indonesia. The West has realized the importance of the separation of Church and State, but Islamic countries have not been successful in separating God from the government. It is considered a badge of honor to have the word "Islamic" in the name of an Islamic country. Of course, this is all done to control the masses with an iron fist in the name of divine power, consequently giving Mullahs complete authority to suck cash from both the rulers and the masses.

ELECTORAL DEMOCRACIES*

NO.	COUNTRY	NO.	COUNTRY	NO.	COUNTRY
1	Albania	40	Guatemala	79	Papua New Guinea
2	Andorra	41	Guyana	80	Paraguay
3	Antigua & Barbuda	42	Hungary	81	Peru
4	Argentina	43	Iceland	82	Philippines
5	Australia	44	India	83	Poland
6	Austria	45	Indonesia	84	Portugal
7	Bahamas	46	Ireland	85	Romania
8	Bangladesh	47	Israel	86	St. Kitts and Nevis
9	Barbados	48	Italy	87	St. Lucia
10	Belgium	49	Jamaica	88	St. Vincent & the Grenadines
11	Belize	50	Japan	89	Samoa
12	Benin	51	Kiribati	90	San Marino
13	Bolivia	52	Latvia	91	Sao Tome & Principe
14	Bosnia-Herzegovina	53	Lesotho	92	Senegal
15	Botswana	54	Liberia	93	Serbia
16	Brazil	55	Liechtenstein	94	Seychelles
17	Bulgaria	56	Lithuania	95	Sierra Leone
18	Canada	57	Luxembourg	96	Slovakia
19	Cape Verde	58	Macedonia	97	Slovenia
20	Chile	59	Malawi	98	South Africa
21	Columbia	60	Maldives	99	South Korea
22	Comoros	61	Mali	100	Spain
23	Costa Rica	62	Malta	101	Suriname
24	Croatia	63	Marshall Islands	102	Sweden
25	Cyprus	64	Mauritius	103	Switzerland
26	Czech Republic	65	Mexico	104	Taiwan
27	Denmark	66	Micronesia	105	Tanzania
28	Dominica	67	Moldova	106	Tonga
29	Dominican Republic	68	Monaco	107	Trinidad & Tobago
30	East Timor	69	Mongolia	108	Turkey
31	Ecuador	70	Montenegro	109	Tuvalu
32	El Salvador	71	Namibia	110	Ukraine
33	Estonia	72	Nauru	111	United Kingdom
34	Finland	73	Netherlands	112	United States
35	France	74	New Zealand	113	Uruguay
36	Germany	75	Nicaragua	114	Vanuatu
37	Ghana	76	Norway	115	Zambia
38	Greece	77	Palau		
39	Grenada	78	Panama		

*Alphabetical List of Electoral Democracies, Data from 2011 Freedom House Report.

CHAPTER 9

TERRORISM, JIHADISM AND OUR OPTIONS

"The Wahabis profess a life of exceeding austerity, and what they practice themselves they rigorously enforce on others. They hold it as an article of duty, as well as of faith, to kill all who do not share their opinions and to make slaves of their wives and children. Women have been put to death in Wahabi villages for simply appearing in the street."

—WINSTON CHURCHILL, 14 JUNE 1921

ANALYSIS

IN THE AFTERMATH OF SEPTEMBER 11, 2011 we felt violated and insecure, and our lifestyles have changed forever. Billions of dollars were lost by businesses, billions of dollars were spent on new security systems and trillions of dollars were spent on two wars. Al-Qaeda became the number one national enemy followed by the Taliban and other terrorist organizations.

Terrorism has an old history, and its purpose is to use violence in order to impact a favorable political outcome. Jewish killed Romans to oust them from Judea in the first century. The Hashshashin or Assassins murdered Muslim leaders from 11th to 13th century until they were crushed by the Mongols. With the advances in global media coverage, the recent phenomenon of modern terrorism depends on this method to create fear among citizens. Terrorism has existed for ages in one form or another throughout the history of humanity. Terrorism by non-State actors started in the 20th century. The rise of guerrilla warfare by the Irish, Basque and Zionists were the first acts used before and after World War II. The Islamic leaders during the colonialism era incited Muslims to rise up against the infidels and started using Mullahs to do their bidding. The Kurds divided among Turkey, Syria, Iran and Iraq were the first group to use terrorist activities in their struggle to gain independence.

In the 1960's and 1970's, the PLO popularized tactics of hijacking planes. In 1972, they killed Israeli athletes during the 1972 Munich Olympics to bring attention to their cause. In the 21st century, the Islamic movements use terrorism as a favorite method of killing in the name of God under the guise of jihad. While nationalistic terrorism has declined precipitously, the religiously inspired terrorism is on the rise and is the most alarming threat today, considering that the terrorist's claim that fighting them is fighting directly with God. Invoking of the divine allows terrorist leaders to recruit from a large supply of unemployed young minds who are subjected to extensive brainwashing and promised a ticket to heaven in exchange for their earthly life along with demise of other innocents both non-Muslims and Muslims. Since 2011, Taliban have killed over 40,000 Muslims in Pakistan who do not follow their brand of Islam.

Some of the Mullahs are now promoting that God has divided the world into two houses: "House of Peace" (Dar-al-Islam) and "House of War (Dar-al-Harb). The first one is dominated by Muslims and the second by non-Muslims. Therefore, it is a Muslim's duty to wage war in order to bring non-Muslims into the House of Peace. They believe that God commands it. In his famous book *The Muqaddimah*, Muslim scholar Ibn Khaldun declares, *"In the Muslim community, holy war is a religious duty, because of the obligation to convert everybody to Islam either by persuasion or by force."* [1]

This insidious thinking is a major factor in the ascent of the terrorist movements in Islam. However, a growing number of Muslim scholars are saying not so fast by quoting this verse from Quran (2:256) *"Let there be no compulsion in religion."* [2]

The al-Qaeda and Taliban Terrorists include the well- educated and the uneducated, western educated and madrassa educated, rich and poor. The educated and rich, however, have been successful in manipulating the illiterate and poor to join their repugnant causes. The indoctrination lies and innuendos warp the mind to such a fury that the zeal to die for God while killing innocents blurs all realities. The idea and thought that God would reward someone with 72 virgins for destroying the precious life that He has given to each human being is incomprehensible.

There is considerable confusion that exists among both liberal and extremist Muslims today. While liberals will condemn terrorist activities by using verses of the Quran that support their reasoning for tolerance, the Extremists will find in the same Quran verses an interpretation supporting their heinous objectives. Here are few examples from Quran, first the verse that clearly forbids the killing of innocents (Quran 5:32): *"We ordained for the Children of Israel that if any one slew a person–unless it be for murder or for spreading mischief in the land–it would be as if he slew the whole people: and if any one saved a life, it would be as if he saved the life of the whole people. Then although there came to them Our messengers with clear signs, yet, even after that, many of them continued to commit excesses in the land.* [3]

The above verse clearly equates the killing of one innocent life to the whole of mankind, which is accepted by the majority of Muslims and ignored by the terrorists.

Here is one verse of the Quran used by the terrorists to justify their wicked acts (Quran 9:5): *"But when the forbidden months are past, then fight and slay the Pagans wherever ye find them, an seize them, beleaguer them, and lie in wait for them in every stratagem (of war); but if they repent, and establish regular prayers and practise regular charity, then open the way for them."* [4]

The Progressive Muslims argue that the above verse was for the specific period in the past when Muslims were trying to survive the onslaught of Meccan pagans. Unfortunately, the terrorists have been successful in drowning out the voices of reason. The autocratic environment promotes the suffocation of political dialogue and progress toward open society. The Progressive majority is unable to overcome the Extremist minority since rulers view them as a direct threat to their own seat of power. The destruction created by the Extremists provides these rulers with an avenue to further tighten their grip by proclaiming a threat to national security. So the vicious cycle continues.

Additionally, the autocratic system leads to the decimation of opposition. Most of the opposition leaders never get to mature in the political process and end up spending much of their lives in prisons or in hiding. Once the dictator is overthrown, there is no one to guide the country on the path to success, and the opposition embarks on revenge, attempting to decimate the other side. The recent Arab Springs clearly shows this dilemma. Egypt, Libya and Tunisia (and pretty soon Syria) are all in political doldrums and have been unsuccessful in addressing issues of the nation. Since the overthrow of Saddam Hussein in 2004, Iraq still has not been able to fully become democratic, wherein the opposition is allowed to mature and become a viable institution in the process of governing. There is no hope for Afghanistan to become a democratic state in near future and rid itself of terrorists.

The West felt relieved when the Soviet Superpower gave up in 1991 after decades of tit-for-tat scenarios. There was hope that peace would last at least for a few decades. The Americans' lone status at the top of the Superpowers became an eyesore for many. Rational and intellectual minds would point toward China to one day take on the American might but never the rag-tag, dubious and scruffy groups like al-Qaeda. No other nation then or now could fight with the USA and win the battle, let alone the war. Terrorist groups, with their main objective to kill civilians indiscriminately, make it difficult for civilized societies to fight them efficiently due to their fundamental nature of the principles of freedom.

In Iraq and Afghanistan, the American military quickly defeated both armies. Then, our forces were dragged down by the terrorists. Our respect for human life, in combination with hesitant political leaders, generally ends up tying the hands of military planners, generals and soldiers. Avoiding collateral damage and civilian deaths limits our ability to fight and provides the terrorists with a free hand to pursue their evil agenda. Maybe this was the reason— to stamp out the fear of terrorism— that Alexander the Great, the Mongols, Ottomans, Mughals, various Chinese dynasties and European Kings killed almost everyone, young and old, children and women, after defeating the enemy. Today, we would call it State-Sponsored Terrorism.

Unfortunately, we will be dealing with this deformed mental state and barbarism of terrorists for many years to come. The proliferation of modern, lethal and nuclear weapons requires an urgent response from the civilized nations to join together as a cohesive group to fight the terrorists wherever they exist and stamp out this evil in our midst.

THE TERRORIST MINDSET

So what do the terrorists want to achieve by destroying lives in the name of a mutual God of many faiths? For the Muslim terrorists (not the majority Muslims), there is only one goal, i.e., to create an Islamic Caliphate and live under Sharia Law. The Caliphate these Extremists want to create has never existed in the history of Islam. The first four Caliphs, who ruled for 32 years, had a terrible time controlling their subjects, and as a result three of them were murdered.

The recent experimentation of the Taliban and their leader Mullah Omar created hell on earth in Afghanistan, and the events of that period are well documented. Their tyrannical regime's claims to fame were making a beard compulsory for men, keeping women locked up, destroying the economy, the astronomical rise in a poor class and the flogging or beheading of any-one who disagreed with their barbaric and self-created version of Islam.

The terrorists have killed hundreds of thousands in Iraq, Afghanistan and Pakistan. The terrorists are basically cowards who victimize innocent citizens, and in the simplest form, they are bullies. At a minimum, Muslim scholars must declare fatwa against suicide bombings and unite in con-demning these as acts of terror. Muslims should start an internal debate on the items listed below in order to rid themselves of individuals with the Violent Mindset who commit these atrocities in the name of religion against anyone living either in their lands or foreign lands:

1. Allow Islam to change with the times through inquiry and evalua-tion of all doctrines.

2. Allow Islam to learn from other religions or dogmas.

3. Allow minorities total religious freedom.

4. Allow integration of civil laws with the Sharia law.

5. Disallow Jihad, House of War.

6. Allow women the same rights as men.

7. Allow freedom of speech and expression in pursuit of life and liberty.

Taliban have killed over 40,000 innocent citizens since 9/11 in Pakistan through suicide bombings and shootings. After 9/11, the U.S. forces quickly removed the Taliban from power; however, the terrain in Afghanistan and adjacent Pakistan provided them with natural hideouts and caves and along with al-Qaeda, they roamed freely between the rugged hills.

When Pakistani President Musharraf decided to align with the USA, the Taliban created Tehrik-i-Taliban Pakistan (TTP), which is currently led by a Mehsud tribe from South Waziristan. TTP has vowed to bring down the Pakistan government and create havoc internally in Pakistan. There are several other groups aligned with the TTP, including the Punjabi Taliban. The second group was led by the Haqqani tribe and is aligned with the Afghani Taliban, who is busy carrying out terrorist acts against NATO and the Afghan government. Their stated goal is to expel all "infidels," but in reality, it includes all minority Muslims.

The situation in Pakistan is rather complex and precarious. The country can be compared to a ship in the ocean with no captain at the helm and a mutiny brewing on board. Each terrorist has his gun drawn, and bullets are being fired indiscriminately in all directions. Pakistan is an ideal place for the terrorists to operate and a difficult place for innocent citizens to live.

The Musharraf government tried to negotiate with a few of the terrorist groups in 2007 and 2009, but both attempts failed miserably. The Pakistani Military launched an attack against them in South Waziristan and Swat but have not been able to finish the job. The Pakistani military leaders continue to prepare for the ultimate battle with India, which is a totally preposterous notion since the TTP is wreaking havoc and severely impacting civilians and businesses alike. There is a growing element of Extremists in the Pakistani military that support the Taliban and other jihadi groups with the goal of using them against India. There are certain political leaders that believe they can buy their way by directly negotiating with the Taliban once NATO forces leave Afghanistan. On the other hand, in crowded Madrassas there is no shortage of future Taliban recruits. There are an estimated 3 to 5 million Afghani refugees in Pakistani camps, providing a fresh ongoing supply of recruits to the Taliban. Pakistani religious parties, mostly led by the ignorant Mullahs, continue to inflame hatred in the name of Islam and have been successful in bringing out thousands of confused and unemployed Pakistani citizens onto the street, where people die and property is destroyed.

Pakistan is a poor country, but it owns over 100 nuclear weapons. This would be equivalent to a middle class U.S. citizen buying an Abrams tank and parking in their front yard, knowing full well that he or she cannot afford the tank and that it was a pretty dumb idea to begin with. Statistics from the Pakistani English newspaper Dawn tell the tale of economic state of affairs. The average per capita income for 2011 was $1,254 and was mainly attributed to the $12 billion remittance from Pakistanis working overseas, mostly in the Middle East. From Pakistani Ministry of Finance the budget numbers Dr. Abdul Hafeez Sheikh for 2011 were: [5]

Total governmental Income = $26.7 Billion
Total governmental Expenditures = $39.9 Billion
Total governmental Deficit = $13.23 billion
The yearly military budget = $6.5 billion (24% of Income)

Since 2001, the USA has been providing between $1–2 billion per year to Pakistan, and it is barely surviving as a nation.

Ayesha Siddiqa has served as professor of Military Science at Johns Hopkins University. She wrote a book in 2007 titled *Military Inc.: Inside Pakistan's Military Economy*, which presents some interesting facts: [6]

- The top brass retire with assets "between $2.5 and $6.9 million."
- The military-controlled businesses are valued at "$15 billion."
- The military controls over "100 million" acres of land.

This unchecked military control of a large percentage of GDP and industry has made them a mighty and powerful force in internal politics. The military has ruled Pakistan for 33 years out of the 65 years since its separation from India. The reign of strongmen (Ayub Khan, Yahya Khan, Zia-ul-Haq and Pervez Musharraf) speaks volumes on why democracy has not taken hold in Pakistan. While the military may have brought temporary stability at times, its impact on the civil institution has been devastating. The political systems could never develop fully. Moreover, just like the military, when civilian government comes to power, it uses authoritarian methods to silence the voices of the opponents. When opposition comes to power, they waste time settling scores instead of building strong socio-economic systems.

Ms. Siddiqa further states, *"Since the country's socio-political system is predominantly authoritarian and has a pre-capitalist structure, the ruling classes are not averse to using military force to further their personal, political and economic interests. The elite therefore continue to strengthen the armed forces and contribute to the evolution of the military fraternity into a class."* [7]

However, the political parties and military cooperate thoroughly in the effort to keep the "phantom threat of India" alive in the Pakistani psyche. The distorted history books have created a class who feels that India belongs to Muslims and Pakistan. Therefore, it is their duty to figure out a scheme to dominate India through war and then through forced conversions. Pakistan has fought three wars with India, in 1948, 1965 and 1971, along with many border skirmishes under the pre-text of Kashmir. They lost all of the wars. (The Kashmir region is claimed by both India and Pakistan. At the time of partition in 1947, Raja of Kashmir chose to become part of India, but Pakistan felt that the Muslim Kashmiri majority wanted to join with Pakistan. The United Nations has passed several resolutions since 1948, but the stalemate continues to this day between the two neighbors.) The 1971 war resulted in the breakup of East Pakistan, which became Bangladesh.

A developing country with a per-capita income of around $1,300 per year does not need an army of a million plus men (includes active, reserve and paramilitary). The Pakistani military's fascination with fighting India is an illogical approach. India is on its way to becoming a power in Asia both economically and militarily, and Pakistan would be well served in resolving all outstanding issues with India, especially Kashmir.

Pakistan was born out of mother India, and almost all Pakistanis are of Indo-Aryan origin. Pakistan has numerous cultural similarities with India and a common historical bond that cannot never severed. Pakistanis are not Arabs. This is true no matter how much falsehood has been created in the school textbooks or spread by the Mullahs in order to fleece the public monetarily and religiously.

Ironically, if Pakistan had stayed part of India, there would have been over 500 million Muslims in India, which is still a minority albeit a substantially large minority. Indian Muslims are treated well and have ample opportunities to advance in art, science, business and government. It is also in India's interest to act as a big brother and lead the efforts in resolving issues with Pakistan. A federation among India, Pakistan, Bangladesh and Sri Lanka can create a powerful economic block with a population of around 1.7 billion and a GDP of approximately $2.3 trillion. Cheap labor, familiarity with the English language, strengths in the medical and computer sciences, mathematics and process re-engineering skills mixed with the home-grown hungry consumer market are all the ingredients needed to catapult the Sub-Continent back to the glory days of its past.

THE DANGERS OF NUCLEAR WEAPONS

Pakistan has over 100 nuclear weapons, and Iran is close to acquiring nuclear capability. There looms a possibility of these weapons of mass destruction falling into the hands of terrorists or jihadi organizations. With their ultimate desire to win the ticket to heaven, the rest of the world is facing a perilous situation. The terrorists do not have their hands on these weapons; however, if they ever do, they will not hesitate for a second before using them on the citizens of this world, regardless if they are Muslims or non-Muslims. The corresponding response could also add to the devastation, and it would take many decades to recover. Indeed, that would be the darkest day since the beginning of time. However, embarking on a journey to avoid such a catastrophe is possible and within our reach if we start now. Delay in formulating a response should be unthinkable, and the civilized societies must work together to avoid the occurrence of such a day.

So, what can peace-loving people all over the world do? The United States is the only superpower, with China trailing behind. The 11 years in Afghanistan have produced mixed results for America. We may have reduced the threat of the Taliban, but they are not completely eliminated. With Osama bin Laden gone, al-Qaeda still lingers on and is now active in African Maghreb. During the 2012 presidential debate, Mitt Romney remarked, *"We cannot kill our way out of this mess."* We need a comprehensive strategy against this menace, and the USA alone cannot fight this battle. There needs to be a concerted effort by countries representing all of the inhabited continents, i.e., the Americas, Europe, Asia, Africa and Australia. This should include a two-pronged strategy, underlined below:

International Alliance – The USA, having the most experience and knowhow, should take the lead in forming an alliance against worldwide terrorism. The organization could be called "United Against Terrorism" (UAT) and should be totally independent from the United Nations. In all reality, the UN has become more of a social and humanitarian group and is not capable of dealing with terrorism. The UAT should be open to only a select few countries, representing all the continents, few strong economies, religious diversification, etc. The arbitrarily suggested countries are the USA, China, Russia, UK, India, France, Germany, Japan, Turkey, Kenya, South Africa, Indonesia, Argentina and Brazil. These countries represent over four billion people of the world and roughly 80% of the world GDP.

Each UAT member should contribute money, personnel and material and collaborate jointly in policing, pursuing, spying, deploying and conducting military operations wherever necessary against the non-State actors committed to violence and terrorists. The purpose is to create peace, harmony and order in this world. This force could consist of several hundred thousand, half of which could be trained as a counter terrorist force with the ability to be deployed anywhere at short notice. The goal is not to threaten the sovereign nations but to eliminate the Extremists with their agenda of destruction.

Nuclear Weapons In The Hands Of The Jihadi

The largest danger that we face from the Extremists is in the form of a nuclear device. As stated earlier, barring some miracle, Pakistan may fall apart, thus generating a chain reaction that includes nuclear weapons falling into the hands of Extremists. Keep in mind that these Extremists hate anyone who does not follow their wicked dogma. Since terrorists see India next door as one of the biggest threats, hopefully India alone is able to contain the situation; however, that may be easier said than done when the enemy is a coward in hiding and has nukes. In the hands of the wrong party, the nukes will be a disaster for humanity. The scenario below illustrates such an event:

> "If Al-Qaeda was to rent a van to carry the ten-kiloton Russian weapon into the heart of Times Square and detonate it adjacent to the Morgan Stanley headquarters at 1585 Broadway, Times Square would vanish in the twinkling of an eye. The blast would generate temperature reaching into the tens of millions of degrees Fahrenheit. The resulting fireball and blast wave would destroy instantaneously the theater district, the New York Times building, Grand Central Terminal, and every other structure within a third of a mile of the point of detonation. The ensuing firestorm would engulf Rockefellers Center, Carnegie Hall, The Empire State Building and Madison Square Garden, leaving a landscape resembling the World Trade Center site." "On a normal workday, more than half a million people crowd the area within a half-mile radius of Times Square. A noon detonation in midtown Manhattan could kill them all. Hundreds of thousands of others would die from collapsing building, fire, and fallout in the ensuing hours." [8]

If terrorists attack the USA and Israel, the nations will retaliate justifiably and use a lethal force of their own to contain further damage. Either way, it will be a messy and chaotic situation with no easy answers. Not so long ago, Americans were faced with a nuclear threat from the Soviets. The USA and Soviets considered each other rational and observable enemies. The U.S. was able to monitor Soviet airfields with U2 spy planes, and the assurance of mutual destruction kept both sides from ever using their nuclear weapons. Even to this day, nuclear deterrence remains a key strategy among the USA, China and Russia. "Deterrence" has been used successfully so far by dissuading one side from using nuclear weapons because a launch would elicit an equal or higher response from the opposition, ultimately decimating both sides.

However, as the proliferation of nuclear weapons continues, the deterrence policy becomes weaker. This leaves us with a strong possibility that in the very near future we may face a rogue nation or a terrorist group with different sets of values, especially al-Qaeda. Deterrence will continue to work only as long as all sides remain rational and fear death. Many extremist groups, however, are undeterred by any credible threat of retaliation, regardless of how large that threat might be. Furthermore, history is filled with examples of irrational leaders and decisions that have led to war. Nuclear weapons combined with human fallibility not only make nuclear war possible but also inevitable. The situation that we find ourselves in now is the most complex that has ever existed when considering the survival of the human race.

A nuclear weapon uses atomic fission to split an atom into two or more parts, creating a colossal explosion. The explosive yield is measured in TNT (Trinitrotoluene) kiloton or megaton. One kiloton equals one-thousand tons of TNT, and a megaton equals to one-million tons of TNT. One U.S. ton is equal to 2,000 lbs., thus a kiloton would be equal to 2,000,000 lbs. or 400,000 sticks of dynamite each weighing 5 lbs. The "Little Boy" bomb used at Hiroshima was estimated to be around 12–18 kiloton or a destructive power equal to 12,000–18,000 tons of dynamite. The "Fat Man" dropped on Nagasaki was 20–22 kiloton, or 20,000–22,000 tons of dynamite.

The temperature that a nuclear weapon reaches upon detonation is between 50 and 150 million degrees Fahrenheit at the center, whereas the sun reaches a temperature of around 15 million degrees Fahrenheit. A 10–15 kiloton bomb, easily packed into a van, would create unimaginable devastation in any large U.S. city, incinerating and vaporizing all that is near and turning everyone within a half mile into charcoal. There is no sense in describing the destruction further, as we all know it is quick and total. The civilized nations must do everything possible to avoid nukes ever being used. There is no good that can come out of a nuclear explosion. Here is a list of nuclear stockpiles from nucleardarkness.org:

STATUS OF WORLD NUCLEAR FORCES 2010 * [9]

COUNTRY	STRATEGIC	NON-STRATEGIC	OPERATIONAL	STOCKPILE
Russia	2,600	2,050	4,650	12,000
United States	2,126	500	2,626	9,400
France	300	n/a	~300	300
China	180	?	~180	240
United Kingdom	160	n/a	<160	185
Israel	80	n/a	n/a	80
Pakistan	70–90	n/a	n/a	70–90
India	60–80	n/a	n/a	60–80[i]
North Korea	<10	n/a	n/a	<10
Total:	~5,600[k]	~2,550[k]	~7,900[k]	~22,300[k]

*"All numbers are estimates and further described in the **Nuclear Notebook** in the Bulletin of the Atomic Scientists, and the nuclear appendix in the **SIPRI Yearbook**. Additional reports are published on the **FAS Strategic Security Blog**. Unlike those publications, this table is updated continuously as new information becomes available. Current update: **April 6, 2010**. The total numbers may not add up due to rounding and uncertainty about the operational status of the four lesser nuclear weapons states and the uncertainty about the size k = Numbers may not add up due to rounding and uncertainty about the operational status of the four lesser nuclear weapons states and the uncertainty about the size of the total inventories of three of the five initial nuclear powers."

After the conclusion of the Cold War and the collapse of Soviet Union, the world's amassed a combined stockpile of nuclear weapons that totals approximately 22,300. Of these weapons 95% are possessed by the U.S. and Russia. Below are the explanations from the Nuclear Darkness website:

"7,900 nuclear warheads are now considered deployed and operational (ready for immediate use). 7275 of these warheads reside in the nuclear arsenals of the U.S and Russia."[10]

"A total of approximately 2,000 U.S. and Russian strategic nuclear warheads are kept on high alert, quick-launch status. They are mounted on long-range land and sea-based ballistic missiles, and kept ready to launch with only a few minutes warning. They can reach their targets anywhere on Earth in 30 minutes or less." [11]

"The exact number of nuclear weapons in each country's possession is a closely held national secret. Despite this limitation, however, publicly available information and occasional leaks make it possible to make best estimates about the size and composition of the national nuclear weapon stockpiles." [12]

Iran is now bent on acquiring a nuclear weapon that will lead to a supremacy race in the Middle East between Shia Persians and Sunni Arabs, which could have a horrendous impact on all other earthly creatures. Once the cat is out of the bag, no nation or superpower alone will be able to put it back in. The issue here is not who has the nuclear weapon but who is willing to use it to further their own irrational causes. Imagine nukes in the hands of people who believe in killing "infidels." The civilized world cannot fight with this sort of irrational thinking.

Iran, with its rich cultural heritage and a large intellectual base, is better off working towards becoming an economic powerhouse than pursuing the military might of the era of Cyrus the Great.

Nuclear Pakistan

Pakistan, a country with $1,300 per capita income, developed its nuclear capability to neutralize India. As stated earlier, Pakistan was portioned out of India in 1947. Pakistan has every right to protect its sovereign status; however, it is a poor country with an unstable government dependent upon handouts from the USA, IMF, World Bank and host of other nations. According to The Express Tribune article dated March 6, 2013, *"Pakistan has reached a critical balance of payments predicament and will need another package from the International Monetary Fund before the end of the year to avert a crisis, one of the country's biggest lenders to the country said on Wednesday. The Asian Development Bank's country director, Werner Liepach, also told Reuters in an interview Pakistan will need up to $9 billion from the IMF to cushion the economy."* [13]

Pakistanis working overseas (mostly in the Middle East) contribute significantly to the treasury. According to an ARY News article dated January 26, 2013: *"Presently, there is only one major source of foreign inflows and that is home remittances sent by overseas Pakistanis. The inflow of workers' remittances* *offered considerable support to the current account as remittances posted a growth of 13 percent to $7.1 billion in the first half of FY13, sources said."* [14]

Since its independence, Pakistan has shown neither the capacity nor the capability to pull itself out of the economic misery that it is facing and will continue to face. It is a corrupt society from top to bottom with a pervasive tribal and feudal mentality. The military has been able to provide only a few periods of stability since its inception.

Pakistan consists of four provinces (states): Punjab, which is the largest with 54% of the population; Sind; Baluchistan, which is rich in natural resources and the largest in area with 40% of the land; and Khyber Pakhtunkhwa, which is Pushtun and terrorist dominated. Both Baluchistan and Khyber Pakhtunkhwa comprise a 1,500-mile border with Afghanistan.

Each province speaks a different dialect and has somewhat different culture, but they are brought together in the name of religion. Pakistan can be compared to the former Yugoslavia, which was comprised of Serbs, Croats, Bosnians, Slovenes, Albanians, Macedonians, etc. The danger is that Pakistan may follow the way of Yugoslavia, and when considering the nuclear devices, the situation could be catastrophic for all of us.

What can we do? We must bring Saudi Arabia and Iran, the two stalwarts of the Sunni and Shia branches of Islam respectively, into our fold. They both are in the race for their branch of Islam to win, but this is not the time of religious dogma supremacy; it is time for peace.

We are in a pickle of a dilemma, and no one person, group or nation has the answer. At the same time, being a superpower, it is our duty to work on keeping world order by working with other nations with a vested interest in peace and prosperity. We cannot ignore the Muslim world and Extremist mindset; they will not go away. The problem is not a lack of understanding but a fear of acting. We may be repeating the past that earned us World War II.

Nuclear weapons in the wrong hands are the real game changer. The wrongful deaths of 3,000 Americans on 9/11 caused us to engage in two wars that have cost us close to $2 trillion. Nuclear terrorism against us will result in the loss of several hundreds of thousands or even a million Americans. We will demand justice, and the American government would rightfully respond in kind. Just imagine the events that would unfold right in front of our eyes. As Americans, we will and must support our leaders to annihilate the enemy. However, the impact on our daily lives would be devastating. We would have to become a police state to fight the next danger. Our civil liberties would have to take a back seat for the sake of national interest, and the freedom that we love so dearly would be left to the annals of folklore.

No one has the foresight to predict the right solutions or outcomes; however, we do have friends in the Muslim world who do not support the evil ways of the terrorists. They must help us. We need leaders who will get the right people to work together on this. There are thousands of Muslim immigrants who will die in defending America and its values. We have to get them involved to fight the battles that we must win.

The Violence In Pakistan

Pakistan is a failed state or pretty near to it. The Islamic parties, though not successful at the ballot, are controlling the agenda. Their gap in education, deficiency in intellectual capital, zero economic growth, corruption by both the government and military, weak civilian population and strong military, sectarian violence to kill all minorities, ignorant passion for jihad, and distortion of history by denying Indian roots and adopting Arab roots are all masala for a very bad tasting dish.

FATALITIES IN TERRORIST VIOLENCE IN PAKISTAN 2003–2012 AS OF OCTOBER 21, 2012

Data from South Asia Terrorism Portal (www.satp.org). [15]

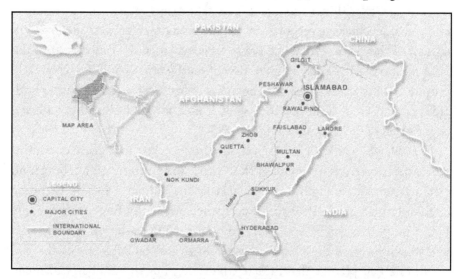

YEAR	CIVILIANS	SECURITY FORCE PERSONNEL	TERRORISTS/ INSURGENTS	TOTAL
2003	140	24	25	189
2004	435	184	244	863
2005	430	81	137	648
2006	608	325	538	1471
2007	1522	597	1479	3598
2008	2155	654	3906	6715
2009	2324	991	8389	11704
2010	1796	469	5170	7435
2011	2738	765	2800	6303
2012	2402	605	2276	5283
Total	14,550	4,695	24,964	44,209

The Drone Debate

Unnatural loss of life anywhere is always tragic. Drone attacks have killed key al-Qaeda and Taliban terrorists but also innocent civilians. There is an intense debate within Pakistani circles that drone attacks have produced more suicide attacks in response by the terrorist organizations against civilians since they believe that the Pakistan government is complicit with the USA military. The Pakistani government on the other hand has frequently protested these attacks as an infringement on its sovereignty. Whether both governments are together on the use of drones or not, the benefits achieved and the loss of life cannot be denied.

In 2014, when NATO forces pull out, drone strikes may cease or continue; no decision has been made by the American administration. There is no clear agreement among the Pakistanis that the Taliban will stop bombing civilian targets inside Pakistan if and when American forces leave. Some Pakistani politicians believe that bringing back the army in the barracks will somehow make the Taliban cease their attacks on Pakistani civilians.

No one can predict the Taliban's behavior, but the Taliban's ultimate agenda of creating a theocratic state may lead to the conclusion that these suicide attacks will continue until Taliban are fully defeated or turn peaceful by renouncing violence. Unfortunately, the civilized world will have to fight this wickedness for years to come.

The tables below compare Drone Attacks and Taliban Suicide Attacks:

TABLE 1 [16]

AMERICAN DRONE ATTACKS IN PAKISTAN

YEAR	ATTACKS	DEAD	INJURED
2008	63	967	2,137
2009	87	1,305	3,723
2010	68	1,187	2,926
2011	45	676	1,462
2012	22	203	25
Total	285	4,338	10,273

From GEO TV broadcast Aaj Kamran Kay Sath-16 Oct 2012-Part 1
Data is as of October 12, 2012

TABLE # 2 [(17)]

TALIBAN TERROR ATTACKS IN PAKISTAN

YEAR	ATTACKS	DEAD	INJURED
2008	2,148	2,267	4,500
2009	2,586	3,021	7,300
2010	2,113	2,913	5,800
2011	1,986	2,391	4,400
2012	650	1,200	2,000
Total	9,483	11,792	24,000

TALIBAN SUICIDE ATTACKS IN PAKISTAN

YEAR	ATTACKS	DEAD	INJURED
2008	63	967	2,137
2009	87	1,305	3,723
2010	68	1,187	2,926
2011	45	676	1,462
2012	22	203	25
Total	285	4,338	10,273
Grand Total	9,768	16,130	34,273

From GEO TV broadcast Aaj Kamran Kay Sath-16 Oct 2012-Part 1
Data is as of October 11, 2012

Since the American administration does not acknowledge drone attacks within Pakistan, it is difficult to verify the actual numbers. The numbers shown in Table 1 are the best estimate available.

Taliban terror attacks include bombing without the use of a suicide bomber. Since these crimes are committed against the Pakistani civilian population, the numbers can be verified by the police and civil authorities.

The Dangers In Pakistan

Pakistan has become an enigma in the war against terrorism. There is a stalemate in the political infrastructure. The elected government is weak, and the military is the de-facto final decision maker. After Pakistan's creation in 1947, America was considered a friend and loved by the majority of Pakistanis. The turn to fundamentalism and the War on Terrorism has shifted the opinions of the majority of Pakistani against the USA. The educated and business class would like to see a better relationship with the USA, while the Mullahs create hate among the uneducated majority. Despite all of the billions of dollars that the USA has sent to keep Pakistan afloat, America has not bought much goodwill. The dilemma that the civilized world is faced with today is how to create stability both politically and economically in Pakistan while helping it to protect its 100–200 nuclear weapons from falling into terrorist hands.

The economic challenge, lack of good educational institutions and the push to fundamentalism is prohibiting Pakistan from digging itself out of this deep hole that has been getting wider and deeper since late 1970s.

Anjum Niaz opined on October 14, 2012 in the Pakistani newspaper Dawn, writing, *"Presently, there are an estimated 103 million Pakistanis under the age of 25. They are not just a number but a critical mass — 63 per cent of Pakistan. Less than half are literate. And what do they do? Some are enrolled in madrassas where the emphasis is learning the Holy Quran by rote; some others are sole family providers and slog for a minimum wage; others are just 'sitting around' guys who form a groundswell when politicians bus them in for political rallies, demonstrations and protests."* [18]

Professor Satish Kumar is a well-known political commentator and author. He serves as a Director of National Security Research Foundation (NSRF), a New Delhi based think tank. In January 2000, he wrote an article entitled "Militant Islam; The Nemesis of Pakistan." In it, he writes, *"The biggest irony of Pakistan's history is that Islam, which was supposedly the raison d'être of Pakistan, not only failed to hold the country together, but also became the biggest source of its identity crisis. It is in the name of Islam that the country has suffered some of its worst internal conflicts in the last 10 years. And it is in the name of Islam that the country has created an image of being the most potent source of religious terrorism, which poses a threat to peace and stability in large parts of the world."* [19]

It is surprising that Dr. Kumar predicted many of these ills almost 12 years ago. Today, they have been greatly amplified and require Pakistan's leadership to swiftly act. However, the leadership necessary to deal with menace is nowhere to be found, leaving the rest of the civilized people to wonder what can be done.

CHAPTER 10

IS TIME RUNNING OUT?

"You have heard the law that says, 'Love your neighbor' and hate your enemy. But I say, love your enemies! Pray for those who persecute you! In that way, you will be acting as true children of your Father in heaven. For he gives his sunlight to both the evil and the good, and he sends rain on the just and the unjust alike."

—JESUS, MATTHEW 5:43-47

ANALYSIS

IN 2010, THE ESTIMATED WORLDWIDE Muslim population from the Pew Research Center's Forum on Religion & Public Life was 1.6 billion out of the world's total population of 6.9 billion. The Muslim population is projected to rise to 2.2 billion by year 2030, which is a 35% increase over 20 years. Muslims are growing at twice the rate of non-Muslims. Pakistan will become the largest Muslim country, growing from 178 million to a projected 256 million. Indonesia will be the second largest with 239 million (2010 – 205 million), India 236 million Muslims (2010 – 177 million), Bangladesh 188 million (2010 – 147 million) and Egypt 105 million (2010 – 80 million). This will put a tremendous burden on the socio-economic infrastructures of these poor countries, except for Indonesia which is considered a developing country. India, which is a non-Muslim country, will face an overall increase in its population for both Hindus and Muslims and may face economic challenges too.

209

Today, except for a few oil producing countries in the Middle East, North Africa and Central Asia, the majority of the Muslim countries are dependent on economic support from the World Bank, IMF, USA, Europe and a few Arab countries (Saudi Arabia, Qatar, UAE and Kuwait). They are suffering from the lack of visionary leaders, tolerance, democracy, literacy, work ethics, manufacturing base, educational systems, basic opportunities, and moral and ethical values. Furthermore, corruption and un-proportional spending on the military drains the few economic resources at their disposal. This situation led Recep Tayyip Erdogan, Prime Minister of Turkey to make this remark. *"The Muslim world and its subset the countries of the Middle East have been left behind in the marathon of political, economic and human development. For that, there is a tendency to blame others as the primary cause."* [1]

This is a predicament of the Muslim world that the rest of the world cannot easily ignore when it has the potential of affecting the rest of humanity adversely. There are no simple solutions, as it is difficult to force these sovereign nations to follow a certain path that may have worked well elsewhere. All countries that have risen economically had to push from within to reach the pinnacle. For example, the USA's becoming a superpower was engineered by the many American Exceptional Mindsets. Earlier, Great Britain became a superpower on its own. Japan and Germany after World War II rose from the ashes with monetary help from America but still it was the people who did the heavy lifting. (Quran 13:11) *"Allah does not change a people's lot unless they change what is in their hearts."* [2]

Pakistan built nuclear weapons at its own choosing in spite of opposition by Western powers. Instead of following the militaristic path, what if Pakistan had followed the economic path to achieve glory? Pakistan could have built universities to advance in science and technology; factories to produce goods (consumer & industrial) for export; industry to create jobs for the masses to increase the standard of living and affluent citizens to avoid the birth of extremism.

Iran is now following the same path to achieve the glory of its past through a militaristic path. With its rich cultural history, Iran probably has the most potential to become an economic superpower comparable to Japan and Germany. Education, intellect and yearning for learning are deeply rooted. However, the dictatorial regime of the Shah and the autocratic theocratic government in place since 1979 has weakened the human spirit and sapped the Persian energies. Iran must forget the defeat of the antiquity days by Alexander the Great and Arabs in the 6th century, so it can take its rightful place on the world stage through peaceful means.

The oil rich Muslim countries of Saudi Arabia, UAE, Qatar and Kuwait must change their emphasis from consumerism and tall buildings, shopping malls, and big airports to an industrial base with one goal: to manufacture the best products that world has ever seen. This should be combined with an emphasis on innovations, space exploration, advances in medical science and helping poor countries. (Quran 2:177) *"It is not righteousness that ye turn your faces towards east or west; but it is righteousness- to believe in Allah and the Last Day, and the Angels, and the Book, and the Messengers; to spend of your substance, out of love for Him, for your kin, for orphans, for the needy, for the wayfarer, for those who ask, and for the ransom of slaves".* [3]

It goes without saying that there is still hope for the Muslim world granted they wake up, let go of their violent ways and once again, as in the Golden Age of Islam, devour the knowledge that is currently available and being developed by the West and other nations. (Quran 20:114) *""O my Lord! advance me in knowledge."."* [4]. Build the best educational institutions for higher learning and provide free tuitions to the needy. (Quran 45:13) *"And He has subjected to you, as from Him, all that is in the heavens and on earth: behold in that are Signs indeed for those who reflect."* [5]

Even though Prophet Muhammad had no formal schooling due to his circumstances, he recognized the importance of human intelligence and intellect in the pursuit of higher knowledge. *"A person who follows a path for acquiring knowledge, Allah will make easy the passage to Paradise for him."* [6] What knowledge terrorists are gaining by killing innocents, none whatsoever as they fall deeper in the abyss of ignorance. Prophet Mohammad emphasized the pursuit of knowledge on many occasion, *"A Muslim will not tire of knowledge until he reaches Heaven."* [7]

The Exceptional Mindset in the Muslim world should erect structures that support the mind and foster the intellect and the genius that can create prosperity and peace. They should seriously consider rooting out the talk of wars, dogmas, rhetoric and violence, as they are not Islamic and lead to the precipitous ignorance holding Muslims from reaching Heaven.

COMPARATIVE DATA

On the economic front, Muslim nations are clearly lacking, especially if one takes out oil revenues that reach close to one trillion dollars by some estimates. Let us look at a few numbers to evaluate the condition of the Muslim nations.

POPULATION

- *World*   *- 6.9 billion (Pew Forum 2010 data)*
- *Muslim*   *- 1.6 billion (Pew Forum 2010 data)*
- *Muslim %*   *- 23.47%*

One out of five persons on this planet is a Muslim. As stated earlier, Muslims are increasing at a rate that is twice that of non-Muslims. This will dramatically increase the demand for food, shelter, jobs, and health care that a majority of Muslim nations today are not equipped to handle. This will result in an economic failure, leading to an astronomical rise to chaos and violence.

MANUFACTURING

- *World*   *- $10 trillion (World Bank National Accounts Data)*
- *Muslim*   *- $687 billion (World Bank National Accounts Data)*
- *Muslim %*   *- 6.86%*

These World Bank "Statistics by Country" cover from 2003 to 2009. The Muslim manufacturing of roughly 7% output is pretty low. The USA manufacturing output is $2.3 trillion with a population of 300 million, Japan's is $1.7 trillion with a population of 127 million, China's is $1.4 trillion with a population of 1.3 billion and Germany's is $470 billion with a population of 82 million. The fundamental reasons for low output are: a lack of good educational systems, a war-centric mentality, chaining masses to the distorted, a lack of freedom and basic economic, social and democratic infrastructure. According to an article by Dr. Farrukh Saleem, a Pakistani columnist compares Muslims to other groups in his article "*Why are Muslims so Powerless,*" "*Every fifth human being is a Muslim; for every single Hindu there are two*

Muslims, for every Buddhist there are two Muslims and for every Jew there are one hundred Muslims. Ever wondered why Muslims are so powerless?" [8]

Dr. Saleem puts the reason clearly on lack of education *"There are 57 member-countries of the Organisation of Islamic Conference (OIC), and all of them put together have around 500 universities; one university for every three million Muslims. The United States has 5,758 universities and India has 8,407. In 2004, Shanghai Jiao Tong University compiled an 'Academic Ranking of World Universities', and intriguingly, not one university from Muslim-majority states was in the top-500."* [9]

GROSS DOMESTIC PRODUCT (GDP) [10]

- *World*   *- $70 trillion (International Monetary Fund, 2011 estimates)*
- *Muslim*   *- $5.7 trillion (International Monetary Fund, 2011 estimates)*
- *Muslim %*   *- 8.1%*

In comparison with the GDP of other countries, the USA is $15 trillion, China $7.3 trillion, Japan $5.8 trillion and Germany $3.6 trillion. Canada, with a population of around 30 million, has a GDP of $1.7 trillion or 30% of entire Muslim GDP. [11]

MILITARY SPENDING [12]

- *World*   *- $1.5 trillion (SIPRI Military Expenditures, 2010 data)*
- *Muslim*   *- $146 billion (SIPRI Military Expenditures, 2010 data)*
- *Muslim %*   *- 9.47%*

According to SIPRI data for 2010, Saudi Arabia spent the most among Muslim countries with $46 billion, followed by Turkey at $18 billion, United Arab Emirates at $16 billion, Iran at $7 billion, Algeria at $5.5 billion and Pakistan at $5 billion. Obviously, these numbers are much lower when compared to the USA with its $711 billion, China with $143 billion, Russia with $72 billion and the United Kingdom with $63 billion. The difference is that the non-Muslim countries have resources and a well-developed infrastructure (economic, educational and science) to support their military spending. However, the Muslim countries' notion of becoming a mighty military force will not be supported without first developing strong industrial, economic, manufacturing, scientific and educational infrastructures. The $146 billion currently wasted can be put to better use but due to the absence of Exceptional Mindset, unfortunately this waste will continue.

According to Organization of the Islamic Conference (OIC), *"In 2011, having accounted for 22.8 per cent of the world total population, the 57 OIC member countries produced only 10.9 per cent of the world total GDP – expressed in current USD and based on PPP."* [13]

The Muslim world should clearly see from the numbers above that they are lagging individually or collectively. Each Muslim nation needs a new mindset and a 180-degree reversal of their current misdirection. In the short run, it is fine to build tall modern buildings and big malls with ski slopes (Dubai, Abu Dhabi, Saudi Arabia) on the strength of a single product: "OIL." In the long run, however, buildings and malls do not produce the infrastructures discussed earlier. The consumerism alone does not create a productive citizenry that can keep a nation strong. Citizens must not be trained as consumers but must also be engaged in earning a self-worth through the fruit of their labor and intellect. This can only be achieved through becoming a peaceful nation, allowing freedom of speech, tolerance, equal women rights and the promotion of education with an emphasis on science and technology.

20TH CENTURY MUSLIM LEADERS

In over a hundred years, Muslims have produced only a few leaders who were forward thinkers and had an Exceptional Mindset: Kemal Ataturk, the secular founder of modern Turkey; Mohammad Ali Jinnah, the secular founder of Pakistan; and Anwar al-Sadat of Egypt. Anwar al-Sadat did the unthinkable when he flew to Israel in November 1977 in search of peace. The peace came, and Sadat signed a peace accord with Prime Minister Menachem Begin in March 1979. Sadly, Sadat was assassinated in 1981 for walking the right path and showing the courage as a statesman.

Unfortunately, the Muslim world has been endowed with autocratic, greedy, corrupt, inept and sometimes megalomaniac leaders. A few of them are discussed below in no particular order:

Muammar Gaddafi of Libya came to power in 1969 and died a violent death in 2011. Ruling over 40 years, he was a megalomaniac and could not separate himself from power. The Libya that had once been ruled by the Phoenicians, Greeks, Romans and Moors discovered oil in 1959 and soon became the richest country in Africa. Gaddafi had ample resources to make Libya an economic powerhouse, but instead he became a dictator with very little individual civil rights afforded to his countrymen. He was in the process of grooming one of his sons to take over after his death.

Saddam Hussain of Iraq officially came to power in 1979, but he had been a strongman years earlier. He was an autocrat and a tyrant who killed thousands of Iraqi Shia and Kurds. He fought an eight year war with Iran (1980–1988), lost and was defeated badly in the first gulf war. He was hanged in 2003 after the second defeat by the USA. He was grooming one of his sons to take over after his death. Listed below are some of the numbers from the disastrous Iraq–Iran war.

Iraq–Iran War Casualties and Economic Losses–*"During the eight years between Iraq's formal declaration of war on September 22, 1980, and Iran's acceptance of a cease-fire with effect on July 20, 1988, at the very least half a million and possibly twice as many troops were killed on both sides, at least half a million became permanent invalids, some 228 billion dollars were directly expended, and more than 400 billion dollars of damage (mostly to oil facilities, but also to cities) was inflicted, mostly by artillery barrages."* [14]

General Zia-ul-Haq of Pakistan came to power in 1977 after deposing Prime Minister Zulfiqar Bhutto. Zia hanged Bhutto in 1979 after a mockery of a trial. In the name of Islam, Zia created jihadi movements and ruled with an iron-fist for eleven years until he died in a mysterious plane crash in 1988. To this day, Pakistan has not recovered from the extremist movements set in motion by Zia.

Yasser Arafat of the PLO was born in Egypt and established the FATAH movement in 1959 while working in Kuwait as a civil engineer. The PLO was created in 1964 during an Arab League Summit in Cairo. He was an intelligent man but an inept leader who fought with both Muslims and Jews. King Hussain of Jordan expelled the PLO in 1970 during Black September after Arafat tried to set up a parallel government in Jordan. In June 1983, Syrian dictator Hafez al-Assad expelled Arafat from Syria and put him on a plane to Tunis. At the time, Arafat blamed his expulsion on a Syria-Libyan plot to take over the PLO. Arafat died from a mysterious illness while being treated at Percy Military Hospital of Paris, France. His body has been ex-humed recently to determine if poisoning was the cause.

Hafez al-Assad was a Syrian dictator that gained power in 1971 and ruled until June 2000. He belonged to a minority Alawite sect, an offshoot of the Shia Islamic sect. Hafez al-Assad eliminated all political dissidents through torture and execution. He is accused of killing between 10,000–25,000 civilians in Hama in 1982. He occupied Lebanon from 1976 to 1985. Surprisingly, he joined the U.S.-led first Gulf War against Saddam in 1990–1991. His son Bashar al-Assad succeeded after his death. During the Syrian civil war that started in March 2011 it is estimated that Bashar and his military are responsible for over 60,000 Syrians killed, over a million displaced and hundreds of cities destroyed with the total damage reaching billions of dollars.

Hosni Mubarak of Egypt became President after Anwar Sadat was as-sassinated in October 1981. He was a good man who turned corrupt and greedy, and he was ousted from power in 2011. He was grooming his son to take over after his death. ABC News reported in 2011 that the "experts be-lieved the personal wealth of Mubarak and his family to be between US $40 billion and $70 billion acquired through military contracts made during his time as an air force officer." [15]

Asif Ali Zardari is the current president of Pakistan. He grew up in a modest family and acquired most of his money while his late wife Benazir Bhutto served twice as Prime Minister of Pakistan. He is currently worth $1.8 billion. In June 2012, Pakistani Prime Minister Mr. Gilani was disqual-ified by the Supreme Court of Pakistan on charges of "contempt of court" when he refused the Court's demand to send a letter to Swiss authorities to reopen a money laundering case against President Zardari. Mr. Zardari had spent time in prison from 1997 to 2004 on the charges of corruption and money laundering.

Nawaz Sharif held the position of Prime Minister of Pakistan twice in the 1990's. He was deposed by military strongman General Pervez Musharraf. Sharif is worth around $1.4 billion. He came from a middle upper class fam-ily, however, and has profited handsomely along with his politician brother Shahbaz. The struggling family business grew from one single struggling foundry to a conglomerate of 30 businesses engaged in textile, sugar, paper, and steel with estimated revenue of over a half a billion dollars.

The Dawn Newspaper dated July 16th, 2012 reported that a money laundering case has been filed by the National Accountability Bureau (NAB) of Pakistan in the amount of $32 million against the Sharif brothers.

Gaddafi, Zia, Saddam, Assad and Mubarak all had a chance to make their countries great. They either grabbed power through force or were unwilling to give up power peacefully while promoting their sons to take over. The irony is that the current crop of Muslim leaders is neither better nor has the interest of their citizens.

Europeans came out of the dark ages without any previous model to follow. Even though it took them a few hundred years, Europeans and later Americans were able to set the systems in motion that made their countries strong and uplifted their citizens economically. Japan, China, South Korea, Singapore, Vietnam, Hong Kong, Thailand, etc. have copied the western model to prosperity. Why can't Muslim leaders do the same? With the Internet Age, every little detail about the western economic model is available on the web.

What is keeping them from learning and modifying the various economic growth models at their disposal? Is it corruption? Is it culture? Is it greed? Is it the illiteracy rate? Is it the Mullah Community? Is it a lack of democratic systems? Is it autocratic regimes? Is it the war mentality? Is it a superiority complex? Is it an inferiority complex? Is it suffocation of freedom? Is it the lack of individual rights? Is it a combination of all of the above? Whatever the answer or answers may be, in the absence of viable leaders, Muslims will have to find answers to their lack of progress and undesirable economic conditions. The rulers are either incapable or not willing to change the lot of their subjects.

Muslims can follow the peaceful message of Islam instead of Ignorance, which has resulted in the mushrooming of the Violent Mindset. Today's Muslim world is quick to blame everyone except themselves for all their misfortunes. For over a hundred years now, they have contributed nothing to the modern world except misery, corruption and violence. Their dictators, despots and tyrants have squandered trillions of dollars; killed millions of their own citizens through war or poverty; have stolen billions of dollars from their own citizens; and have created a Muslim image, justifiably, of that of a monster.

Collectively, Muslims lack the critical mass of Exceptional Mindset. Intellectualism is frowned upon in the Muslim world. The sectarian hatred within the Muslim world is killing scores of people daily. Muslims have not invented anything of value since the 1300s. The governments are corrupt; public servants are stealing public property; educational systems are promoting ignorance; individual rights are trampled daily; the mind is not free and so is rotting; thirty-nine countries out of the forty-seven Muslim countries are run by the dictators; art and literature is frowned upon; compassion, kindness and respect, the true message of Islam, is rejected openly. Unless Muslims look in the mirror and stop blaming others for their sordid state, they will never get out of the rabbit hole that they have pushed themselves into.

Muslims have not managed well in their own countries. Pakistan lost Bangladesh (formerly East Pakistan) because of their mistreatment of Bengalis. It was Pakistani soldiers who raped thousands of Bengali women and murdered hundreds of thousands of Bengali children and men. Saudis and Bahrainis are killing Shias; the Taliban are killing Shia in Pakistan; Bashar al-Assad is killing Sunnis in Syria; and in Iraq, Shia and Sunni are killing each other. There is a cloud of darkness over the Muslim world that can only be lifted after foreswearing violence and by finding compromises to resolve issues not only among themselves but also with their worldly outlook.

Prophet Mohammad came to rid the dwellers of the desert from ignorance, but Muslims seem oblivious to this. Muslim dictators and Mullahs are using hate-baiting in pursuit of their own selfish and destructive causes.

WEALTH COMPARSION OF MUSLIM LEADERS VERSUS WESTERN LEADERS

Muslim rulers treat their countries as their personal property since they achieve power through the back door or through heredity. One wonders how is it possible for them to plunder and loot the property of their own citizens without fear of God or the Islamic religion they practice. Compare their wealth with the Western leaders who are elected by their citizens and can be removed through ballots of citizen voting. It is interesting to note that Queen Elizabeth, one of the oldest and well-established monarchies, is worth far less than many of the rulers of the Muslim world.

The same freedoms and liberties that we hold precious as Americans are withheld from the good Muslims of countries where they are held captive by the Extremists who ironically in turn enjoy their twisted freedoms and liberties by force feeding their beliefs to the masses.

MUSLIM LEADER WEALTH [16]

1. *Hosni Mubarak, former president of Egypt– $70 billion*

2. *Mahathir Mohammad, former Prime Minister of Malaysia– $44 billion*

3. *Colonel Gaddafi, former leader of Libya– $35 billion plus*

4. *President Suharto, former president of Indonesia– $35 billion*

5. *Sultan Haji Hassanal Bolkiah, Sultan of Brunei– $20 billion*

6. *King Abdullah Bin Abdul-Aziz, King of Saudi Arabia– $18 billion plus*

7. *Sheikh Khalifa bin Zayed Al Nahyan, Abu Dhabi– $15 billion*

8. *Zine el-Abidine Ben Ali, former president of Tunisia– $7.8 billion*

9. *Sheikh Mohammed bin Rashid Al Maktoum, ruler of Dubai– $4 billion*

10. *Hamid bin Khalifa al-Thani, Emir of Qatar– $2.5 billion*

11. *Mohammed VI, King of Morocco– $2.5 billion*

12. *Saddam Hussein, deceased President of Iraq– $2 billion*

13. *Asif Ali Zardari, President of Pakistan– $1.8 billion*

14. *Yasser Arafat, deceased leader of PLO– $300 million*

THE WESTERN LEADERS' WEALTH [17]

1. *Queen Elizabeth of United Kingdom– $450 million*

2. *Tony Blair former Prime Minister of United Kingdom– $3 million*

3. *Jacques Chirac former President of France– $9 million*

4. *King Juan Carlos of Spain– $5 million*

5. *Junichiro Koizumi former Prime Minister of Japan– $2 million*

6. *Gerhard Schroder former Chancellor of Germany– $1 million*

7. *Jimmy Carter, former president of USA– $5 million*

8. *Ronald Regan former President of USA– $4 million*

9. *George H. W. Bush former President of USA– $20 million*

10. *Bill Clinton former President of USA– $17.4 to $53.7 million*

11. *George W. Bush former President of USA– $15 million*

12. *Barack Obama, President of USA– $10.1 million*

It is important for Muslims all over the world to put to rest the silly conspiracy theories that are abound and promoted to brainwash their minds. The world is not against them; the "Conspirators" are their own rulers.

CONTRADICTORY MUSLIM BEHAVIOR

It is ironic that if a Muslim is killed by a non-Muslim they will rise up while they murder many in their own backyard without remorse or ill feelings. Sunnis are killing Sunnis and Shias, but no shame is ever expressed by the killing party.

Due to high unemployment in Muslim countries, demonstrations against worthless causes are a routine affair. The Israeli–Palestinian conflict, pictures or a movie about Prophet Mohammad or derogatory remarks about Islam are the hot buttons that will bring unemployed Muslims onto the street. They throw stones and fire bombs. They destroy buses and shops that provide them transportation and goods. These violent demonstrations always produce a few deaths, several injured and millions of dollars' worth of property loss.

If someone asks them why are you doing this, the angry response is that Americans and Jews are killing Muslims. They are not interested in the actual cause or logical reasoning but never shy away from the full display of their brutality. The reasons for this irrational behavior include: brainwashing from their early childhood; the distortion of history, in which Muslims no matter how inept, deserve to rule the world; and violence sanctioned by the Mullah instead of peace.

Startlingly, Muslims are not welcomed by other Muslim countries for permanent immigration. Most of them go as laborers and few are given white collar jobs. In the Arab world, most non-Arab Muslims are called "Beggars" (Maskeen). A visa is difficult to get, as is a job, and marriage to a local Muslim girl is out of the question. In order to start a business, a local sponsor is required, and becoming a citizen of that brotherly Arab country is impossible. In reality, most of them are treated worse than animals.

Compare this to America, Canada and Western Europe where Muslims are treated well. They can start or buy a business, can be admitted to a top university, join the military, marry a local girl, become a citizen, can be elected to a public office, buy a fancy house and even acquire a National Football Team. The Jacksonville Jaguars football franchise in Jacksonville, Florida is owned by Shahid Khan, an American Pakistani. So why is it that a good number of Muslim immigrants harbor ill feelings toward their new country, America, when they are treated so much better than they would be in their own birth country or for that matter any Muslim country on this planet, is most puzzling!

Not all but quite a few Muslim-Americans espouse negative feelings toward the USA with the understanding that there is a difference between constructively criticizing (fine) and wishing ill feelings (not fine). It is incomprehensible that a person or persons who came to this country voluntarily and freely took the "Oath of Allegiance" in order to become a U.S. citizen would carry venom on their tongues against their new adopted country. Are they hypocrites or is hypocrisy part of the Muslim Psyche?

They enjoy all the benefits accorded to a citizen of our democratic society, both monetary and social. Then the question is: why do they harbor negative feelings? The one most common response given is the American support of Israel or the Jewish people and ignoring of Palestinian people. This is a totally absurd, irrational and illogical answer.

There is no doubt that if the American government eliminates visa requirements, most of Mullahs who preach hate, thump their chests and burn American flag would be the first in line with their passports to get visas stamped for the USA. These Muslims are hypocrites, double faced and churlish people who have totally lost touch with reality. Most of them follow no real teachings of Islam or commonly accepted human mores. They are brainwashed to commit violence for all the wrong causes without any rationalization.

PART VI

CHAPTER 11

THE JEWISH MYTH
AMONG MUSLIMS

"Energy is the basis of everything. Every Jew, no matter how insignificant, is engaged in some decisive and immediate pursuit of a goal... It is the most perpetual people of the earth..."

—JOHANN WOLFGANG VON GOETHE,
GERMAN DRAMATIST, NOVELIST AND POET (1749–1832)

ISRAEL AND THE JEWISH MYTH

OVERALL, MUSLIMS HAVE NEGATIVE FEELINGS towards Israel and Jewish people even though until 100 years ago the relations among both were friendly. Is it the Israeli–Palestinian conflict, several defeats suffered in the hands of Israeli military or the not-so-kind treatment of West Bank civilians by the Israeli Government? The issues are complex, and solutions seem to be even more elusive. America is a superpower and has its own agenda designed by its elected officials.

American Muslims must become loyal to this country and express their feelings at the ballot box. They may have nostalgic feelings about the old country they left behind but must not espouse negative feelings against America solely based on the support of Israel. The world was not created for only Muslims; there are other religions and ethnic groups, and American policies are not driven based on the interest of Muslims alone.

Here are some of the facts about Jews versus Muslims that hopefully will provide a better understanding:

1. The worldwide Jewish population is around 15 million vs. 1.6 billion Muslims

2. One in every 514 people in the world is Jewish vs. 1 in every 23 is Muslims

3. There is only one Jewish country vs. 47 Muslim countries in the world who are unable to manage themselves properly

4. Jews represent .02% the world population vs. 23% for Muslims

5. There are 6 million Jews living in Israel and the Arab population is over 300 million Muslims

6. Israel population 6 million, revenues $68.29 billion (2011 est.) and Expenses $75.65 billion (2011 est.)

7. Pakistan population 177 million, revenues $26.7 billion (2011 est.) and Expenses $39.9 billion (2011 est.)

8. Iran population 75 million, revenues $110.9 billion (2010 est.) Expenses 89.98 billion (2010 est.)

9. Egypt population 83 million, revenues $46.82 billion (2010 est.) and Expenses $64.19 billion (2010 est.)

10. Per capita income of Pakistan $1,300, Egypt $6,600, Iran $13,000 and Israel $32,000

It can be clearly seen that Israel, with only 6 million people, is more capable and productive than Pakistan, Iran and Egypt. If one takes out the oil production of Iran then Iran is even worse off in comparison. It is difficult to comprehend why Muslims blame everything on Jewish conspiracies. One should always look in the mirror first, and it is more of an inferiority complex that leads to these foolish assumptions.

Iran is one of the oldest civilizations with a splendid past. It is rich with culture and folklores that generally make the nation strong. It has an abundance of intellectuals and an educated elite class; however, it has fallen prey to the same disease affecting other Muslim countries with Mullahs. It has embarked upon a costly path to glorification by acquiring nuclear weapons instead of becoming an industrial giant through the production of automobiles, TVs, smart phones, heavy machinery, etc.

Egypt is also rich in history with the fabulous riches of the Pharaoh, Cleopatra's charms, the land of the fertile Nile and the spectacular Pyramids; however, it is totally dependent on the aid it receives from the USA ($2–3 billion per year), World Bank, IMF (International Monetary Fund) and tiny Qatar (population less than 2 million) to survive. What happened? Former President Mubarak hung on for 32 years and was grooming his son to take over. Was he a President or a King? Now the replacement government is more interested in practicing religion than surviving. Egypt needs to adopt a mindset wherein the answer does not lie in Sharia but in higher education, production, science and technology. Furthermore, setting up factories to deliver the best automobiles, TVs, smart phones or heavy machinery may not surpass the miracles of Pyramids but at least it would woo the users.

So, let us go back to the Jews, whom the majority of Muslims blame for their wretched state of affairs. The Jews do not actively seek the conversion of others to their religion. Only two religious groups, the Muslims and Christians, are in a race to convert everyone on this planet. Overall, the numbers for Jews are either constant or declining. The Christian population in Europe and American is at a zero birth. Only devout Catholics in Central and South America, Asia and Africa are producing more children. Here is an interesting study from the Pew Forum on global population. According to Pew, "*The world's Muslim population is expected to increase by about 35% in the next 20 years, rising from 1.6 billion in 2010 to 2.2 billion by 2030, according to new population projections by the Pew Research Center's Forum on Religion & Public Life. Globally, the Muslim population is forecast to grow at about twice the rate of the non-Muslim population over the next two decades – an average annual growth rate of 1.5% for Muslims, compared with 0.7% for non-Muslims. If current trends continue, Muslims will make up 26.4% of the world's total projected population of 8.3 billion in 2030, up from 23.4% of the estimated 2010 world population of 6.9 billion.*" [1]

There are over 44 million Muslims in Europe and 2.6 million in the USA. Muslims have all the tools in these civilized societies to progress, prosper and become enlightened. They have been given an opportunity in these free countries to advance both economically and intellectually. As evident from the beginning of time, the world was designed for people who can compete and get ahead, and there is an opportunity that should not be missed by harboring illogical feelings.

Both Israelis and Palestinians have to work together to find a permanent solution. There is no doubt that the misery experienced by the citizens of West Bank and Gaza inflames hatred and passion. There is no solution in violence and unequal treatment. Thousands of children and women were killed because men do not have enough sense to cease the bloodshed. It is time to try a new approach towards achieving everlasting "peace" by renouncing all violence in the land considered "holy" by all: Jews, Christians and Muslims.

THE JEWISH HISTORY

Jewish history is full of trials and tribulations. By reading it, one realizes that Jews have been oppressed by Christians and Muslims since the 4th century. It would be helpful for the Muslim world to read Jewish history. By analyzing their plight and their need for the migration to the land of their ancestors, it makes sense why Jews need their own state.

Jewish history is nearly 6,000 years old and started in the south Mediterranean, encompassing land surrounding the Tigris, Euphrates and Nile rivers and the countries of Babylon, Egypt, Canaan (present day Israel, Jordan, Lebanon and Palestine). Jews consider themselves descendants of the ancient people of Israel in the land of Canaan. Their lineage goes back to Noah, Abraham, Isaac, Jacob and Moses and from the 12 tribes from the sons of Jacob, Reuven, Shimon, Levi, Yehuda, Yissachar, Zevulun, Dan, Gad, Naftali, Asher, Yosef and Benyamin.

After a famine in Canaan, 11 sons settled in Egypt with their tribes at the behest of their 12th brother Yusuf. As the story is told by Judaism, Christianity and Islam, Joseph (Yusuf, Yosef) was sold by his brothers due to their jealousy and open fondness shown to him by their father Jacob. Joseph ended up in Egypt as a slave but rose to become a high ranking official in Pharaoh's court. In Egypt, the prosperity of Jews did not last for long, and eventually they were enslaved by the Pharaoh for 400 years.

Moses came from the Levi tribe and is recognized as a Prophet by the Jews, Christians and Muslims. He freed the Jews from Egyptian bondage. It is mentioned in the Bible and Quran, the Nile River was parted, and Moses led his people to the ancestral land of Canaan. The event is known as the Exodus and *"marks the formation of Israel as a political nation in Canaan, in 1400 B.C.E."* [2]

According to the Bible, prior to conquering Canaan, Jews wandered in the Sinai desert for 40 years. They received the Ten Commandments, and Moses had a famous encounter with God at Mount Sinai. Canaan provided a homeland to the Jews and ultimately resulted in the founding of three Abrahamic religions (Judaism, Christianity and Muslims) and a long era of conflicts that still exists today.

Around 1000 B.C.E., Saul (Talut in Quran) established the Israeli Kingdom that continued with David (Daud in Quran) and his son Solomon (Suleiman in Quran), who built the temple. Jerusalem, considered holy by all three Abrahamic religions, first appears in the book of Joshua (Yusha ibn Nun in Quran). *"During its long history, Jerusalem has been destroyed twice, besieged 23 times, attacked 52 times, and captured and recaptured 44 times."* [3]

With the Roman conquest of the southern Mediterranean, Jews were either sold into slavery or found themselves as second class citizens in the Roman Empire. The early Christians blamed Jews for the crucifixion of Christ. Therefore, they were not treated well. Once Rome became Christian, the Christians worked diligently to convert Jews to Christianity. While Jews were trying to protect themselves from the Roman and Byzantine Empires, Islam exploded into prominence. By 636, Levant (Israel, Jordan, Lebanon and Syria) had become part of the Muslim world. Ironically, Jews were treated better in the Muslim world than in the Christian Byzantine Empire, as a great number of Jews fled Christian Byzantine territories to Islamic territories. This amicable situation between the Jews and the Muslims would last well into the early 19th century. *"The size of the Jewish community in the Byzantine Empire was not affected by attempts by some emperors (most notably Justinian) to forcibly convert the Jews of Anatolia to Christianity, as these attempts met with very little success."* [4]

Jews (identifiable by the Judenhut they were required to wear) were massacred by Christian knights during the First Crusade in France and Germany, as illustrated in this French Bible from 1250: *"Along with the Arabs and the Turks, the Jews were among the most vigorous defenders of Jerusalem against the Crusaders. When the city fell, the Crusaders gathered the Jews in a synagogue and burned them. The Jews almost single-handedly defended Haifa against the Crusaders, holding out in the besieged town for a whole month (June-July 1099)."* [5] It is a well-accepted fact that Jews were overall treated better by Muslims than Christians.

James Carroll wrote, *"Jews accounted for 10% of the total population of the Roman Empire. By that ratio, if other factors had not intervened, there would be 200 million Jews in the world today, instead of something like 13 million."* [6]

Jews were by and large persecuted in Europe, frequently massacred and exiled from the European Christian world, especially during crusades. Their properties were seized, and they were expelled and banished from France, Austria and England. This led them to migrate to Poland and other Eastern European countries. Finally, Christian rulers saw Jews as suppliers of capital, and money lending fell in the hands of Jews, allowing them some protection in society.

The ejection of the Moors from Spain by Catholics also caused the Jewish expulsion as a result of the Spanish Inquisition. These Jews mainly ended up in the Muslim Ottoman Empire and were treated with respect. In the Ottoman Empire, Jews quickly became masters of trade, finance and diplomacy. *"In the 16th century especially, the Jews were the most prominent under the millets, the apogee of Jewish influence could arguably be the appointment of Joseph Nasi to Sanjak-bey (governor, a rank usually only bestowed upon Muslims) of the island of Naxos."* [7]

Adolf Hitler, Christian by birth with his Nazi party, carried out the most heinous crime of the 20th century by exterminating over six million European Jews. To avoid this persecution, Jews fled to the USA, Palestine, Soviet Union and other parts of the world. The Holocaust affected Jews gravely, but it also created a feeling of shame and empathy for the Jewish people. This led to the creation of the Jewish state of Israel.

During the late 1800s, the Zionism movement gave credence to a Jewish state to fulfill the biblical prophecies. Theodor Herzl was behind this charge. Because the Ottoman Empire chose the wrong side and Levant was lost to the British and French, the creation of Israel became a viable option with the Balfour Declaration of 1917. On May 14, 1948, Israel became an independent country, and the Jewish dream of returning home after seventeen hundred years was achieved.

It would be unfair not to mention that millions of Palestinians were displaced, and their properties were seized by the Jews migrating from Europe after World War II. Unfortunately for Palestinians, they never had good leaders who could face the new reality on the ground. The Muslim propensity for violence did not lend itself to a positive solution. In order to deal with the violence, Israel has at times responded with belligerency. The bottom line is that the violence needs to end. Palestine and the Muslim world need to accept Israel and renounce all violence against Jews and all human beings.

The Muslim arguments that Jews are involved in a conspiracy against them and control all of the media while manipulating the message are nothing but pure rhetoric. Muslims can work to become better conspirators, and with their 1.5 billion population, they can buy or create media giants, wherein they can present their point of view effectively in this era of the Internet, YouTube and Facebook.

The Muslim psyche to declare Jews as citizens non-grata is based on a false assumption. The teachings against Jews in Muslim schools and Madrassas are reprehensible. Jews have been persecuted for centuries, displaced all over the world, do not believe in converting anyone and have only one country of their own. Let them live in peace.

PART VII

CHAPTER 12

FINAL THOUGHTS

"The road must be trod, but it will be very hard. And neither strength nor wisdom will carry us far upon it. This quest may be attempted by the weak with as much hope as the strong. Yet it is oft the course of deeds that move the wheels of the world: Small hands do them because they must, while the eyes of the great are elsewhere."

—J.R.R. TOLKIEN, THE FELLOWSHIP OF THE RING

IT IS EASY FOR MUSLIMS to boast about the "Golden Age" and the inventions of over 1,000 years ago. When you inquire about recent inventions, there is generally a feeble smile followed by some irrational answer. In the past, I was asked a similar question and found no answer; so I started to research this dilemma. After an extensive search, I have painfully come to a conclusion that Muslims gave up the desire to "innovate" many centuries ago. Why? There are many explanations. Let us examine the background and few of the reasons.

There is no doubt that the Muslim period until 12th century was open and creative, as proven by the Golden Age. The Muslim world became rigid after the Mongol destruction of Baghdad in 1258. It slowly became theocratic, autocratic and unadoptable to the changes all around its realm. Muslims were forbidden to ask questions since all answers could be found in the Islamic doctrines, notably in the rote memorization of the Quran and Hadith. Critical thinking that leads to reason and investigation was no longer the accepted mode of higher intellect and was considered heresy.

Interestingly, the Ottoman and Mughal Empires along with the Moors of Spain totally failed to recognize the gradual European rise from the dark ages to enlightenment. They either felt secure in their domains or did not have the Exceptional Mindset to evaluate their looming downfall and the rise of the West.

- Muslim world inventions since the 15th century are ZERO.
- USA and West inventions since the 15th century are in the THOUSANDS.
- Jewish inventions since 15th century are in the HUNDREDS.
- Muslim world Nobel Prizes in Sciences are TWO.
- USA & West Nobel Prizes in Sciences are over FIVE HUNDRED.
- Jewish Nobel Prizes in Sciences are over EIGHTY.

This is no insult intended to the Muslim world, as I have personally been embarrassed by the lack of innovations. Muslims need to look in the mirror and take the necessary corrective action. They are as capable as anyone else if they can fully understand how to use the wisdom given to them by their Creator.

Message To The Immigrant Muslims

A number of Muslim immigrants moving to the West are not integrating well, either through their own choosing or the lack of viable opportunities of the host country (mostly in Europe). The USA is the exception to this rule, and the majority of legal immigrants attain equal rights comparable to the natural born citizen right away. Most Muslims coming to this country are well educated, respect American values and practice good citizenship.

In today's world of jihad and the resulting violence, the people seeking truth should understand the debate on both the Progressive and Extremist fronts within the Muslim world. We already know the intentions of the Extremists with their goal of Islamic Caliphates versus other Progressive Muslims arguing for interpreting religious codification and doctrines to make them compatible with the ever-changing world.

However, we should all be concerned about the small number that enjoy all the economic benefits that America has to offer yet harbor negative feelings toward this country and have been unable to cut the loyalty cord with the country they left behind. They took an "Oath of Allegiance" when they became citizens but feel no shame in wishing bad for America. These people have the potential of doing harm to this country and its people through terrorist activities.

The Muslim immigrants to America and Europe need to open their minds. They cannot continue to enjoy all the economic benefits while criticizing their new homeland. The total freedom in the new homeland does not mean that you can enjoy all the fruit that the tree provides while hating the tree. It is our duty to protect and love the tree.

Immigration to America is voluntary. No one is forced to immigrate to America, and we all came voluntarily out of our own free will. Why don't Muslims immigrate to Saudi Arabia, Iran, Egypt, Algeria, or Pakistan? The answer is very simple: those countries do not want other Muslims, and very few economic opportunities to flourish exist. Most of the immigration to the rich Muslim countries is by laborers who are afforded few rights and no chance of ever becoming citizens with full rights.

The harboring of negative feelings towards the new country is unethical and detrimental to themselves, their children and grandchildren. In the secular countries of the West, one is free to practice their faith and has many avenues at their disposal to express their disagreements. Whereas in most Muslim countries, Christians cannot build a church, Jews cannot build a synagogue and Hindus cannot build a temple. Right now, minorities are suffering in the majority of Muslim countries.

No country or government is perfect. As a superpower, the USA has global goals that may not always make all the citizens happy; nonetheless, one cannot deny that overall the USA is a paradise on earth and has done much more good in promoting cause of humanity.

Muslims can learn from the election of President Barrack Obama. It was not long ago that black Americans had no rights and were treated as second-class citizens. In less than fifty years, after self-correction through the civil right movement and support by the majority of whites, the first black person became a president of a superpower. Can Muslims honestly say that in Shia Iran, a Sunni can become a leader? Can they say that in Wahhabi Saudi Arabia, a Shia can become a leader? Of course, the answer is a resounding NO!

The Muslims living in all the Western countries need to follow the teachings of peace, compassion and moral righteousness lavishly promoted by Moses, Jesus and Mohammad.

Just as the Irish, Italian, German, Indians, and Chinese have done before them, Muslims must integrate and assimilate to become productive citizens of their new land. Muslims living in the USA should respect diversity and speak out and condemn the killing of innocent human beings and the terrorism committed by the jihadi.

Most Americans are kind, loving, charitable and the most giving people in the world; Muslim immigrants and citizens should be thankful every day for their open and accepting arms.

In Conclusion

It is no coincidence that I have come to accept and promote the USA as a great country. My story is based on my personal journey over time. My contentions are based on the experiences that I have encountered since coming to America in 1973. These are the fundamental reasons that have brought me to this reality:

1. My experiences with the Angels of the American Mid-West and their unconditional love and help.

2. The values that most Americans follow are the teachings of God.

3. The philosophy of the "Melting Pot," which has created a genuine cosmopolitan environment.

4. The common language of English that binds us all.

5. The individual freedom that most immigrants did not have in their country of origin.

6. The entrepreneurial spirit that allows anyone to achieve the "American Dream."

From the bottom of my heart and with every fiber of my being, every second that I spend in this great nation is a blessing that I will never take for granted. It was bestowed to me from the same loving compassionate God that created the Mid-West angels and friends that molded and nurtured me along the way.

I am proud and deeply humbled to be a citizen of the USA and will do anything I can to keep this country strong, diverse and a constant "beacon of hope" for the challenging world we live in.

In closing, my only wish is that this book is a small step in the search for peace or at the least a starting point for understanding and honest conversation among us all.

Appendices

LIST OF AMERICAN AND EUROPEAN INVENTIONS

AMERICAN INVENTIONS FOR A BETTER LIFE

1. Swim Fins: Invented by Benjamin Franklin, 1717 (USA)

2. Mail Order: Invented by Benjamin Franklin, 1744 (USA)

3. Lightning Rod: Invented by Benjamin Franklin, 1749 (USA)

4. Lightning Conductor: Invented by Benjamin Franklin, 1752 (USA)

5. Swivel Chair: Invented by Thomas Jefferson, 1776 (USA)

6. Bifocals: Invented by Benjamin Franklin, 1784 (USA)

7. Cotton Gin: Invented by Eli Whitney, 1793 (USA)

8. Fire Hydrant: Invented by Frederick Graff Sr., 1801 (USA)

9. Vapor-Compression Refrigeration: Invented by Oliver Evans, 1805 (USA)

10. Coffee Percolator: Invented by Benjamin Thompson Rumford, 1806 (USA)

11. Circular Saw: Invented by Tabitha Babbitt, 1813 (USA)

12. Morse Code: Invented by Alfred Vail and Samuel Morse, 1832 (USA)

13. Combine Harvester: Invented by Hiram Moore, 1834 (USA)

14. Steam Shovel: Invented by William Otis, 1835 (USA)

15. Wrench: Invented by Solymon Merrick, 1835 (USA)

16. Solar Compass: Invented by William Austin Burt, 1835 (USA)

17. Circuit Breaker: Invented by Charles Grafton Page, 1836 (USA)

18. Telegraph Code: Invented by Samuel F.B. Morse, 1837 (USA)

19. Vulcanized Rubber: Invented by Charles Goodyear, 1839 (USA)

20. Rotary Printing Press: Invented by Richard Hoe, 1843 (USA)

21. Pressure Sensitive Tape: Invented by Dr. Horace Day, 1845 (USA)

22. Printing Telegraph: Invented by Royal Earl House, 1846 (USA)

23. Printing (Rotary): Invented by Richard Hoe, 1846 (USA)

24. Gas Mask: Invented by Lewis Haslett, 1847 (USA)

25. Safety Pin: Invented by William Hunt, 1849 (USA)

26. Jackhammer: Invented by Jonathan J. Couch, 1849 (USA)

27. Safety Pin: Invented by Walter Hunt, 1849 (USA)

28. Fire Alarm Box: Invented by Dr. William Channing, 1851 (USA)

29. Burglar Alarm: Invented by Edwin T. Holmes, 1851 (USA)

30. Elevator: Invented by Elisha G. Otis, 1852 (USA)

31. Burglar Alarm: Invented by Reverend Augustus Russell Pope, 1853 (USA)

32. Sewing Machine: Invented by Isaac Merritt Singer, 1853 (USA)

33. Electric Stove: Invented by George B. Simpson, 1859 (USA)

34. Escalator: Invented by Nathan Ames of Saugus, 1859 (USA)

35. Vacuum Cleaner: Invented by Daniel Hess, 1860 (USA)

36. Light Bulb: Invented by Joseph Swan, 1860, (USA)

37. Ratchet Wrench: Invented by J.J. Richardson, 1863 (USA)

38. Peanut Products: Over 450 products by George Washington Carver, 1864-1943 (USA)

39. Rotary Printing Press (Web): Invented by William Bullock, 1865 (USA)

40. Motorcycle (Steam-Powered) : Invented by Sylvester Howard Roper, 1867 (USA)

41. Paper Clip: Invented by Samuel B. Fay, 1867 (USA)

42. Barbed Wire: Invented by Lucien B. Smith, 1867 (USA)

43. Ticker Tape: Invented by Edward A. Calahan, 1867 (USA)

44. Refrigerator Car: Invented by J.B. Sutherland, 1867 (USA)

45. Tape Measure: Invented by Alvin J. Fellows, 1868 (USA)

46. Pipe Wrench: Invented by Daniel C. Stillson, 1869 (USA)

47. Can Opener (Rotary): Invented by William W. Lyman, 1870 (USA)

48. Sandblasting: Invented by Benjamin Chew Tilghman, 1870 (USA)

49. Railway Air Brake: Invented by George Westinghouse, 1872 (USA)

50. Jeans: Invented by Levi Strauss and Jacob Davis, 1873 (USA)

51. Barbed Wire: 1873: Invented by Joseph F. Glidden, 1873 (USA)

52. QWERTY: Invented by Christopher Sholes, 1874 (USA)

53. Fire Sprinkler (Automated): Invented by Henry S. Parmelee, 1874 (USA)

54. Mimeograph: Invented by Thomas Alva Edison, 1875 (USA)

55. Carpet Sweeper: Invented by Melville R. Bissell, 1876 (USA)

56. Telephone: Invented by Alexander Graham Bell, 1876 (USA)

57. Classification of Data for Libraries: Invented by Melvil Dewey, 1876 (USA)

58. Phonograph: Invented by Thomas Alva Edison, 1877 (USA)

59. District Heating: Invented by Birdsill Holly, 1877 (USA)

60. Cash Register: Invented byJames Ritty, 1879 (USA)

61. Photographic Plate: Invented by George Eastman, 1879 (USA)

62. Electric Lamp: Invented by Thomas Alva Edison, 1879 (USA)

63. Cash Register: Invented by James Ritty, 1879 (USA)

64. Metal Detector: Invented by Alexander Graham Bell, 1881 (USA)

65. Iron (Electric): Invented by Henry W. Seely, 1881 (USA)

66. Fan (Electric): Invented by Schuyler Skaats Wheeler, 1882 (USA)

67. Electric Fan: Invented by Schulyer Wheeler, 1882 (USA)

68. Skyscraper: Invented by William Le Baron Jenney, 1882 (USA)

69. Electric Flat Iron: Invented by H.W. Seeley, 1882 (USA)

70. Thermostat: Invented Warren S. Johnson, by 1883 (USA)

71. Solar Cell: Invented by Charles Fritts, 1883 (USA)

72. Skyscraper: Invented by William Le Baron Jenney, 1884 (USA)

73. Fountain Pen: Invented by Lewis E. Waterman, 1884 (USA)

74. Adding Machine: Invented by William Burroughs, 1885 (USA)

75. Photographic Film: Invented by George Eastman, 1885 (USA)

76. Telephone Directory: Invented by R. H. Donnelley, 1886 (USA)

77. Screen Door: Invented by Hannah Harger, 1887 (USA)

78. Gramophone Record: Invented by Emile Berliner, 1887 (USA)

79. Comptometer: Invented by Dorr Felt, 1887 (USA)

80. Kinetoscope: Invented by William Kennedy Laurie Dickson, 1888 (USA)

81. Drinking Straw: Invented by Marvin Stone, 1888 (USA)

82. Revolving Door: Invented by Theophilus Van Kannel, 1888 (USA)

83. Ballpoint Pen: Invented by John J. Loud, 1888 (USA)

84. Photography (On Film): Invented by John Carbutt & George Eastman, 1888 (USA)

85. Payphone: Invented by William Gray, 1889 (USA)

86. Tabulating Machine: Invented by Herman Hollerith, 1890 (USA)

87. Smoke Detector: Invented by Francis Robbins Upton and Fernando J. Dibble, 1890 (USA)

88. Rotary Dial: Invented by Almon Brown Strowger, 1891 (USA)

89. Bottle Cap: Invented by William Painter of Baltimore, 1892 (USA)

90. Dimmer: Invented by Granville Woods, 1892 (USA)

91. Zip Fastener: Invented by Whitcomb L. Judson, 1893 (USA)

92. Medical Glove: Invented by William Stewart Halsted, 1894 (USA)

93. Razor (Safety): Invented by King C. Gillette, 1895 (USA)

94. Fly Swatter: Invented by Robert R. Montgomer, 1900 (USA)

95. Assembly Line: Invented by Ransom Olds, 1901 (USA)

96. Air Conditioning: Invented by Willis Carrier, 1902 (USA)

97. Offset Printing Press: Invented by Washington Rubel, 1903 (USA)

98. Airplane: Invented by Wilbur and Orville Wright, 1903 (USA)

99. Windshield Wipers: Invented by Mary Anderson, 1903 (USA)

100. AC Power Plugs and Sockets: Invented by Harvey Hubbell, 1904 (USA)

101. Paper Shredder: Invented by Abbot Augustus Low, 1909 (USA)

102. Traffic light (Electric) : Invented by Policeman Lester Wire, 1912 (USA)

103. Electric Stove: Invented by Lloyd Groff Copeman, 1912 (USA)

104. Supermarket: Invented by Clarence Saunders, Piggly Wiggly, 1916 (USA)

105. Cloverleaf Interchange: Invented by Arthur Hale, 1916 (USA)

106. Light Switch (Toggle): Invented by William J. Newton and Morris Goldberg, 1916 (USA)

107. FM Radio: Invented by Edwin Howard Armstrong, 1918 (USA)

108. Flowchart: Invented by Frank Gilbreth, 1921 (USA)

109.   Garage Door: Invented by C.G. Johnson, 1921 (USA)

110.   Radial Arm Saw: Invented by Raymond De Walt, 1922 (USA)

111.   Instant Camera: Invented by Edwin H. Land, 1923 (USA)

112.   Food Frozen: Invented by Clarence Birdseye, 1923 (USA)

113.   Invented by William Petersen, 1924 (USA)

114.   Masking Tape: Invented by Richard G. Drew, 1925 (USA)

115.   Garage Door Opener: Invented by C.G. Johnson, 1926 (USA)

116.   Power Steering: Invented by Francis W. Davis of Waltham,
        1926 (USA)

117.   Liquid-Fuel Rocket: Invented by Dr. Robert H. Goddard,
        1926 (USA)

118.   Garbage Disposal: Invented by John W. Hammes, 1927 (USA)

119.   Electric Razor: Invented by Col. Jacob Schick, 1928 (USA)

120.   Sunglasses: Sam Foster, 1929 (USA)

121.   Frozen Food: Invented by Clarence Birdseye, 1929 (USA)

122.   Launderette: Invented by J.F. Cantrell, 1934 (USA)

123.   Black Light: Invented by William H. Byler, 1935 (USA)

124.   pH Meter: Invented by Arnold Orville Beckman, 1935 (USA)

125.   Phillips-Head Screw:–Invented by Henry F. Phillips, 1935 (USA)

126.   Richter Magnitude Scale: Invented by Charles Richter and Beno
        Gutenberg, 1935 (USA)

127.   Programming Languages: Invented by A Alonzo
        Church and Stephen Cole Kleene, 1936 (USA)

128.   Compact Fluorescent Lamp: Invented by George Inman,
        1936 (USA)

129.   Digital Computer: Invented by George Stibitz, 1937 (USA)

130.   Sunglasses (Polarized) : Invented by Edwin Land, 1937 (USA)

131.   Fiberglass: Invented by Russell Games Slayter, 1938 (USA)

132.   Xerography: Invented by Chester Floyd Carlson, 1938 (USA)

133.   Teflon: Invented by Roy Plunkett, 1938 (USA)

134.   Twist Tie: Invented by T and T Industries, Inc., 1939 (USA)

135.   First Digital Computer: Invented by John Vincent Atanasoff, 1939 (USA)

136.   Automated Teller Machine: Invented by Luther George Simjian, 1939 (USA)

137.   Deodarant, Invented by Jules Montenier, 1941 (U.S)

138.   Remote Control: Invented by Robert Adler, 1941 (USA)

139.   Microwave Oven: Invented by Percy Spencer, 1945 (USA)

140.   Cruise Control: Invented by Ralph Teetor, 1945 (USA)

141.   Space Observatory: Invented by Lyman Spitzer, 1946 (USA)

142.   Filament Tape: Invented by Cyrus Woodrow Bemmels, 1946 (USA)

143.   Credit Card: Invented by John C. Biggins, 1946 (USA)

144.   Electric Blanket: Invented by Simmons Co., 1946 (USA)

145.   Bipolar Junction Transistors: Invented by John Bardeen and Walter Brattain, 1947 (USA)

146.   Transistor: Invented by John Bardeen and Walter Brattain, 1947 (USA)

147.   Defibrillator: Invented by Dr. Claude Beck, 1947(USA)

148.   Supersonic Aircraft: Piloted by Chuck Yeager, Made by Bell Aircraft Company, 1947 (USA)

149.   Hand Dryer: Invented by A George Clemens, 1948 (USA)

150.   Transistor: Invented by John Bardeen, William Shockley and Walter Brattain, 1948 (U.S)

151.   Cable Television: Invented by John Walson and Margaret Walson, 1948 (USA)

152. Video Game: Invented by Thomas T. Goldsmith Jr. and Estle R. Mann, 1948 (USA)

153. Radiocarbon Dating: Invented by Willard F. Libby, 1949 (USA)

154. Atomic Clock: Invented by 1949 - The United States National Bureau of Standards, 1949 (USA)

155. Crash Test Dummy: Invented by Samuel W. Alderson, 1949 (USA)

156. Compiler: Invented by Grace Hopper, 1949 (USA)

157. Aerosol Paint: Invented by Ed Seymour, 1949 (USA)

158. Leaf Blower: Invented by Dom Quinto, 1950 (USA)

159. Teleprompter: Invented by Hubert Schlafly, 1950 (USA)

160. Cooler: Invented by Richard C. Laramy, 1951 (USA)

161. Correction Fluid: Invented by Bette Nesmith Graham, 1951 (USA)

162. Nuclear Power: Atomic Energy Commission to produce electricity for households, 1951 (USA)

163. Airbag: Invented by John W. Hetrick, 1952 (USA)

164. Barcode: Invented by Norman Joseph Woodland, 1952 (USA)

165. Artificial Heart: Invented by Dr. Forest Dewey Dodrill, 1952 (USA)

166. WD-40: Invented by Norm Larsen, 1953 (USA)

167. Carbonless Copy Paper: Invented by Lowell Schleicher and Barry Green, 1953 (USA)

168. Zipper Storage Bag: Invented by Robert W. Vergobbi, 1954 (USA)

169. Door (Automatic Sliding) : Invented by Dee Horton and Lew Hewitt, 1954 (USA)

170. Cardiopulmonary Resuscitation: Invented by James Elam, 1954 (USA)

171. Nuclear Submarine: Invented by Admiral Hyman Rickover, 1955 (USA)

172.   Hard Disk Drive: Invented by Reynold Johnson, 1955 (USA)

173.   Videotape: Invented by Charles Ginsburg and Ray Dolby, 1956 (USA)

174.   Wireless Microphone: Invented by Raymond A. Litke, 1957 (USA)

175.   Laser: Invented by Gordon Gould, 1957 (USA)

176.   Air-Bubble Packing: Invented by Alfred Fielding and Marc Chavannes, 1957 (USA)

177.   The First Personal Computer (IBM 610): Invented by IBM Labs, 1957 (USA)

178.   The Integrated Circuit: Invented by Jack Kilby and Robert Noyc, 1958-59 (USA)

179.   Doppler Fetal Monitor: Invented by Dr. Edward H. Hon, 1958 (USA)

180.   Integrated Circuit: Invented by Jack Kilby, 1958 (USA)

181.   Weather Satellite: Invented by NASA, 1959 (USA)

182.   Laser: Invented by Dr. Charles H. Townes, 1960 (USA)

183.   Child Safety Seat: Invented by Leonard Rivkin, 1960 (USA)

184.   Magnetic Stripe Card: Invented by Forrest Parry, 1960 (USA)

185.   Global Navigation Satellite System : Invented by Richard Kershner, 1960 (USA)

186.   Combined Oral Contraceptive Pill: Invented by Dr. Gregory Pincus, 1960 (USA)

187.   Spreadsheet (Electronic): Invented by Richard Mattessich, 1961 (USA)

188.   Biofeedback: Invented by Neal Miller, 1961 (USA)

189.   Communications Satellite: Invented by John Robinson Pierce, NASA, 1962 (USA)

190.   Light-Emitting Diode: Invented by Nick Holonyak Jr., 1962 (USA)

191.   Jet Injector: Invented by Aaron Ismach, 1962 (USA)

192. Laser Diode: Invented by Robert N. Hal, 1962 (USA)

193. Glucose Meter: Invented by Leland Clark and Ann Lyons, 1962 (USA)

194. Computer Mouse: Invented by Douglas Engelbart, 1963 (USA)

195. Balloon Catheter: Invented by Dr. Thomas Fogarty, 1963 (USA)

196. Plasma Display: Invented by Donald Bitzer, H. Gene Slottow and Robert Willson, 1964 (USA)

197. Liquid Crystal Display (Dynamic Scattering Mode) : Invented by George H. Heilmeier, 1964 (USA)

198. Kevlar: Invented by Stephanie Kwolek, 1965 (USA)

199. Hypertext: Invented by Ted Nelson, 1965 (USA)

200. Cordless Telephone: Invented by Teri Pal, 1965 (USA)

201. Minicomputer: Invented by Wesley A. Clark and Charles Molnar, 1965 (USA)

202. Compact Disc: Invented by James Russell, 1965 (USA)

203. Calculator (Hand-Held): Invented by Jack Kilby, 1967 (USA)

204. Virtual Reality: Invented by Ivan Sutherland, 1968 (USA)

205. Lunar Module: Invented by Tom Kellyas, 1969 (USA)

206. Laser Printer: Invented by Gary Starkweather, 1969 (USA)

207. Wide-Body Aircraft: Invented by Joe Sutter, The Boeing Company, 1969 (USA)

208. Taser: Invented by Jack Cover, 1969 (USA)

209. Mousepad: Invented by Jack Kelley, 1969 (USA)

210. Markup Language: Invented by Jerome H. Saltzer, 1969 (USA)

211. Wireless Local Area Network: Invented by Norman Abramson, 1970 (USA)

212. Personal Computer: Invented by John Blankenbaker, 1971 (USA)

213. Microprocessor: Invented by Ted Hoff, Federico Faggin, 1971 (USA)

214. Floppy Disk: Invented by David L. Noble, 1971 (USA)

215. String Trimmer: Invented by George Ballas, 1971 (USA)

216. E-mail: Invented by Ray Tomlinson, 1971 (USA)

217. Video Game Console: Invented by Ralph H. Baer, 1972 (USA)

218. Global Positioning System: Invented by B. Parkinson, M. Birnbaum, B. Rennard, and J. Spilker, 1972 (USA)

219. Magnetic Resonance Imaging: Invented by Dr. Raymond Damadian, 1972 (USA)

220. Catalytic Converter (Three-Way): Invented by John J. Mooney and Carl D. Keith, 1973 (USA)

221. Mobile Phone: Invented by Douglas H. Ring and W. Rae Young, 1973 (USA)

222. Voicemail: Invented by Stephen J. Boies, 1973 (USA)

223. Heimlich Maneuver: Invented by Henry Heimlich, 1974 (USA)

224. Post-It Note: Invented by 3M, 1974 (USA)

225. Universal Product Code: Invented by George Laurer at IBM, 1974 (USA)

226. Digital Camera: Invented by Steven Sasson, 1975 (USA)

227. Gore-Tex: Invented by Wilbert L. Gore, Rowena Taylor, and Gore's son, Robert W. Gore, 1976 (USA)

228. Popcorn Bag: Invented by William A. Brastad, 1978 (USA)

229. Polar Fleece, Malden Mills, Polartec LLC, 1979 (USA)

230. Control-Alt-Delete: David Bradley, 1981 (USA)

231. Space Shuttle: George Mueller, 1981 (USA)

232. Graphic User Interface: Alan Kay and Douglas Engelbart, 1981 (USA)

233. CD-ROM: Invented by James T. Russel, 1982 (U.S)

234. Internet: (Not the World Wide Web) Paul Baran, Bob Kahn and Vinton Cerf, 1983 (USA)

235. LCD Projector: Gene Dolgoff, 1984 (USA)

236. 3-D Printer: Invented by Chuck Hall, 1986 (USA)

237. Luggage (Tilt-and-Roll): Robert Plath, 1988 (USA)

238. Nicotine Patch: Murray Jarvik, Jed Rose and Daniel Rose, 1988 (USA)

239. Firewall: William Cheswick and Steven M. Bellovin, 1988 (USA)

240. ZIP File Format: Phil Katz for PKZIP, 1989 (USA)

241. DNA Computing: Leonard Adleman, 1994 (USA)

242. Segway PT: Dean Kamen, 1994 (USA)

243. Scroll Wheel: Eric Michelman, 1995 (USA)

244. JavaScript: Brendan Eich, 1995 (USA)

245. Adobe Flash: Jonathan Gay, 1996 (USA)

246. Torino Scale: Richard P. Binzel, 1999 (USA)

247. iBOT: Dean Kamen, 1999 (USA)

248. Artificial Eye (Working): Invented by William H Dobelle, 2000 (USA)

249. iPhone: Invented by Steve Jobs & John Casey, Apple Computers, 2000 (USA)

250. Nanowire Battery: Dr. Yi Cui, 2007 (USA)

251. Bionic Contact Lens: Babak Parviz, 2008 (USA)

AMERICAN BUSINESS AND AGRICULTURE INVENTIONS

1. Reaper: Invented by Henry Ogle, 1826 (USA).

2. Tractor (1st Gasoline Pwered Engine): Invented by John Froelich, 1892 (U.S)

3. Tractor (Caterpillar): Invented by Benjamin Holt, 1900 (USA)

4. Bulldozer: Invented by James Cummings and J. Earl McLeod 1923 (U.S)

American Entertainment Inventions

1. Record (long-playing): Invented by Dr. Petter Goldmark, 1948 (USA)

2. Phonograph: Invented by Thomas Edison, 1877 (U.S)

3. Video Game Console: Invented by Magnavox, 1972 (U.S)

4. Car Radio: Invented by William Lear and Elmer Wavering, 1929 (USA)

5. Gramophone: Invented by Thomas Edison, 1878 (USA)

6. Microphone: Invented by Alexander Graham Bell 1876 (USA)

7. Phonograph: Invented by Thomas Alva Edison, 1878 (USA)

8. Record (Long-Playing): Invented by Dr. Petter Goldmark 1948 (USA)

9. Jukebox: Invented by Hobart C. Niblack, 1927 (USA)

10. Film (Musical): Invented by Dr. Lee de Forest, 1923 (USA)

11. Film (Talking): Invented by Warner Bros., 1926 (USA)

European Inventions And Discoveries

1. Crane: Invented in Ancient Greece, 515 BC (Greece)

2. Iron Working: Invented in Hallstatt, Austria, c. 1000 BC (Austria)

3. Lathe: Invented by the Greeks, c. 1500 BC (Greeks)

4. Segmental Arch Bridge: Invented in the Roman Republic, 1st c. BC (Italy)

5. Crankshaft: Invented in Augusta Raurica, Roman Empire 2nd c. (Italy)

6. Water Wheel: Inventen in The Hellenistic Kingdoms, 3rd c. BC (Greece)

7. Paddle Wheel Boat: Invented in the Roman Empire, 4th–5th c (Italy)

8. Eyeglasses: Invented in Italy, 1286 (Italy)

9. Printing Press: Invented by Johannes Gutenberg, 1440 (Germany)

10. Printing Press: Invented by Johannes Gutenberg, 1455 (Germany)

11. Chain Drive: Invented by Leonardo da Vinci, 1493 (Italy)

12. Telescope (1st refracting): Invented by Hans Lippershey, 1608 (Germany)

13. Slide Rule: Invented by William Oughtred, 1621 (England)

14. Clock (Pendulum): Invented by Christian Huygens, 1657 (Netherlands)

15. Laws of Gravitation and Motion: Invented by Isaac Newton, 1687 (England)

16. Steam Engine: Invented by Thomas Savery, 1698 (England)

17. Alcohol Therometer: Invented by Daniel Gabriel Fahrenheit, 1709 (Dutch-German)

18. Steam Engine (Piston): Invented by Thomas Newcomen, 1712 (England)

19. Blood Pressure Measurement: Invented by Stephen Hales, 1733 (England)

20. Chronometer: Invented by John Harrison, 1735 (England)

21. Centigrade Temperature Scale: Invented by Anders Celsius, 1742 (Sweden)

22. Steam Engine (Condenser): Invented by James Watt, 1765 (Scotland)

23. Ship (Steam): Invented by J.C. Perier, 1775 (France)

24. Watch (Self-Winding): Invented by Abraham-Louis Breguet, 1791 (France)

25. Gas Lighting: Invented by William Murdock, 1792 (Scotland)

26. Electric Battery: Invented by Volta, 1800 (Italian)

27. Chlorinated Water: Invented by William Cumberland Cruikshank, 1800 (England)

28. Locomotive: Invented by Richard Trevithick, 1804 (England)

29. Railway Steam Locomotive: Invented by Richard Trevithick, 1804 (England)

30. Canning of Food: Invented by Nicolas Appert, 1810 (France)

31. Rubber (Waterproof): Invented by Charles Macintosh, 1819 (Scotland)

32. Generator: Invented by Michael Faraday 1831 (England)

33. Cement: Invented by Joseph Aspdin, 1824 (England)

34. Electromagnet: Invented by William Sturgeon, 1824 (England)

35. Photography (On Metal): Invented by Joseph Nicéphore Niepce, 1826 (France)

36. Propeller (Ship): Invented by Francis Smith, 1827 (England)

37. Photography (On Paper): Invented by W. H. Fox Talbo, 1835 (England)

38. Motorcycle: Invented by Edward Butler, 1848 (England)

39. Refrigerator: Invented by Invented by James Harrison, 1851 (Australia)

40. Rubber Tires: Invented by Thomas Hancock, 1857 (England)

41. Electric Motor (DC): Invented by Zenobe Gramme, 1873 (Belgium)

42. Streetcar (Electric): Invented by Ernst Werner von Siemens, 1879 (Germany)

43. Telegraph: Invented by Sir William Cook, 1837 (England)

44. Steel Production: Invented by Henry Bessemer, 1885 (England)

45. Ship (Turbine): Invented by Hon. Sir Charles Parsons, 1894 (England)

46. Cinema: Invented by Auguste and Louis Jean Lumicre, 1895 (France)

47. Radio Telegraphy (Over 1 km): Invented by Lord Ernest Rutherford, 1895 (British-New Zealand)

48. Radioactivity: Invented by Antoine Bacqucrel, 1896 (France)

49. Steel: Invented by Harry Brearley, 1913 (England)

50. Helicopter: Invented by Corradino d' Ascanio, 1930 (Italy)

51. Jet Engine: Invented by Sir Frank Whittle, 1937 (England)

52. Microscope (Electron): Invented by Vladimir Kosme Sworykin, 1939 (Russia)

53. First Program Controlled Computer: Konrad Zuse, 1941 (Germany)

54. World Wide Web: Invented by Sir Tim Berners-Lee, 1989 (England)

TRAVEL INVENTIONS

1. Airplane: Invented by Orville Wright and Wilbur Wright, 1903 (USA)

2. Gyro-Compass: Invented by Elmer A. Sperry, 1911 (USA)

3. Radar: Invented by Dr. Allbert H. Taylor and Leo C. Young, 1922 (USA)

4. Rocket Engine: Invented by Robert H. Goddard, 1926 (USA)

5. Rubber (Vulcanised): Invented by Charles Goodyear, 1841 (USA)

6. Submarine: Invented by David Bushnell, 1776 (USA)

7. Balloon: Invented by Jacques Montgolfier and Joseph Montgolfier, 1783 (France)

8. Airship (Non-Rigid): Invented by Henri Giffard, 1852 (France)

9.   Airship (Rigid): Invented by Graf Ferdinand von Zeppelin, 1900 (Germany)

10. Automobile (Steam): Invented by Nicolas Cugnot, 1769 (France)

11. Automobile (Gasoline): Invented by Karl Benz, 1855 (Germany)

Medical Inventions And Discoveries

1.   Hippocratic Medicine: Hippocrates, Father of Western Medicine is born, c. 460 BCE (Greece)

2.   Spectacles: Invented by Roger Bacon, 1249 (England)

3.   Microscope: Invented by Zacharius Jannssen, 1590 (Dutch)

4.   Blood Cells: Discovered by Anton van Leeuwenhoek, 1670 (Dutch)

5.   Bacteria Observed: Discovered by Anton van Leeuwenhoek, 1683 (Dutch)

6.   First Smallpox Inoculations: By Giacomo Pylarini, 1701 (Italy)

7.   Flexible Urinary Catheter: Benjamin Franklin, 1752 (USA)

8.   Beginning of Pathology as a Science: Discovered by Giovanni Battista Morgagni, 1761 (Italy)

9.   The Cure for Scurvy: Discovered by 753 James Lind, 1773 (England)

10. Bifocal Lens: Invented by Benjamin Franklin, 1780 (USA)

11. Vaccination for Smallpox (First Vaccine): Invented by Edward Jenner, 1796 (England)

12. Homeopathy: Discovered by Samuel Hahnemann, 1810 (Germany)

13. The Stethoscope: Invented by René Laënnec, 1816 (France)

14. First Successful Blood Transfusion: Invented by James Blundell, 1818 (England)

15. Ether Used as a General Anesthetic: Invented by Crawford W. Long, 1842 (USA)

16. Nitrous Oxide: Invented by Dr. Horace Wells, 1844 (USA)

17. Washing Hands Stops the Spread of Disease: Discovered by Ignaz Semmelweis, 1847 (Hungary)

18. Ophthalmoscope: Invented by Hermann von Helmholtz, 1851 (Germany)

19. Hypodermic Syringe: Invented Charles Gabriel Pravaz, 1853 (France)

20. Syringe: Invented by Charles Gabriel Pravaz, 1853 (France) and Alexander Wood (Scotland) 1853

21. Germs as a Cause of Disease: Discovered by Louis Pasteur, 1857 (France)

22. Bacteria Causes Disease: Discovered by Louis Pasteur, 1857 (France)

23. Cells Come From Other Cells: Discovered by Rudolf Virchow, 1858 (Prussia-Germany Empire)

24. Sphygmomanometer: Invented by Etienne-Jules Marey, 1860 (France)

25. Antiseptic System: Invented by 1865 Joseph Lister, 1865 (England)

26. Genes: Discovered by Johann Gregor Mendel, 1866 (Austria)

27. Antiseptic: Discovered by Dr. Joseph Lister, 1867 (England)

28. Cancer Recognized as Uncontrolled Cell Division: Discovered by Wilhelm Waldeyer, 1867 (Germany)

29. Practice of Surgery: Invented by Joseph Lister, 1867 (England)

30. First Diagnosis of Multiple Sclerosis: Discovered by Jean Martin Charcot, 1868 (France)

31. Cholera Vaccine: Discovered by Jaume Ferran I Clua, 1879 (Spain)

32.   Anthrax Vaccine: Discovered by Louis Pasteur, 1881 (France)

33.   Rabies Vaccine: Discovered by Louis Pasteur, 1882 (France)

34.   TB bacillus: Discovered by Robert Koch, 1882 (Germany)

35.   First Contact Lenses: Invented by F.E Muller, 1887 (Germany)

36.   Tetnus and Diptheria Vaccines: Discovered by Emil von Behring, 1890 (Germany)

37.   Asprin: Invented by Felix Hoffman, 1899 (Germany)

38.   Rubber Gloves Enter the Operating Room: Invented by William Stewart Halsted, 1889 (USA)

39.   Psychonalysis: Founding Father, Sigmund Freud, 1895 (Austria)

40.   X-Rays: Invented by Wilhelm Conrad Röntgen, 1895 (Germany)

41.   Cause of Malaria: Discovered by Ronald Ross, 1897 (England)

42.   Typhoid Vaccine: Discovered by Almroth E. Wright, 1898 (England)

43.   Cause of Yellow Fever: Discovered by Walter Reed, 1900 (USA)

44.   Four Blood Groups: Discovered by Karl Landsteiner, 1901 (Austria)

45.   Blood Classifications: Discovered by Karl Landsteiner, 1901 (Austria)

46.   Electrocardiograph: Invented by Willem Einthoven, 1901 (Netherlands)

47.   Discovery of Vitamins: Discovered by Sir Frederick G. Hopkins, 1906 (England)

48.   Vitamin A: Discovered by Elmer V. McCollum and M. Davis, 1913 (USA)

49.   Vitamin B: Discovered by Elmer V. McCollum, 1916 (USA)

50.   Vitamin C: Discovered by Albert Szent-Györgyi and Charles Glen King, 1920 (USA).

51.   Vitamin D: Discovered by Sir Edward Mellanby, 1920 (USA)

52. The Band-Aid®: Earle Dickson for, Johnson & Johnson, 1921 (USA)

53. Insulin: Discovered by Frederick Banting and Charles Best, 1921 (Canada)

54. Vitamin E: Discovered by Sir Herbert McLean Evans, 1922 (USA)

55. Electroencephalogram (EEG): Hans Berger, 1924 (Germany)

56. Penicillin: Discovered by Alexander Fleming, 1928 (Scotland)

57. Iron Lung: Invented by Philip Drinker, 1929 (USA)

58. Vitamin K: Discovered by Henrik Dam (Denmark) and Edward Adelbert Doisy, 1929 (USA)

59. Streptomycin: Invented by Selman A. Waksman, 1943 (USA)

60. Open Heart Surgery: Invented by Alfred Blalock, 1944 (USA)

61. Influenza Vaccine: Discovered by Dr. Thoman Francis, 1945 (USA)

62. Cortisone: Invented by Louis Frederick Fieser, 1948 (USA)

63. Holter Monitor: Invented by Norman Holter, 1949 (USA)

64. Cardiac Pacemaker: John Hopps, 1950 (Canada)

65. Structure of DNA: Discovered by James Watson, Francis Crick and Rosalind Franklin, 1953

66. Heart-Lung Machine: Invented by John H. Gibbon, 1953 (USA)

67. X-Ray Diffraction to study DNA: Rosalind Franklin, 1953 (England)

68. Kidney Transplant: Dr. Joseph E. Murray, 1955 (USA)

69. Balloon Embolectomy Catheter: Thomas Fogarty, 1963 (USA)

70. CAT Scan: Invented by Sir Godfrey N. Hounsfield, 1967, (England)

71. Pneumonia Vaccine: Invented by Maurice Hilleman, 1977 (USA)

72. Mumps, Measles, Chickenpox, Hepatitis A & B, & Meningitis Vaccines: Maurice Hilleman, 1948-58 (USA)

73. Artificial Kidney Dialysis Machine: Willem J. Kolff, 1985 (Netherlands)

74. Dolly the Sheep, The First Clone: Ian Wilmut and Keith Cambell, 1996 (England)

Military/War Inventions

1. Catapult: Before 421 BC, (Ancient Greece Including Sicily)

2. Spears: 400 ka (Germany)

3. Cannon (Iron): c. 1320 (Germany)

4. Columbiad: Invented by George Bomford, 1812 (USA)

5. Revolver: Invented by Samuel Colt, 1835 (USA)

6. Maynard Tape Primer for Muskets: Invented by George Bomford, 1845 (USA)

7. Repeating Rifle (Lever Action): Invented by Walter Hunt, 1860 (USA)

8. Machine Gun (Hand-Cranked): Invented by Richard Gatling, 1861 (USA)

9. Spar Torpedo: Invented by E. C. Singer, 1864 (U.S)

10. Machine Gun: Invented by Stevens Maxim, 1884 (U.S)

11. The Maxim Gun: Invented by Hiram Stevens Maxim, 1884 (U.S)

12. Semi-Automatic Shotgun: Invented by John Moses Browning, 1898 (U.S)

13. The Tank: Invented by Ernest Swinton, 1915 (England)

14. Bazooka: Invented by Edward Uhl, and Colonel Leslie Skinner, 1942 (USA)

15. Atom Bomb: Invented by 1945.Julius Robert Oppenheimer, 1945 (U.S)

NOTES

PART I

CHAPTER 1 – MY BEGINNINGS

1. Ethnogue, Summary by language family "Ethnologue list of language families."

2. Ethnogue, Summary by language size "Ethnologue list of languages by number of speakers."

PART II

CHAPTER 2 – THE EXCEPTIONAL MINDSET

1. Dr. Niall Ferguson, "Six Killer Apps," historian and professor at Harvard. Presentation April 2, 2012 in Vancouver.

2. Dr. Carol S. Dweck, "Mindset: The New Psychology of Success," (New York: Random House, 1998).

3. Al-Faraaid, "Laws of Inheritance," Bukhari, Book 8, Volume 80, Hadith 747.

CHAPTER 3 – AMERICANS AND EUROPEANS AT THE TOP

1. David Landes, "The Wealth and Poverty of Nations," (New York: W.W. Norton & Company, Inc., 1998), p. 54.

2. The Guardian, "Mysteries of Computer from 65BC are Solved," November 29, 2006.

3. Clifford Ando, "Imperial Ideology and Provincial Loyalty in the Roman Empire," (Berkeley: University of California Press, 2000), pp. 86–87.

4. Herbert Butterfield, "The Origins of Modern Science, 1300–1800," (New York: The Macmillan Company, 1957), p. viii.

5. Steven Shapin, "The Scientific Revolution," (Chicago: University of Chicago Press, 1996) p. 1.

6. Jerry Brotton, "The Renaissance: A Very Short Introduction," (Oxford University Press, 2006).

7. Suzanne Austin Alchon, "A Pest in the Land: New World Epidemics in a Global Perspective," (University of New Mexico Press, 2003), p. 21.

8. Angus Maddison, "The World Economy: Historical Statistics," (Paris: Development Centre, OECD, 2003), pp. 256–262, Tables 8a and 8c.

9. Robert E. Lucas, Jr., "Lectures on Economic Growth," (Cambridge: Harvard University Press, 2002), pp. 109–110.

10. Bernard C. Beaudreau, "Mass Production, the Stock Market Crash and the Great Depression," (New York, Lincoln, Shanghi: Authors Choice Press, 1996).

11. David A. Wells, "Recent Economic Changes and Their Effect on Production and Distribution of Wealth and Well-Being of Society," (New York: D. Appleton and Co., 1890).

12. Paul Kennedy, "The Rise and Fall of the Great Powers," (New York: Vintage, 1987), p. 149

13. Mortality. www.britannica.com. Retrieved February 15, 2013.

14. BBC News, "A millennium of health improvement," 1998-12-27. Retrieved February 15, 2013. http://news.bbc.co.uk/2/hi/health/241864.stm

15. Thomson Prentice, "Health, history and hard choices: Funding dilemmas in a fast fast-changing world," (World Health Organization:

Indiana University Presentation, August 2006). http://www.who.int/global_health_histories/seminars/presentation07.pdf

16. Gordon Wood, "The Radicalism of the American Revolution," (New York: Vintage, 1992), pp. 278–9.

17. Thomas Edison in a statement to a reporter during the first public demonstration of his incandescent, 31 December 1879. Quoted in Chronology of Americans and the Environment (2011) by Chris J. Magoc, p. 46.

18. Demography of England. http://en.wikipedia.org/wiki/Demography_of_England.

19. Geography of the United Kingdom. http://en.wikipedia.org/wiki/Geography_of_the_United_Kingdom

20. List of largest empires. http://en.wikipedia.org/wiki/List_of_largest_empires

21. Charles Dickens, William Harrison Ainsworth, Albert Smith, "Bentley's Miscellany, Volume 43," (London: Richard Bentley) p. 111.

22. Bernard Lewis, "I'm Right, You're Wrong, Go To Hell," Atlantic Magazine, May 2003.

23. Ibid.

24. The Top Countries in all Fields, "Scientific Papers and Citations," Essential Science IndicatorsSM from Thomson Reuters, time period: 2001-August 31, 2011.

25. Dr. Edgar Choueiri, "Igniting the Arab Scientific Revolution," Ibn Rushd Fund for Freedom of Thought.

26. Dr. Saleem H. Ali, www.saleemali.newsvine.com/_news/2010/02/14/3895511-nobel-laureates-and-the-muslim-world

27. Ibid.

28. The Holy Quran, Abdullah Yusuf Ali, (New York: Tahrike Tarsile Quran, Inc., 1988), 7:57.

29. Ayn Rand, "Capitalism: The Unknown Ideal," (New York: Signet, 1967)

30. James Adams Truslow, "Epic of America," (Safety Harbor, FL, 2001), pp. 214-215.

31. Gibson Campbell and Kay Jung, "Historical Census Statistics on Population Totals by Race, 1790 to 1990, and by Hispanic Origin, 1790 to 1990, for the United States, Regions, Divisions, and States," Population Division Working Paper No. 56. (Washington, DC: Population Division, U.S. Bureau of the Census 2002).

32. John Higham, "Strangers in the Land: Patterns of American Nativism, 1860–1925," (New Brunswick: Rutgers University Press, Second edition, 1988).

33. Digital History, "Landmarks in Immigration History," http://www.digitalhistory.uh.edu/historyonline/immigration_chron.cfm

34. Confucius, Chinese philosopher, "The Analects, Book IV, Chapter XVI."

35. Aristotle, Greek philosopher, student of Plato and teacher of Alexander the Great.

36. Mathew 16:26, 60-100.

37. The Holy Quran, Abdullah Yusuf Ali, (New York: Tahrike Tarsile Quran, Inc., 1988), 4:173

38. Giovanni Pico della Mirandola 1463-1494, Italian Renaissance Neo-Platonnist philosopher, scholar and humanist in "Oratio de hominis dignitate", 1487.

39. Galileo Galilei, 1564-162, Italian physicist and astronomer.

40. Voltaire 1694-1778, French philosopher, a crusader against tyranny and bigotry.

41. Thomas Paine (1737-1809), "Age of Reason 1794," Opening page.

PART III

CHAPTER 4 – THE PAKISTAN THAT WAS!

1. 2005–06 Economic and Social Indicators of Pakistan

2. Pak Tribune, The Promising Pakistan, 17 November, 2011. Retrieved February 15, 2013 www.paktribune.com/speakouts/The-Promising-Pakistan-196.html

3. Esposito, John L. 1987. "Islam: Ideology and Politics in Pakistan," in Ali Banuazizi and Myron Weiner (eds.), The State, Religion, and Ethnic Politics: Pakistan, P. 37 Iran, and Afghanistan, pp. 360-1. (Lahore: Vanguard Publishers).

4. The Herald (Karachi, Pakistan), "Zia and Politics: Attitude and Impact," August 1999, p.54.

5. Veena Kukreja, "Contemporary Pakistan: Political Processes, Conflicts and Crises," (New Delhi; Sage Publications, 2003), p.169.

6. The Herald (Karachi, Pakistan), "Zia and the End of Civil Society," August 1999, p. 63.

7. Nadeem F. Paracha, "Be Critical," Dawn Newspaper, September 13, 2012.

8. Ibid.

9. Ibid.

PART IV

CHAPTER 5 – THE HISTORY OF ISLAM

1. The Holy Quran, Abdullah Yusuf Ali, (New York: Tahrike Tarsile Quran, Inc., 1988), 96:1-3

2. The Prophet Mohammad Last Sermon at Mount Arafat, Mecca. www.islamicity.com/mosque/lastserm.HTM

3. Khalid Yahya Blankinship, "The End of the Jihad State, the Reign of Hisham Ibn 'Abd-al Malik and the collapse of the Umayyads," (State University of New York Press, 1994), p. 37.

4. Vartan Gregorian, "Islam: A Mosaic, Not a Monolith," (Brookings Institution Press, 2003), pp. 26–38.

5. Ibid.

6. Hillel Ofek, "Why the Arabic World Turned Away from Science?" New Atlantis Journal, September 2, 2011.

7. Pervez Hoodbhoy, "Science and the Islamic World: The Quest for Rapprochement," Physics Today, August 1, 2007, Volume 60, Number 8: 49.

8. Montgomery W. Watt, "The Faith and Practice of al-Ghazali," (London: George Allen & Unwin), p. 32-33.

9. Pervez Hoodbhoy, "Islam and Science; "Religious Orthodoxy and the Battle for Rationality," (London: Zed Publication, 1991), p. 107.

10. Will and Ariel Durant, "The Story of Civilization; Our Oriental Heritage," (New York: Simon and Schuster, 1935).

11. Ibid.

12. Sir Henry Miers Elliot, "The history of India, as told by its own historians: the Muhammadan period," (London: Trubner And Co. 1869 Volume II), p. 98. www.Elibron.com

13. Jorge Flores/Antonio Vasconcelos de Saldanha (eds.), Os Firangis na Chancelaria Mogol. Copias Portuguesas de Documentos de Akbar (1572-1604), (New Delhi: Embaixada de Portugal, 2003).

14. Harbans Mukhia, "The Mughals of India," (Hoboken, New Jersey: Wiley-Blackwell, 2004), pp. 25–26.

15. Alan Palmer, "The Decline and Fall of Ottoman Empire (New York: Fall River Press, 1992), p. 21.

16. Ibid. p. 6.

CHAPTER 6 – ISLAMIC DOCTRINES

1. The Holy Quran, Abdullah Yusuf Ali, (New York: Tahrike Tarsile Quran, Inc., 1988), 6:38.

2. Abdullahi Ahmed An-Na'im, "Toward Islamic Reformation," (New York: Syracuse University Press), p.52. Charles Howard Candler Professor of Law, School of Law, Emory University, Atlanta, Georgia.

3. Ibid, p. 283.

4. Fazlur Rahman Malik, former professor of Islamic Studies at the University of Chicago and McGill University.

PART V

CHAPTER 7 – THE MUSLIM WORLD SINCE WORLD WAR II

1. James R. Woolsey (former Director of Central Intelligence), "Defeating the Oil Weapon," Commentary; September 2002, Volume 114, Issue 2, p. 29.

2. Nancy H. Dupree, "An Historical Guide To Afghanistan," (Afghan Air Authority, Afghan Tourist Organization, 1977).

3. Neamatollah Nojumi, "The Rise of the Taliban in Afghanistan: Mass Mobilization, Civil War and the Future of the Region," (New York: Palgrave, 2002), p. 260.

4. Elaine Sciolino, "State Dept. Beomes Cooler to the New Rulers of Kabul," New York Times, October 23, 1996.

5. Zaffar Abbas, "Pakistan's undeclared war," BBC, September 10, 2004. http://news.bbc.co.uk/2/hi/south_asia/3645114.stm]

CHAPTER 8 – EXTREMISM IN THE MUSLIM WORLD

1. Karen Pfeifer, "Petrodollars at Work and in Play in the Post-September 11 Decade," Middle East Research and Information Project, MER 260 – 9/11/11.

2. Mohammad Sageer, "When Petro-Dollar Speaks." www.faithfreedom. org/oped/MohdSageer40210.htm

3. Karen Pfeifer, "Petrodollars at Work and in Play in the Post-September 11 Decade," Middle East Research and Information Project, MER 260 – 9/11/11.

4. Andrew Mango, "Ataturk: The Biography of the founder of Modern Turkey," (New York: Overlook TP, 2002), p. 404

5. Syed Qutb, "Milestones," (Chicago: Kazi Publication, 2007), pp. 130, 134.

6. Eman Al Nafjan, "Teaching Intolerance," Foreign Policy magazine. May-June 2012.

7. Saudi Arabia's Curriculum of Intolerance, Center for Religious Freedom, (Washington, D.C.: Freedom House, 2006) www.freedomhouse.org/report/special-reports/saudi-arabias-curriculum-intolerance

8. "Jihad Against Jews and Crusaders," World Islamic Front Statement. Al-Qaeda declaration of Jihad, February 23, 1998. http://www.fas.org/irp/world/para/docs/980223-fatwa.htm.

9. Majid Khadduri, "War and Peace in the Law of Islam," (Baltimore: John Hopkins University Press, 1955), p. 56.

10. Abdullah Saeed and Hassan Saeed, "Freedom of Religion, Apostasy and Islam," (Burlington VT: Ashgate Publishing Company, 2004), pp. 38–39.

11. The Guardian, "Islamic scholar attacks Pakistan's blasphemy laws," January 20, 2010.

12. A 1944 quote from Muhammad Ali Jinnah, Founder of Pakistan.

13. A quote from Mustafa Kemal Atatürk, Founder of Modern Turkey.

14. The Holy Quran, Abdullah Yusuf Ali, (New York: Tahrike Tarsile Quran, Inc., 1988), 2:256

15. Reza Aslan, (Associate professor of creative writing at the University of California, Riverside), "Rejected by Religions, but Not by Believers," Room for Debate, The Opinion Page. New York Times, October 5, 2012.

16. Arch Puddington, "Freedom in the World 2011" Report, Freedom House.

CHAPTER 9 – TERRORISM, JIHADISM AND OUR OPTIONS

1. Ibn Khaldun, "The Muqaddimah," (Princeton University Press, 1967), p. 183.

2. The Holy Quran, Abdullah Yusuf Ali, (New York: Tahrike Tarsile Quran, Inc., 1988), 2:256

3. Ibid. 5:32

4. Ibid. 9:5

5. Dr. Abdul Hafeez Sheikh, former Minister of Finance, Federal budget submitted on June 3, 2011. www.finance.gov.pk.

6. Ayesha Siddiqa (former Deputy Director in audit Defence Services, Pakistan), "Military Inc.: Inside Pakistan's Military Economy," (London: Pluto Press, 2007).

7. Ibid.

8. Allison, Graham, "Nuclear Terrorism," The Ultimate Preventable Catastrophe. (New York: Owl Books, Henry Holt and Company, LLC, 2005), pp. 3-4.

9. Status of World Nuclear Forces 2010, SIPRI Yearbook. http://www.nucleardarkness.org/globalnucleararsenal/ statusofworldnuclearforces/

10. Ibid

11. Ibid

12. Ibid

13. The Express Tribune with the International Herald Tribune, "Pakistan in a critical balance of payments situation: AD, "March 6, 2013.

14. ARY News, "Pakistan to pay loan installment to IMF next month," January 26, 2013.

15. Data from South Asia Terrorism Portal. Fatalities in Terrorist Violence in Pakistan 2003–2012 as of October 21, 2012. (www.satp.org).

16. Table 1 Data from GEO TV broadcast, "Aaj Kamran Khan Kay Sath" October 16, 2012.

17. Table 2 Data from GEO TV broadcast, "Aaj Kamran Khan Kay Sath" October 16, 2012.

18. Anjum Niaz opined on October 14, 2012 in the Pakistani newspaper Dawn,

19. Dr. Satish Kumar, (Director of National Security Research Foundation (NSRF), a New Delhi based think tank), "Militant Islam: The Nemesis of Pakistan," Article originally written January 2000. http://www.newageislam.com/NewAgeIslamRadicalIslamismAndJihad_1.aspx?ArticleID=1326, April 15, 2009.

CHAPTER 10 – Is Time Running Out?

1. Recep Tayyip Erdogan, Prime Minister of Turkey. Speech at Harvard University, Kennedy School of Government, January 30, 2003.

2. The Holy Quran, Abdullah Yusuf Ali, (New York: Tahrike Tarsile Quran, Inc., 1988), 13:11

3. Ibid. 2:177

4. Ibid. 20:114

5. Ibid. 45: 13

6. Prophet Mohammad, from the Collections of Muslim.

7. Prophet Mohammad.

8. Dr. Farrukh Saleem, "Why Muslims are so from the website Studying Islam, www.studying-islam.org/articletext.aspx?id=1054]

9. Ibid

10. Gross Domestic Product (GDP), 2011 estimates. International Monetary Fund.

11. Central Intelligence Agency. The World Factbook. www.Indexq.org/economy/gdp.php

12. Military Expenditure, 2010. Stockholm International Peace Research Institute (SIPRI).

13. Statistical, Economic and Social Research and Training Centre for Islamic Countries (SESRIC) "2012 Annual Economic Report," Organization of the Islamic Conference (OIC).

14. History Channel. The Reader's Companion to Military History. Edited by Robert Cowley and Geoffrey Parker. (New York: Houghton Mifflin Harcourt Publishing Company, 1996). www.history.com/topics/iran-iraq-war.

15. Kim Susanna, "Egypt's Mubarak likely to retain vast wealth," ABC News. February 2, 2011.

16. Muslim Leaders Wealth, http://en.wikipedia.org/wiki/List_of_heads_of_state_and_government_by_net_worth

17. The Western Leaders Wealth, http://en.wikipedia.org/wiki/List_of_heads_of_state_and_government_by_net_worth

PART VI

CHAPTER 11 – THE JEWISH MYTH AMONG MUSLIMS

1. The Pew Forum. "The Future of the Global Muslim Population: Projections for 2010-2030," January 27, 2011. www.pewforum.org/The-Future-of-the-Global-Muslim-Population.aspx

2. Commentary on Genesis 30:24. The Anchor Bible, Volume 1, Genesis. (New York, Doubleday and Company, Inc., 1964).

3. Mandy Katz, "Do We Divide the Holiest Holy City?" Moment Magazine. May 8, 2012.

4. George Ostrogorsky, "History of the Byzantine State," (New Brunswick, New Jersey: Rutgers University Press, 1986).

5. Joseph E. Katz, "Continuous Jewish Presence in the Holy Land," www.EretzYisroel.Org. Retrieved February 16, 2013.

6. James Carroll, "Constantine's Sword: The Church and the Jews," (New York: Houghton Mifflin Harcourt, 2001), 26

7. Dmitri Gondicas and Charles Issawi, "Ottoman Greeks in the Age of Nationalism," (Princeton: Darwin Press, 1999)

APPENDIX I – LIST OF AMERICAN AND EUROPEAN INVENTIONS

From Wikipedia, the free encyclopedia

Timeline of United States inventions (before 1890)
Timeline of United States inventions (1890–1945)
Timeline of United States inventions (1946–1991)
Timeline of United States inventions (after 1991)
(From Wikipedia–http://en.wikipedia.org/wiki/
Timeline_of_historic_inventions)

CPSIA information can be obtained
at www.ICGtesting.com
Printed in the USA
LVHW080337040919
629881LV00011B/182/P